SEEKING TALENT FOR CREATIVE CITIES

The Social Dynamics of Innovation

P9-CPY-515

With the growth of knowledge-based economies, cities across the globe must compete to attract and retain the most talented workers. *Seeking Talent for Creative Cities* offers a comprehensive and insightful analysis of the diverse, dynamic factors that affect cities' ability to achieve this goal.

Based on a comparative national study of sixteen Canadian cities, this volume systematically evaluates the concerns facing workers operating in a range of creative endeavours. It draws on interviews, surveys, and census data collected over a six-year research program conducted by experts in business, public policy, urban studies, and communications studies to identify the characteristics and features of particular city-regions that influence these workers' mobility and satisfaction. *Seeking Talent for Creative Cities* represents a rigorously empirical test of popular wisdom on the true relationship between urban development and economic competitiveness.

(Innovation, Creativity, and Governance in Canadian City-Regions)

JILL L. GRANT is a professor in the School of Planning at Dalhousie University.

Innovation, Creativity, and Governance in Canadian City-Regions

Series editor: David A. Wolfe

The series on *Innovation, Creativity, and Governance in Canadian City-Regions* presents the research results of a six-year, sixteen-city study of the social dynamics of innovation, creativity, and civic governance in Canadian cities. The first three volumes in the series provide detailed analyses of each of the three research themes carried out across a selection of large, mid-sized, and small Canadian cities, and the fourth one integrates the key findings across all themes for the individual cases.

While the cases covered are primarily Canadian, the volumes present the material in an international and comparative context that addresses ongoing intellectual and policy debates concerning urban economic development and civic governance. As such, the series offers important new insights that contribute to our contemporary understanding of the relationship between urban social dynamics and economic performance.

Seeking Talent for Creative Cities

The Social Dynamics of Innovation

EDITED BY JILL L. GRANT

UNIVERSITY OF TORONTO PRESS
Toronto Buffalo London

ISBN 978-1-4426-4734-3 (cloth)
ISBN 978-1-4426-1544-1 (paper)

Printed on acid-free, 100% post-consumer recycled paper with vegetable-based inks.

Library and Archives Canada Cataloguing in Publication

Seeking talent for creative cities : the social dynamics of innovation/edited by
Jill L. Grant.

(Innovation, creativity, and governance in Canadian city-regions)
Includes bibliographical references.
ISBN 978-1-4426-4734-3 (bound). – ISBN 978-1-4426-1544-1 (pbk.)

1. Cities and towns – Canada – Growth – Case studies. 2. Sociology, Urban –
Canada – Case studies. 3. Cultural industries – Canada – Case studies.
4. Diffusion of innovations – Canada – Case studies. 5. Municipal government –
Canada – Case studies. I. Grant, Jill, editor of compilation II. Series: Innovation,
creativity, and governance in Canadian city-regions (Toronto, Ont.)

HT127.S43 2014   307.760971   C2013-906138-X

University of Toronto Press acknowledges the financial assistance to its
publishing program of the Canada Council for the Arts and the Ontario Arts
Council.

Canada Council   Conseil des Arts
for the Arts   du Canada

ONTARIO ARTS COUNCIL
CONSEIL DES ARTS DE L'ONTARIO
50 YEARS OF ONTARIO GOVERNMENT SUPPORT OF THE ARTS
50 ANS DE SOUTIEN DU GOUVERNEMENT DE L'ONTARIO AUX ARTS

University of Toronto Press acknowledges the financial support of the Government of Canada through the Canada Book Fund for its publishing activities.

Contents

Tables

Figures

Foreword to the Series

**Innovating in Urban Economies: Economic Transformation
in Canadian City-Regions**

Innovation and creative capacity are essential determinants of economic prosperity in a globalizing, knowledge-based economy. Although the process of globalization has led to numerous predictions of the "death of distance," growing evidence suggests that the contemporary global economy make cities more – not less – important as sites of production, distribution, and innovation. Over the past decade, recognition has grown that even the most global of economic activities remain fundamentally rooted in city-regions as critical sites for organizing economic activity. More significantly, the social dynamics of city-regions are crucial in shaping economic outcomes (Gertler 2001).

The interactive and social nature of the innovation process makes city-regions the appropriate scale at which social learning processes unfold. Knowledge transfer between highly skilled people happens more easily in cities, while talent flows within and between cities are a critical means for the dissemination of innovative ideas. In a country with diverse and strongly differentiated regional economies, relationships between economic actors, organizations, and institutions at the local and regional scale are crucial factors affecting national prosperity. The concentrations of talented people and skilled occupations in urban centres are seen as critical sources of the creative and innovative ideas which generate growth in city-regions. And leading urban regions are no longer prepared to be passive objects at the hands of globalizing forces associated with the spread of information technologies, but are taking control of their own economic future through efforts aimed at the "strategic management" of their own economies (Audretsch 2002). From this perspective, many of the key foundations of economic success in a globalizing, knowledge-based economy are the social qualities and properties of urban places.

The papers collected in this series report on the research results of a six-year study of the social dynamics of economic performance in Canadian city-regions by members of the Innovation Systems Research Network (ISRN). The ISRN itself was an innovative experiment in knowledge management that came into existence in 1998 through the leadership of the Social Sciences and Humanities Research Council and its partners, the National Research Council and Natural Sciences and Engineering Research Council. The ISRN is a collaborative, multi-disciplinary network of university-based researchers analysing how innovation processes unfold in different regions and localities across the country. Since its inception in 1998, the network's research has focused on how the interaction among the major components of the regional innovation system shape the process of innovation and social learning that is critical for Canada's success in the knowledge-based economy. Its primary objectives have been: (1) to understand the process by which regional networks foster the production and circulation of knowledge that is critical to the innovation process, and (2) to deepen our understanding of the role of public policy in facilitating (or impeding) this process (Holbrook and Wolfe 2005).

The goal of the ISRN's first research program from 2001 to 2005 was to determine the prevalence and success of local industrial clusters across Canada and to analyse how the formation and growth of these clusters contribute to local economic growth and innovative capacity. Underlying this objective was a set of fundamental conceptual questions: how do local assets and relationships between economic actors enable firms – in any industry – to become more innovative? Under what circumstances does "the local" matter, and how important are local sources of knowledge and locally generated institutions (public and private) in strengthening the innovative capabilities of firms and industries? What is the relative importance of non-local actors, relationships, and flows of knowledge in shaping the development trajectories of localized innovation and growth?

The results of that five-year project made a distinctly Canadian contribution to the study of industrial clusters. The international literature on clusters and regional innovation systems recognizes that in a global marketplace, local input factors and inter-firm dynamics are critical to a firm's ability to innovate and thereby gain competitive advantage. But, as noted above, a critical question addressed in the ISRN study concerns the relative importance of local versus non-local factors in cluster performance and the relationship between the two sets of factors. The ISRN case studies provided important insights into these questions. They documented a balance between the relative impact of local and non-local relationships and knowledge flows – in other words, the dynamic tension between the local "buzz" and global "pipelines" that circulate knowledge between clusters (Bathelt, Malmberg, and Maskell 2004). They underlined the sectoral specificity of industrial clusters – clusters in different sectors draw upon different knowledge bases which influence both the innovation process within the clusters and the underlying relationship between the cluster and the research infrastructure which supports it. The case studies also highlighted the centrality of a strong, dynamic talent base, or "thick" labour market for the success of most clusters. The ability to draw upon a plentiful supply of labour with the skills required by cluster firms is often the most critical factor that attracts them to, and anchors them in, a specific geographic location (Wolfe 2009a).

Finally, the case studies suggested that some of the most successful clusters have profited from the development of strong social networks at the community level and the emergence of dedicated, community-based organizations. These entities link leaders in the individual clusters to a broader cross-section of the community. They appear to be supported by new institutions of civic governance that identify problems impeding the growth of the cluster and help mobilize support across the community for proposed solutions. The research also found some evidence to suggest that size is a critical variable in the success of civic engagement, with some of the larger urban centres encountering greater difficulty in achieving effective degrees of mobilization (Wolfe and Nelles 2008).

The results of the first ISRN project led to the overwhelming conclusion that many of the most significant factors which underlay the performance of individual clusters were not specific to the cluster itself. The research thus led to the conclusion that the social characteristics, dynamics, and relationships within the wider city-region are important determinants of economic performance. This led the members of the network to undertake a second Major Collaborative Research Initiative (MCRI), with funding from SSHRC and other partners, to investigate the social dynamics of innovation and economic performance, with the city-region as the primary unit of analysis. The second MCRI project from 2006 to 2011 set out to analyse what were believed to be three key determinants of the economic performance at the local level: the broader dynamics of innovation and knowledge flows, the role of creativity and talent, and the contribution made by new forms of civic governance in Canadian city-regions (Wolfe 2009b).

The study involved detailed investigations of all three of these themes – innovation, talent, and governance – in a sample of sixteen large, mid-sized, and small Canadian cities across eight provinces, resulting in more than fifty case studies in all. Each case was examined using a common research methodology, primarily based on in-depth interviews with key participants in critical sectors in the local economy using common interview guides. The key questions for each theme were largely the same, but were structured to reflect the researchers' detailed knowledge of their own local economy and institutions.

This series of four volumes presents the results of a selection of the case studies conducted under each of the themes. The present volume considers factors affecting how talented and creative people are attracted to and retained in Canadian city-regions. Other volumes in the series deal with the role of knowledge flows in the dynamics of innovation, the significance of civic governance in stimulating economic performance, and the social dynamics and character of innovation systems.

David A. Wolfe, Series editor

REFERENCES

Audretsch, D.B. 2002. "The innovative advantage of US cities." *European Planning Studies* 10 (2): 165–76. http://dx.doi.org/10.1080/09654310120114472.
Bathelt, H., A. Malmberg, and P. Maskell. 2004. "Clusters and knowledge: Local buzz, global pipelines and the process of knowledge creation." *Progress in Human Geography* 28 (1): 31–56. http://dx.doi.org/10.1191/0309132504 ph469oa.
Gertler, M.S. 2001. "Urban economy and society in Canada: Flows of people, capital and ideas." *Isuma: Canadian Journal of Policy Research* 2 (3): 119–30.
Holbrook, J.A., and D.A. Wolfe. 2005. "The Innovation Systems Research Network: A Canadian experiment in knowledge management." *Science & Public Policy* 32 (2): 109–18. http://dx.doi.org/10.3152/147154305781779623.

Wolfe, D.A. 2009a. "Introduction: Embedded clusters in a global economy." *European Planning Studies* 17 (2): 179–87. http://dx.doi.org/10.1080/09654310802553407.

Wolfe, D.A. 2009b. *21st century cities in Canada: The geography of innovation.* Ottawa: Conference Board of Canada.

Wolfe, D.A., and J. Nelles. 2008. "The role of civic capital and civic associations in cluster policies." In *Handbook of Research on Innovations and Cluster Policies*, ed. Charlie Karlsson, 374–92. Cheltenham, UK: Edward Elgar Publishers.

Preface

New Economic Development Strategies and the Search for Talent

The early years of the twenty-first century witnessed the rise of a new philosophy of economic development that portrayed the search for talented and creative workers as a prerequisite to innovation and urban growth within what Allen Scott (2007) called cognitive-cultural capitalism: an economy that increasingly relies on high technology, service industries, and cultural products. The ascendance of creative cities discourse – influenced extensively by the work of Richard Florida (2002) and Charles Landry (2000) – unleashed a global competition for *talent*: the creative and highly skilled workers whose abilities and ideas spark others in this new knowledge economy. With theorists writing volumes about the importance of attracting and retaining talented workers, and governments implementing strategies seeking to turn their communities into talent magnets or creative cities, researchers recognized an opportunity and need to evaluate current conditions to understand the factors that affect the location choices that talented workers make in deciding where to live.

In 2005 David A. Wolfe of the Munk Centre at the University of Toronto assembled a highly respected team of national scholars and an international research advisory board to conduct an ambitious program of research trying to understand the social dynamics of economic performance in Canada. With funding from the Major Collaborative Research Initiatives program at the Social Sciences and Humanities Research Council of Canada and from a range of other sources, the team launched a comprehensive multi-year study of sixteen Canadian cities in eight provinces (Wolfe 2009). This book presents some of the results from one of the project themes: namely, it explores the primary factors and processes that contribute to attracting and retaining talented and creative workers in the Canadian city-regions studied. Although not all the cities examined in the research program are profiled here, the chapters present findings from seven provinces: from Atlantic to Western Canada. The cases feature reports from Canada's largest city – Toronto (Ontario) – and small cities such as Moncton (New Brunswick) and Kingston (Ontario). The chapters illuminate the effects of relative size, relative location, regional economy, lifestyle concerns, and occupational sectors as factors influencing the kinds of choices talented workers make and the features they cite in explaining those choices.

Chapters are organized to offer useful comparisons and contrasts. Part I includes two chapters that offer synthetic summaries of project findings from all of the city-regions studied. In chapter 1, Meric S. Gertler, Kate Geddie, Carolyn Hatch, and Josephine Rekers draw the overall lessons from the research program and relate them to literature in the field to highlight the contribution the Canadian research makes to wider theoretical understandings of talent mobility and to regional economic development policy in cities large or small. Tara Vinodrai, in chapter 2, presents findings from census and other quantitative data to illustrate differences across occupations and among the Canadian city-regions.

Parts II and III present case studies from particular city-regions. The chapters in Part II reflect on the search for the so-called super-creatives: that is, talented workers in the cultural and creative sectors. Several chapters focus on dynamic arts and culture sectors in Toronto, Canada's largest and most diverse city-region. Deborah Leslie, Mia Hunt, and Shauna Brail consider the role that cultural diversity plays in Toronto's ability to attract and retain artists in chapter 3. In chapter 4, Charles Davis, Jeremy Shtern, Michael Coutanche, and Elizabeth Godo explore the social dynamics of innovation among screenwriters based in Toronto. Brian Hracs and Kevin Stolarick turn their attention to Toronto musicians in chapter 5, developing a theoretical model to explain mobility choices. In the final entry in the section, chapter 6, Jill Grant, Jeff Haggett, and Jesse Morton examine the role that isolation plays in mobility choices for musicians in Halifax (Nova Scotia). While the Toronto case suggests that centrality and city size simultaneously enhance and jeopardize creative activities, the Halifax results show some ways that cultural workers may link smaller and more peripheral locations to creative engagement.

Part III includes three chapters that examine the mobility choices made by science and technology workers: talent that in the Canadian context is highly educated and often very well paid. By contrast with talented workers in the creative industries (who tend to cluster in the largest city-regions), high-tech workers locate where the resources and firms that employ people with their skills are situated: city-regions of various sizes offer some degree of employment for these workers, although some industries cluster in particular locations. Sébastien Darchen and Diane-Gabrielle Tremblay in chapter 7 describe the factors that Montreal (Quebec) students in science and technology programs consider as they plan their future career choices and moves. In chapter 8, Peter Phillips and Graeme Webb find mixed results in their assessment of the role of factors like tolerance and social inclusion in making Saskatoon (Saskatchewan) an attractive place for talented workers in the geo-science field. Camille Ryan, Ben Li, and Cooper Langford offer a case study of Calgary (Alberta) in chapter 9: environmental factors and personal and professional networks prove important to making the city-region attractive to the talented energy-sector workers they surveyed. In the various city-regions, science and technology workers seem to place job quality above other considerations and may attribute lesser value to factors such as night life and cultural diversity.

Two chapters in Part IV profile some of Canada's small city-regions. These locations often face special challenges in attracting and retaining creative talent. In chapter 10, Josh Lepawsky, Heather Hall, and Betsy Donald compare the spatial and social conditions operating in St John's (Newfoundland and Labrador) with those in Kingston (Ontario). Kingston simultaneously benefits and suffers from its close proximity to three major cities (Toronto, Montreal, and Ottawa), while St John's is an isolated regional centre. The contrast illuminates the ways in which relative location affects how talented workers think about their choices. Yves Bourgeois documents Moncton (New Brunswick) in chapter 11: an atypical success story of small city growth, Moncton took advantage of its bilingual workforce to establish a unique niche in the knowledge economy.

Part V allows a member of the project's Research Advisory Board (RAB) to comment on the implications of the research findings. Throughout the research program the RAB members – including Phil Cooke, Kevin Morgan, Allen Scott, Bjørn Asheim, Peter Maskell, and others – provided regular feedback on data and interpretations at the network's annual meetings. In chapter 12, Bjørn Asheim considers some of the ways in which the Canadian findings compare with and advance international understandings of the factors that affect the attraction and retention of talented and creative workers: ultimately, he challenges the notion of the "creative city" and urges scholars and policymakers to use the term with caution.

To what extent do the Canadian findings indicate that place matters in attracting and retaining talented and creative workers? Overall, the results suggest that some basic economic realities have not changed despite the popularity of creative cities discourse: workers say they go where they can find appropriate and meaningful jobs or where they can be successful in their creative practices. Places with economic diversity benefit from an abundance of jobs to entice talent; places with social and cultural diversity provide a milieu that appeals to relatively mobile workers in cultural industries. The data presented here indicate that workers value place quality, but also demonstrate that workers find attractive qualities in many kinds of places. Workers in most places and most industries reported good things about their city-regions. Whether they lived in large city-regions or small ones, they often said that their community was "just the right size" and "a good place to raise a family." Overall, the research exposes the kind of spatial and social sorting that goes on within the workforce in a country where the policy environment enables job mobility but the vast geography imposes high costs on labour mobility. Those who have certain kinds of ambitions, and the means to relocate, move to particular kinds of places. The talented folks who are most mobile, with skills in demand in all city-regions, have the greatest ability to sort spatially on lifestyle and amenities: hence, the culture junkies may head to Toronto or Montreal, the entrepreneurial types move to Calgary or Waterloo (Ontario), and the surfers and sailors relocate to Vancouver (British Columbia) or Halifax.

Policymakers have launched pell-mell into efforts to brand their cities as creative. Richard Florida has become famous and wealthy offering guidance to those anxious to attract talent and thereby lure investment. As the research reported here notes, however, communities differ widely in their social, economic, and geographic characteristics and assets. Given the widely divergent circumstances they face, it seems highly unlikely that they can benefit from a single economic development strategy or solution. Contemporary economic conditions and cultural practices favour larger, more diverse urban regions: mid-sized and smaller city-regions need to consider local assets and options pragmatically. Moreover, as Scott (2007) notes, the cognitive cultural economy that creates the context within which talent thrives and becomes the target of government policy interventions simultaneously depends on a growing servile class: low paid, poorly educated, disadvantaged workers who do not enjoy the material benefits of the creative economy. Public policy that ignores the negative externalities of strategies employed to seek talent is unlikely to create long-term social dynamics within city-regions that can produce continual innovation and success.

Jill L. Grant

REFERENCES

Florida, Richard. 2002. *The rise of the creative class and how it's transforming work, leisure, community, and everyday life*. New York: Basic Books.

Landry, Charles. 2000. *The creative city: A toolkit for urban innovators*. London: Earthscan.

Scott, Allen J. 2007. "Capitalism and urbanization in a new key? The cognitive-cultural dimension." *Social Forces* 85 (4): 1465–82. http://dx.doi.org/10.1353/sof.2007.0078.

Wolfe, David A. 2009. *21st century cities in Canada: The geography of innovation*. Ottawa: Conference Board of Canada.

Acknowledgments

A national research project inevitably ends with an army of people and institutions whose contributions merit gratitude. First and foremost, the team acknowledges the vital financial and advisory inputs provided by funding agencies and partners in the research. The primary source of funding for the work came from the Social Sciences and Humanities Research Council of Canada through the Major Collaborative Research Initiatives program #412-2005-1001. Throughout the work SSHRC proved immensely supportive of the team's activities.

In addition we appreciate the support of our research partners: Atlantic Canada Opportunities Agency, Health Technology Exchange, National Research Council, Nova Scotia Economic Development, Ontario ministries of Economic Development and Trade, Research and Innovation, and Economic Development and Innovation, Queen's University, Ryerson University, Simon Fraser University, Statistics Canada, Université Laval, University of Toronto, as well as in-kind support from THECIS in Calgary.

The team's annual meetings (King City, ON, 2006; Vancouver and Bowen Island, 2007; Montreal, 2008; Halifax, 2009; Toronto, 2010) would not have proved productive without the contributions of local organizing groups who helped with logistics, policymakers who participated in the knowledge exchange opportunities of the policy events, and local partners mentioned above who provided additional funding.

Several people played pivotal roles in running the research program. Without the intellectual and administrative leadership of David A. Wolfe none of this research could have happened: he assembled the team, led every stage of the work, and ensured that the team delivered what it promised. Meric Gertler offered intellectual guidance at each step of the project. Deborah Huntley, the project manager, provided excellent organizational skills that kept the team on time, on track, and on budget. These three key individuals were joined on the project management committee by Charles Davis, Jill Grant, Adam Holbrook, and Réjean Landry. At and between the annual meetings, the team received guidance and oversight from the project's Research Advisory Board: Bjørn Asheim, Susan Christopherson, Susan Clarke, Philip Cooke, Hervey Gibson, Gernot Grabher, Anders Malmberg, Peter Maskell, Kevin Morgan, Claire Nauwelaers, Tod Rutherford, and Allen Scott.

Teams in each of the city-regions studied, coordinated, and conducted the case-study work. Many city-region teams involved several junior colleagues and students – too numerous to name – who made invaluable contributions to the work. Some began working on the project as doctoral students, graduated to post-doctoral fellows, and ultimately became colleagues and collaborators along the way.

Without the participation of community members from across the country who donated their time and knowledge to the team in agreeing to sit for interviews or complete surveys, none of this work would have been possible. The team sincerely appreciates their willingness to share their wisdom and experience, and hopes that they find the results of the research useful in their efforts to keep their communities vital and progressive.

Final thanks go to Daniel Quinlan and his team at the University of Toronto Press for believing in the importance of bringing this work to a wider audience and for providing assistance along the way to make it possible.

PART I

Seeking Talent for Innovation

1 Attracting and Retaining Talent: Evidence from Canada's City-Regions

MERIC S. GERTLER, KATE GEDDIE, CAROLYN HATCH, AND JOSEPHINE V. REKERS

Introduction: The Social Foundations of Economic Development

Within the last decade, there has been widespread recognition that intangible assets such as knowledge and creativity are the primary drivers of competitive economic success (Maskell and Malmberg 1999). As creative and science-based industries have become among the most dynamic and propulsive forms of economic activity within city-regions, human capital and its ability to innovate is increasingly viewed as a primary factor shaping the geography of economic activity. The highly educated and creative workers who direct this economic activity tend to be geographically clustered, yet potentially mobile, leading city-regions to seek to attract and retain this talent for their economic growth. The ability, then, to develop "regional talent pools of global significance" suggests that a city-region will be able to construct innovation dynamics to drive and maintain local economic productivity, while also being able to pull in other globally mobile capital (Cooke 2005).

But what attracts and keeps talent in certain places? The argument put forth most colourfully by Florida (2002c), but also supported by others during the past decade, is that the social characteristics of particular places attract these desired workers, and thus serve as critical determinants of local economic growth and prosperity (Gertler et al. 2002; Saxenian 2002; Markusen 2006). Places offering a richness of employment opportunities, a desirable quality of life, a critical mass of cultural activity, and social diversity (that is, low barriers to entry for newcomers) exert the strongest pull.

Given the popularity of this argument within academic and policy circles, the Innovation Systems Research Network (ISRN) critically examined issues regarding the social foundations of talent attraction and retention within the framework of a large collaborative research project that investigated the social dynamics of economic performance in Canadian city-regions (2005–10). This major, multi-year, multi-investigator study was designed to explore three related themes: the social dynamics of innovation, the social foundations of talent attraction and retention, and inclusive communities and civic engagement. As the second major five-year project undertaken by ISRN, it built on the network's earlier research on Canadian industrial clusters and regional innovation systems (2000–5).

The ISRN research involved a team of scholars working in communities across Canada who conducted over 600 interviews with workers, employers, and intermediary organizations, based on a common set of questions regarding employment opportunities and experiences, quality of place dimensions, and community characteristics, such as cultural dynamism, openness and tolerance, social inclusion, and cohesion (see appendix A). The aim was to determine the extent to which workers and firms from different sectors of the cognitive-cultural economy were influenced by various factors. The sample sectors were selected using three criteria: sectors that represent a regional specialization,[1] sectors that are fast-growing, and sectors in which highly knowledge-intensive or creative occupations predominate. Investigators in some city-regions focused on a small number of sectors from which to select participants, while others recruited respondents from across several industries (see table 1.1). Within the team, sixteen city-regions were selected from across the country, representing small (100,000–249,999), mid-sized (250,000–999,999) and large (> 1,000,000) cities, which enabled the project to investigate the impact of city size on the nature and strength of relationships between quality of place and economic performance.

In this introductory chapter we present the major findings from the research conducted on the talent theme. However, rather than summarizing the chapters that follow, we draw overall lessons from the research project and seek to frame the findings within the wider literature. The chapter therefore presents a collective, comparative analysis of the sixteen case studies, and the different localities, sectors, and occupational groups that they represent. As such, it arguably constitutes the most comprehensive contribution to current international debates on the role of creative workers and industries in driving the evolution of urban economies.

The chapter proceeds with a discussion of the literature that has asserted, as well as challenged, the view that social dynamics and quality

Table 1.1 Summary of sample sectors by case-study city-region

Case-study city-region	Sample sectors
Calgary, Alberta	advertising/multimedia; architecture/design; consulting/management; consulting/technical; data/storage management; environmental/engineering; health/technical; labour/construction; legal/financial services; media; oil and gas; public relations; retail/customer service; technical/manufacturing
Halifax, Nova Scotia	built environment consulting: business services; health research: biomedical and higher education; music
Hamilton, Ontario	advanced manufacturing; automotive; health science; steel
Kingston, Ontario	higher education
Kitchener-Waterloo, Ontario	ITC: software engineering, software development, computer programming
London, Ontario	health and medical sciences; ICT: digital gaming and creative media
Moncton, New Brunswick	culinary arts; dance and choreography; film and TV; literary arts; management and legal professions
Montreal, Quebec	fashion; music; video gaming; technology education
Ottawa, Ontario	computer science; engineering
Quebec City, Quebec	knowledge-intensive business services (KIBS)
Saint John, New Brunswick	information technology; oil and gas
Saskatoon, Saskatchewan	biotechnology; software
St John's, Newfoundland and Labrador	arts, media and culture; health; higher education; maritime services
Toronto, Ontario	architecture; biomedical technologies; fashion; film; music
Vancouver, British Columbia	architecture; bio-pharma; computer graphics and imaging; film and video production/post-production; fuel cell technology

of place are crucial determinants of economic competitiveness for city-regions. In the third section, we consider the particularities of the Canadian context, and present a schema that reflects factors found significant for differentiating the economic dynamism across our case sites. We do not, however, develop a general model. Our research concludes that one size most definitely does not fit all. However, we draw from the diversity of results derived in the research to add nuance to an understanding of the social dynamics of economic activity and the multiple pathways to economic competitiveness and prosperity. The fourth section therefore details the role of three particular drivers that intersect with the place-based characteristics of Canadian city-regions to shape local economic prospects. We conclude with general observations on the opportunities and challenges for large, mid-sized, and small city-regions, and reflect on the value of the central concept of talent as well as the public policy implications arising from our analysis.

Recent Debates on Creativity, Talent, and Urban Economies: A Brief Overview

That highly skilled and educated workers contribute to the economic growth of the city-regions in which they live is a widely accepted finding, based on studies that correlate the educational attainment of residents and regional development (Glaeser 2000, 2005b). The positive correlation between human capital and economic growth is further strengthened by the willingness of firms to relocate to places with high concentrations of human capital. Studies by Florida (2002b) and Berry and Glaeser (2005) reinforce such findings by illustrating that high concentrations of talented and skilled individuals positively affect regional growth levels. However, at the heart of current debates lies a question regarding how the locational choices of workers intersect with and reinforce those made by firms. The work puts the spotlight once again on an old but still contentious question in economic geography: do people follow jobs or do jobs follow people?

Four theories predominate in the literature on the characteristics of a place that draw talent, thus shaping geographic distributions of human capital. The first suggests that the geographic concentrations of skilled workers result from individuals pursuing high-quality jobs, or a thick labour market (Bartel 1979; Carlino and Mills 1987; Blanchard and Katz 1992). For example, several studies indicate that mobile talented workers chose to live in particular places because of the employment opportunities available there (Shearmur 2007, 2010; Houston et al. 2008; Hansen and Niedomysl 2009).

By comparison, other scholars contend that amenities affect the location decisions and flows of highly skilled knowledge workers (Roback 1982). For example, Glaeser and colleagues argue that a benign climate and particular urban amenities, such as consumer and personal service industries, good public schools, safety from crime, and strong transportation infrastructure appeal to talented workers and consequently impact location decisions and mobility flows (Glaeser 2005a, 2005b;

Glaeser and Gottlieb 2006). In a similar vein, Clark et al. (2002) claim that the very urban amenities that appeal to tourists – namely, restaurants, museums, galleries, and an attractive built form – also serve to attract and retain mobile knowledge workers. Lloyd and Clark (2001) and Shapiro (2006) also point to the importance of lifestyle quality-of-place characteristics such as entertainment, nightlife, and culture in attracting talent.

A third body of work identifies major research universities as an important determinant of the geography of highly skilled individuals (Florida 2002b; Berry and Glaeser 2005). Wolfe and Gertler (2004), for instance, show that post-secondary institutions play a pivotal role in the development of industry clusters, which in turn attract mobile knowledge workers to a region, thus contributing to producing and attracting human capital. Gertler and Vinodrai (2005) characterize universities as "anchors of creativity" that build social cohesion in communities. Florida et al. (2006) suggest that these institutions foster diversity and tolerance, making the communities in which the universities are located more appealing. Wojan et al. (2007) give particular attention to the ability of university towns to draw artists, suggesting such locales will be broadly attractive to highly artistic individuals. In a study of Waterloo, Ontario, Bramwell et al. (2008) find that firms are attracted to and anchored by the local universities in the region, rather than quality-of-life characteristics. However, the ability of a university to attract individuals and firms does not guarantee that it can hold its talent over the long term (Florida et al. 2006). While some regions with great universities have large concentrations of talent, others operate as producers and exporters of human capital and skilled talent to other regions.

Finally, an important stream of research contends that local levels of tolerance and openness to diversity (in terms of the social characteristics of the population and the economic structure of the region) shape the geography of highly skilled individuals (Jacobs 1961; Beckstead and Brown 2003). For example, some argue that demographic diversity influences talent flows (Ottaviano and Peri 2005), while Florida (2002a, 2002b, 2002c) and others (Noland 2005; Florida and Gates 2003) say that cultures of tolerance attract talent that can contribute to higher rates of innovation and regional development. In other words, the more open a place is to new ideas and new people, the stronger the pull it exerts in the global competition for talent. Florida, Mellander, and Stolarick (2010) suggest that these characteristics of place contribute to economic development by making local resources more productive and efficient, acting through four key mechanisms: low barriers to entry for human capital (Florida, Mellander, and Stolarick 2008; Mellander and Florida 2011); knowledge spillovers and human capital externalities (Lucas 1988; Markusen and Schrock 2006; Currid 2007); signals of openness and meritocracy (Inglehart and Norris 2003; Inglehart and Welzel 2005); and resource mobilization (Florida et al. 2010).

A critical response has been evoked by much of the work on talent-driven economic development, and in particular in response to Florida's (2002c) idea of the creative class (Peck 2005; Scott 2006; Shearmur 2007; Storper and Scott 2009; Delisle and Shearmur 2010). Some question the persuasiveness and rigour of the original empirical work (Markusen 2006), challenging the claim that particular qualities of place such as coolness, openness, and social diversity exert a causal influence on the flows of talent. Others more fundamentally critique the class dimensions underpinning this work, arguing that creative class theory caters to a subset of privileged workers at the expense of others and promotes entrepreneurialism, conservative values, and elite interests in the process (Peck 2005; Markusen 2006; Barnes et al. 2006; McCann 2007; Donegan and Lowe 2008). Peck (2005) argues that ideas at the heart of creative class theory drive urban gentrification and inter-urban competition as cities seek to outbid each other in attracting highly skilled and creative workers. Still others question what they consider to be an overly hasty leap from correlation to causality between the location of highly skilled workers and economic growth (Scott 2006; Storper and Manville 2006; Thomas and Darnton 2006; Wojan et al. 2007; Hansen and Niedomysl 2009).

Others suggest that economic development theories based on the broad concept of talent fail to recognize that workers in particular creative occupations or knowledge-intensive industries weigh their location and career choices differently (Markusen 2006; Beckstead et al. 2008). Storper and Scott (2009) conclude that individuals make locational choices based upon a more complex array of factors than the talent-based research suggests. Likewise, recent European studies show only mixed support for the proposition (Hansen and Niedomysl 2009; Asheim and Hansen 2009; Boschma and Fritsch 2009), raising uncertainty about causality and the application of the theory within divergent national contexts and urban systems. The work emphasizes the importance of national variations in economic and social structures and of institutions in shaping the primary relationships of interest (Clifton 2008; Asheim 2009; Asheim and Hansen 2009; Andersen et al. 2010).

Other questions focus on the relevance of "Florida factors" in mid-size and smaller city-regions, the kinds of places that have not attracted the same degree of attention from scholars to this point. Gertler (2001) initially explores the idea of the creative city in the Canadian context, looking at changes in the flow of people, capital, and ideas over time: the research highlights the increasing trend towards income polarization and chronic spaces of exclusion within large Canadian urban centres, phenomena which have the potential to undermine the social characteristics that support a region's economic prosperity. Donald and Morrow (2003) examine the intersection of Florida's talent model and implications for broader social and economic policy in Canada. Gertler et al. (2002) analytically apply the creative city thesis to the Ontario context. Slack et al. (2003) emphasize the importance of the city-region to economic and regional development in Ontario, highlighting many social and economic challenges faced by the province. Further research reveals that, despite persistent efforts, not all locations in the country will necessarily succeed in pursuing talent and amenity-based objectives; in some cases, communities have encountered significant obstacles in developing deep labour markets. For example, Polèse and Shearmur (2006) find that for peripheral regions in Canada, the prospects for sharing in the benefits from interregional and international migration are limited. Many such urban areas are struggling to contend with the loss of home-grown talent to other regions of Canada, as well as the inability to attract and retain well-educated migrants from other regions or countries. Thus, the question of city size and relative location remains central to these debates.

Although recent contributions add significant nuance to theories around talent and urban economic development, one question remains particularly important in the Canadian context: what evidence is there that mid-sized and smaller urban regions demonstrate the same hypothesized relationships between quality of place and economic performance?

Canadian Case-Study Distinctiveness and Drivers for Economic Prosperity: A Schema

Factors such as quality of place are now commonly used by scholars and policymakers to explain a city-region's ability to attract and retain talent, but can we expect these factors to produce the same effects in different types of cities and for different kinds of talent? It stands to reason that the factors and relationships shaping the economic vitality

Figure 1.1 Emerging themes from case studies of Canadian cities

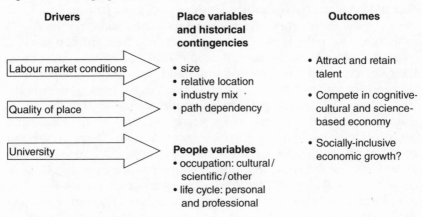

of city-regions are likely to be articulated differently under locally unique sets of conditions. As the Canadian urban system is extraordinarily diverse, it provides a wide variety of sites in which to consider the place-specific nature of these dynamics, and to question the differential ability for city-regions to generate and attract human capital and economic enterprise. Figure 1.1 represents the factors and issues discussed as significant for shaping the economic prospects within the sixteen case-study sites considered in this research project.

Canada is an exceptionally large country whose regions vary greatly in terms of physical environment, climate, history, and local culture. This variation also carries through to city-region diversity within the Canadian urban system. Three differentiating characteristics of Canadian city-regions shape their ability to develop into nodal centres of the cultural-cognitive economy: a city-region's relative location, its economic base, and its demographic structure.

Beginning with relative location, we note that the 5000 kilometres from Vancouver to St John's naturally creates a context wherein certain city-regions are more remote or accessible than others. For example, while Saskatoon and Kingston are of comparable size, Kingston's proximity to other cities in the Quebec City–Windsor corridor affords it a stronger connection to the wider urban system. Lepawsky and colleagues suggest (this volume) that the attractiveness of a place for individual workers and firms must be understood in the context of how a city's relative location influences the flows of people and financial capital. Places deemed better connected, or having place-luck due to their convenient proximity to other major cities, historically have benefitted from logistical advantages, infrastructure, and investments made by multinational firms.

Second, Canadian cities differ significantly according to their local economic base. Certain cities, such as St John's, Calgary, and Vancouver, have a history in staples industries. By contrast, Hamilton, London, Kitchener-Waterloo, Montreal, and Toronto have a base in manufacturing, while Halifax, Kingston, and Ottawa share an industrial past rooted in public- and private-sector services. In other words, the city-regions do not begin from the same starting point in terms of the industrial landscape. The different economic bases and the corresponding skill set of local labour shape each city's economic development opportunities and trajectories. For example, Calgary's finance, management, and business service industries have developed to complement the oil and gas industry. The industrial base also influenced the existing urban landscape, which can provide fertile spaces for emerging industries, such as the old downtown factory and warehouse spaces in cities such as Toronto, Hamilton, and Montreal that now provide a sought-after built environment for artists and cultural industries. However, the existing industrial base, with its attendant infrastructure, does not necessarily provide a supportive context for a smooth transition towards new economic activity. We see this challenge illustrated in Trois-Rivières, where the local material and intellectual infrastructure is oriented towards mature metal and pulp and paper production; consequently, the city-region does not provide adequate support for the emerging high-technology sectors of hydrogen and electro-technologies.

Third, Canadian city-regions vary in their historical population dynamics. Vancouver experienced growth through the influx of business immigrants from Asia in the 1990s, linking the region to the markets and societies across the Pacific, whereas Calgary doubled in population between 1981 and 2006 due to domestic in-migration. Moncton was one of Canada's fastest growing cities in 2001–6 as members of rural francophone communities in New Brunswick migrated to the city, while the population in Saint John decreased due to domestic out-migration in the same period. In Halifax and London, the age-specific nature of interprovincial migration shaped the labour force and local culture, with an increase of 20- to 29-year-olds in Halifax, versus the net out-migration of young adults in London. These demographic changes lead to different priorities for local governments, and also help to produce and reproduce distinct regional cultures, such as Calgary's strong entrepreneurial spirit and maverick character, Halifax's distinct laid-back pace of life, and Montreal's French language and culture. These cultural dimensions contribute to the kinds of amenities and the characteristics of the local labour market available to potential firms and other economic actors, and shape economic development trajectories.

Building on these place-specific characteristics and historical contingencies and the bases that they provide for a city-region's potential to emerge as a strong centre of cognitive-cultural economic activity, we also note important differences within the concept of talent or the types of people that cities are seeking to attract. For instance, we know that people are attracted to cities for different reasons. What we term people variables – such as occupation and stage of life – intersect with the types of labour market conditions and qualities of a place that render it appealing and more likely to attract certain kinds of highly skilled or creative workers. For example, we know that people working in cultural industries tend to prioritize a different set of urban amenities than those employed in science-based sectors.

In the following section we explore how these diverse city-region variables – namely, the relative location, existing industry mix, demographics, city size, as well as different occupational dynamics, career, and life stages of the desired workers – intersect with key drivers of economic vitality and innovation. The three drivers we consider are local labour market conditions, quality of place, and local universities for shaping the capacity of particular places to attract and retain highly educated and creative labour.

Labour Market Conditions: Three Key Dimensions

Across the cases in this research, we find that three dimensions of local labour market conditions underpin a city-region's ability to attract and retain highly educated and creative labour. The first and most often cited consideration is the availability of work opportunities *within* a particular local sector. An urban economy's industrial specialization in one or more closely related industries is commonly linked to the concept of Marshallian dynamics in the urban growth literature (Marshall 1890), in which distinctive local assets and an established presence in a particular industry foster further growth and dynamism in the industry.

Our research shows that breadth and depth of employment opportunities within a given field attract specialized labour. Workers are drawn by the potential for learning and advancement, as well as access to cutting-edge work in their respective fields. For example, Phillips and Webb (this volume; forthcoming) report that biotechnology workers are drawn to Saskatoon because of the range of advanced jobs available in their field. Likewise, Hracs and Stolarick (this volume) find that abundant satisfying work opportunities play a fundamental role in attracting musicians to Toronto. In the Toronto architecture industry, designers are drawn to the city because the sheer density of job opportunities offers considerable scope to advance careers, as architects move between firms to acquire new skills, experience, and contacts (Gertler and Geddie 2008). Similarly, a range of potential work opportunities enables workers to manage the risk associated with periods of unemployment in a chronically cyclical industry, and to improve their pay or working conditions.[2] And a critical mass of firms within the same city neighbourhood fosters the development of collaborative dynamics between companies. Such collaborative engagement not only is a fundamental aspect of project-based work that drives creativity and innovation, but also heightens the general buzz of the industry through the development of local cluster dynamics. This collaborative dynamic further enhances the ability of the city to attract and retain talented labour.

A second dimension of a local labour market that influences the pull and retention of workers is the range and depth of work opportunities *across* sectors. In contrast to the Marshallian effects of industrial specialization, these conditions derive from a diverse and variegated urban economy – commonly referred to as Jacobs dynamics – that present obvious advantages to both firms and workers (Jacobs 1970). The possibility for creative workers to apply standard knowledge from one sector to solve problems or develop new products in another sector helps drive local innovation and economic growth. The availability of talent with experience in other sectors can be of fundamental value in encouraging creativity and enhancing competitive advantage for firms. An abundance of employment opportunities across a range of local industries offers a rich array of potential work experiences as well as some greater insulation from economic downturns for workers.

Leslie and Brail (2009) report that many designers in the Toronto fashion industry also work in film, art, dance, theatre, and costume design. The economic diversity in the local labour market is of paramount benefit to workers in fashion, as Toronto is a hub for so many creative industries. Similarly, designers and programmers in the animation studios in Vancouver and Montreal routinely find work in the electronic games sectors of those same cities (Rantisi and Leslie 2006; Barnes and Hutton

2009). The ability to move fluidly *between* design-related industries and professions enables individual workers to mediate risk, particularly during periods of economic instability. Bourgeois (this volume) notes that in smaller cities such as Moncton, the chance for artists to make a full-time living practising their art in a single artistic field is limited. Therefore, creative workers are impelled to collaborate with artists outside their immediate realm, accelerating the cross-fertilization of ideas.

Third, research from the case studies reveals that temporal dynamics and opportunities for *upward* career mobility shape talent attraction and retention in Canadian city-regions. A local critical mass of employment enhances anticipated future opportunities and a succession of jobs along a career ladder. Findings from several cases suggest that this dimension is often missing in the labour market of small and mid-sized Canadian cities. For example, dancers and choreographers report having to leave Moncton in order to master their field (Bourgeois this volume). Grant and colleagues (this volume) find that Halifax cannot always provide the array of opportunities and infrastructure that musicians might need in order to advance their careers in the industry. And Bradford (2009) notes that in London, the head-office flight of the 1990s reduced prospects for career mobility and availability of senior positions in that city. One research participant in the London study remarks: "There is an innate suspicion of anyone who is successful in London. The attitude is – if you're so good, why aren't you in Toronto?" (Bradford and Ward 2009, 22).

While shallower labour markets in smaller urban regions may not offer the same degree of career mobility found in larger cities in Canada, the case studies reveal that smaller cities can serve an essential function as career incubators. Research shows that narrower labour markets in smaller places offer opportunities to develop wider competencies in given fields, as noted by one interviewee in Moncton who remarked that "small town law firms make you practice every kind of law there is, while big city law firms can require hyper-specialization in a particular field" (Bourgeois 2009, 9). Moreover, the labour market conditions in smaller centres may afford better chances for collaboration, as less entrenched hierarchies can encourage greater creative and artistic freedom. Science-based workers in London appreciate opportunities that are not necessarily available to them in larger cities, promoting one worker to comment that "if I was in Montreal, Toronto or Vancouver, I could not work as I do because they require a PharmaD. The shortage in London creates opportunity for me" (Bradford and Ward 2009, 22). In the St John's music industry, the city is identified as a launching pad to prepare home-grown talent for opportunities in larger centres. Halifax provides a similar incubation function for local musicians and bands, although those hoping to "make it big" might eventually have to relocate to a larger city with more venues and a deeper music industry infrastructure (Grant and Kronstal 2010).

Quality of Place: Personal and Professional Dimensions

Our findings draw attention to four main points. First, the right kind of available job represents an important consideration affecting where highly educated and creative workers choose to live and work, but quality-of-place factors play a complementary role in shaping the mobility of talent. Second, as critics of creative class theory have pointed out, the prevailing literature on talent-based economic development has focused on a fairly narrow set of amenities that reflects middle-class consumption (Peck 2005) and is biased towards large cities. Our work calls for a broader conceptualization of quality-of-place factors and liveability, as well as a more nuanced understanding of the dynamics relevant to smaller cities. Third, the quality of place is often approached and understood by workers through the lens of their professional lives. Because employer and worker roles are frequently blurred in cultural industries, creative talent tends to merge personal and professional quality-of-place concerns. And fourth, evidence from the study points to the overwhelmingly variegated, complex, and subjective nature of regional expectations and preferences. For that reason, variability both in place characteristics such as relative location, city size, and sectoral composition, and in people characteristics – namely, occupational differences, life cycle, and career stage – require careful consideration.

Employees interviewed in the case studies indicate that liveability attributes shape their settlement and career location preferences. In Saskatoon, affordable living is cited as a complementary asset that draws and retains workers in the city's globally competitive biotechnology industry (Phillips and Webb this volume and forthcoming; Phillips et al. 2009). Likewise, smaller, peripheral places like Halifax may generate opportunities for creativity and affordable living that attract musicians (Grant et al. this volume). In London, liveability and lifestyle factors are highlighted by interviewees who discuss the community in light of its affordability, short commute times, good public schools, and sense of personal safety; many endorse it as a good place to raise a family. One recruiter for a local firm asserts: "We use good quality of life to sell London to workers we are trying to recruit who have families. It's a very stable city" (Bradford and Ward 2009, 22). These examples show that although smaller urban settings cannot necessarily compete on big city buzz factors, issues of lifestyle and liveability can play a prominent role. This supports Vinodrai's claim (this volume) that quality-of-place characteristics vary substantially by city size: a broader understanding of liveability is therefore important to analysing talent attraction and retention in smaller cities.

In large part because the personal and professional lives of creatives are difficult to disentangle, the various kinds of scenes, *milieux*, and networks that are fostered in particular places render an environment appealing for these workers. Interviewees in Montreal emphasize that the city's urban form contributes to a strong quality of life due to pedestrian-friendly urban form, short commutes, social interaction, and a sense of community: especially the compact and mixed-use neighbourhoods of Mile End and the Plateau. Rantisi and Leslie (2008) show that the arts and cultural scene is appreciated for its role in fostering impromptu encounters, social networking, and exchange, and driving the creative process. This is also evident in the Toronto fashion industry and film and video production in Vancouver. Dense, mixed-use neighbourhoods facilitate the development of networks that enable designers and other creative workers to attain resources, knowledge, and the word-of-mouth promotion that they require; these tight-knit communities facilitate informal or barter systems of exchange.

In distinction to the role of urban form in facilitating social networking that underpins the creative process, another quality-of-place feature related to affordability is found to be crucial in attracting talent in Montreal. The city's relatively low rents make it possible for designers to afford their own studios or larger live/work spaces and therefore to position themselves to take greater risks in the creative process. These examples suggest that the personal and professional are often inextricably linked in creative professions, thereby influencing quality-of-place preferences for cultural workers.

Another aspect of quality of place highlighted by workers and firms is the presence of a strong regional culture that shapes local business practices. For example, Phillips and Webb (forthcoming) indicate that Saskatoon's environment of informal connections based in social norms may facilitate knowledge transfer and willingness to assist other firms and individuals. There is a widely shared perception in Saskatoon that farmers come together to help one another achieve what they would be unable to do on their own: the classic example (and oft-used metaphor) being a "barn raising." Likewise in Calgary, Ryan and colleagues (this volume) report that "people are pretty open and honest" and that trust creates a foundation for "deals that get done with a handshake." Many Calgary interviewees note the presence of a "maverick culture" and a "let's just do it" attitude among the business community that encourages a highly entrepreneurial spirit.

Research from the case studies indicates that ethnic and cultural diversity not only attracts and retains talent for reasons relating to personal affinity or *consumption* opportunities. Social diversity also provides important benefits from a *production* perspective, particularly as a valuable source of ideas and skills. In this volume, Leslie and colleagues suggest that Toronto's multicultural diversity and cosmopolitanism provide an array of consumption choices for artists and contribute positively to overall quality of life. They find that these characteristics constitute a rich source of artistic inspiration, fostering a multifaceted local creative ecology. Likewise, research on Toronto's fashion industry shows that ethnic diversity not only exerts an attractive pull on design talent, it is a source of valuable skills, as specialized talent like pattern-makers can be found in the local labour market. In a related vein, for cultural and creative workers in Montreal, Rantisi (2009) and Rantisi and Leslie (2008) find that social factors such as bilingualism and cultural diversity are appreciated not only because of the cultural institutions and establishments to which they give rise, but for the ways in which they motivate and inspire the creative process.

Case studies reveal the overwhelmingly varied nature of regional preferences as expressed by workers in different sectors and occupational categories of the creative economy. In Saskatoon, for example, high-technology workers are drawn and retained by professional and commercial aspects of place, namely, salary, cutting-edge work, and affordable living. Similarly, workers in the city's biotechnology sector placed emphasis on career opportunities and reputation of the firm (Phillips and Webb forthcoming). This resonates with research by Vinodrai (this volume), who finds that natural and applied scientists select location based primarily on the quality of the local innovation system rather than other urban characteristics. In our research in Toronto's biotechnology sector we note that workers discussed how much they enjoyed getting out of the city when occasion allowed, as expressed by one star scientist who told us, "The only way I tolerate the city is by going up north to the lakes – we have a cottage up there" (interviews). This complements findings by Darchen and Tremblay (this volume), who contend that science and technology students in Montreal would rather live in the suburbs. By contrast, Vinodrai shows that arts and cultural professionals prefer the city centre; they demonstrate preferences related to vibrant arts and cultural scenes and places that convey openness and diversity (see also Davis et al., and Hracs and Stolarick this volume). Grant and colleagues (this volume) argue that structural changes in the music industry render small cities and more remote locations desirable to one particular occupational class: musicians.

Finally, our research shows that an additional lens through which to understand the social dynamics of talent attraction and retention is that of individual life cycle and career stage. Hracs and Stolarick (this volume) suggest that individuals' expectations evolve over time and are shaped by life cycle, career stage, and lived experience. The importance of family-friendly characteristics such as affordability and a strong public school system, particularly for interviewees in some of the smaller cities in Canada, constitutes one of the most consistent findings regarding quality of place. One recruiter in Kitchener-Waterloo asserts: "If we marry them to a job first, they will then marry a local girl and have kids, then they will end up being married to the region" (Bathelt et al. 2009, 9). Such comments reflect a focused perception of the types of workers considered the target of talent attraction efforts in the region; invoking gender and social reproduction, the respondent quoted suggests that individuals at certain life stages may favour particular places characteristics over others, but these change as personal life circumstances change.

Universities and Local Innovation Systems

Universities emerge as key elements of the local innovation system and major players in attracting and retaining talent, though the particular form of their contribution varies widely among cities. In this section, we outline four roles – discussed in terms of opportunities and limitations – that universities play in terms of their ability to generate, attract, and retain desired talent in a local region.

The first and most frequently cited role is the interaction between universities and local firms to develop a dynamic industrial cluster that serves to retain local graduates and attract talent from elsewhere. Phillips and Webb (forthcoming) show that biotechnology firms in Saskatoon deliberately locate close to the University of Saskatchewan or the nearby research park, Innovation Place, to benefit from knowledge spillovers from research activities. Similarly, interviews with employers and workers in Toronto's biomedical industry underscore the benefit of proximity to the University of Toronto and the cluster of teaching hospitals in the Discovery District. Given the tendency of innovators to occupy dual roles simultaneously – where graduate students, post-doctoral fellows, or professors are also entrepreneurs – locations close to these institutions are of obvious strategic value. One worker notes: "Being downtown where all the hospitals are really helps us to think about the research and the technologies that we're trying to develop. Dealing with clinicians, nurses, doctors, patients on almost a daily basis, a big driving force behind my research is having that clinical component. No other university has eight affiliated teaching hospitals" (Gertler, Vinodrai, and Rekers 2008).

In contrast, several case studies indicate that local educational institutions can underperform or fail to meet expectations in providing support within the regional economy. Bradford and Ward (2009) point out that the universities and health research centres in London remain disconnected from local firms. For instance, interviewees from green manufacturing companies lament that academic and public research organizations have little to offer, being too slow, difficult to deal with, and asking too much in return to justify the effort. The few examples of successful commercialization and spin-offs that have resulted from local university–industry interactions in Kingston suggest that Queen's University is only weakly connected to the surrounding region (Hall and Donald 2009). Despite a concerted effort on the part of universities in Trois-Rivières to engage in research and technology transfer, the region remains "locked into" traditional sectors of pulp and paper and metal transformations (Trépanier et al. 2009).

The second crucial role for universities is their ability to generate talent for the local labour force, which can constitute a vital source of recruitment for local firms. In the Waterloo region, Bathelt et al. (2009, 13) identify the University of Waterloo and Wilfrid Laurier University as key suppliers of talent to local firms, with "this connection reinforced through the cooperative education programs that have been viewed as pillars of the UW success story." Similar examples of institutions providing a fundamental labour force contribution are evident in Toronto's architecture sector (Gertler and Geddie 2008) and Saskatoon's biotechnology industry (Phillips and Webb forthcoming). Research in Vancouver shows that public and private educational institutions contribute significantly to the support of the gaming, new media, film, and television production industries through the development of the local labour force (Barnes and Hutton 2009).

Third, universities are recognized as sources of new talent to a region. By bringing in young adults (albeit often for a period limited to the duration of their studies) and employing experienced administration and academic professionals, they serve as local portals to national and international labour markets. Research in Halifax and Kitchener-Waterloo emphasizes the important role that well-regarded universities play in attracting students and faculty, both national and internationally (Grant 2009; Bathelt et al. 2009). In Ottawa, funded programs draw graduate students in computer science, information technology, and software engineering (Andrew et al. 2009). However not all regions succeed in retaining students after graduation, a trend identified by interviewees in Kingston and London. For example, the president of the University of Western Ontario laments that the university is too often a "pass through," with 85 per cent of students not originally from London leaving after completing their studies (Bradford 2009, 9).

Finally, case-study research reveals that universities play a role to create vibrant and tolerant communities. The influx of international students in Kitchener-Waterloo, for instance, helps to foster a dynamic local market in specialty foods, products, and services, and the presence of vibrant local ethnic communities encourages these students to remain after graduation (Bathelt et al. 2009). In Halifax, the student population supports nightlife and nurtures the local music industry: employers in other sectors recognize the role that a vibrant music scene plays in enhancing quality of life in the region, helping companies to attract and retain workers in various sectors (Grant and Kronstal 2010).

Concluding Reflections: One Size Does Not Fit All

Evidence from the case studies reveals the complex and multifaceted nature of talent attraction and retention dynamics that shape the economic competitiveness and prosperity of Canadian city-regions. While the recent literature has largely framed the central debate as a polarized discussion of jobs versus quality-of-place amenities, we find distinct variations across occupations and sectors. The research reported here shows that highly educated workers in science and technology are drawn to particular places overwhelmingly for economic and professional opportunities. Moreover, it is not simply the presence of an immediate job that is the primary motivating factor, as these individuals tend to adopt a longer-term *career* perspective that includes the possibility of enjoying a range of employment opportunities and advancing up the career ladder. Yet, although the right kinds of jobs and potential career trajectories constitute important motivating factors for workers in these sectors, they may not be sufficient.

The pattern for creative workers in cultural industries is even less clear. On the one hand, several cases find that this particular subset of highly educated and creative talent is similarly motivated by the economic opportunities and commercial aspects of place. Creative workers come to and stay in Montreal for the low rents, while musicians and architects head to Toronto for the density of jobs and sheer scope of opportunities. The ability to use skills and learn across multiple creative sectors attracts design talent to Montreal and Toronto, and software and gaming talent to Montreal and Vancouver. On the other hand, the research also highlights that highly artistic and creative individuals are motivated by factors seemingly unrelated to economic rationale. Cultural workers in Montreal, for instance, appreciate the urban form of certain neighbourhoods that facilitates networking, idea sharing, and close communities. Artists and designers value Toronto's cosmopolitanism and ethnic diversity. Musicians are drawn to and stay in Halifax not merely for the jobs, but also for the supportive audiences, distinctive scenes, and strong identity of place. These characteristics are more about nurturing and inspiring the creative process, and creating a foundation upon which experimentation and creativity may thrive.

A second question explored was whether the relationship between quality of place and economic performance can be found in mid-sized and smaller urban regions in Canada. Findings reveal important variations in the opportunities and challenges associated with city size and labour market concerns of workers and firms. Not surprisingly, the largest cities in Canada offer the greatest range of career opportunities for workers in many sectors of the economy. This valued depth of the labour market may insulate workers from job loss because it offers a larger number of employment opportunities within a field, as well as the opportunity to advance upwards along a career ladder, or to cross over into complementary fields. The trajectory for smaller cities, however, is perhaps somewhat less obvious. In some cases, dynamic labour markets and internationally recognized industries in smaller places exert an attractive pull on globally mobile talent. Such is the case for biotechnology workers who come to and stay in Saskatoon, and high-technology talent who choose to live in Kitchener-Waterloo. These workers are attracted to smaller communities by the availability of cutting-edge jobs in their fields and the quality of the local innovation systems. Yet other examples show that qualitatively different features – namely, the social and physical characteristics of place – constitute the more attractive force for some categories of workers. The relative smallness of St John's can enhance the ability to facilitate strong social networks that may mitigate the risk of job loss and help overcome the precarious boom-bust nature of some highly creative professions (Lepawsky et al. this volume; Greenwood 2009). In Halifax, musicians are drawn by the collaborative community, supportive audiences, and place-specific identity that renders music produced there valuable in export markets. For workers in London, family-friendliness, lifestyle, and liveability attributes are most highly valued. These findings may therefore challenge our starting assumption that city size matters, since highly skilled creative workers are shown to live and work in cities of varying sizes throughout Canada.

What then remains of the central concepts and thesis that motivated the larger study in the first place? What do our collective findings have to say about the legitimacy of the core concepts of talent and creative class and the forces that shape the evolving geography of economic activity and workers in the cognitive cultural economy? First, it is clear that the concepts of talent and creative class require much more systematic unpacking if they are to retain any kind of analytical value. Highly educated and creative workers in different occupations and sectors display widely divergent behaviours influenced by different sets of factors. This makes it impossible to generalize across all forms of creative labour as we try to understand the forces that motivate decisions about where to live and work. Even within each of the subsets of talent types, life-cycle considerations and stage of career have been shown to alter the priorities of creative workers as they contemplate locational decisions.

Second, in reviewing the large number of diverse cases incorporated within this national study, it becomes clear that we have documented a sorting process through which different kinds of talented or creative labour express preferences for different locational choices and, where possible, vote with their feet. Some people prefer the bright lights, cultural buzz, high densities, and social diversity of the big city, while others prefer affordable living spaces, access to recreational spaces, safety, and family-friendly environments, trading off some excitement for access to high-quality research infrastructure. Some crave the wide array of career opportunities available only in the largest, deepest, and most competitive local labour markets, while others opt for the security offered by nearby family and friends and the quiet life. Once we open up the scope of empirical enquiry to include a much broader range of places, the results of the locational sorting process become immediately evident. This insight has important implications of a methodological nature, as it reminds us of the potential influence of survivor bias in shaping the results of our analysis. Because of the sorting and self-selection dynamics described above, particular places will tend to produce and reproduce over time the labour force profile that "fits" their distinctive characteristics, defined in terms of both quality-of-place assets and economic structure. Presumably the types of creative workers who don't fit the local environment will self-select out by choosing to live and work elsewhere. Hence, those remaining in a particular city-region are likely to sing its praises, while those who have left out of frustration or in pursuit of other qualities of place elsewhere are no longer available to be interviewed locally.

Policymakers can draw important lessons from these findings. The case studies reveal that different pathways are possible for city-regions aspiring to participate in the cognitive cultural economy. Yet policymakers need to consider the significant variation among *place* characteristics (such as city size, relative location, industrial structure, and socio-political history) and *people* characteristics (particularly occupational mix and demographic composition of the local labour market). Our research concludes that there is no single course for regional economic development; consequently, practitioners should be cautious about adopting a one-size-fits-all approach. Policy strategists are advised to accentuate and build on the particular inherited assets of their respective regions and pay close attention to local context and variety – in other words, place and people characteristics. Such an approach entails tailoring strategies for future economic prosperity that build on a given community's historical and geographical particularities, while remaining sensitive to the ways in which regional preferences of the local labour market evolve and are shaped over time. The longitudinal, career-based perspective on the factors shaping the mobility of highly educated and creative workers underscores the importance of pursuing opportunities and policy approaches that build on an urban region's strengths, rather than imitating generic and possibly inappropriate policy initiatives from elsewhere.

NOTES

1 Specialization was determined on the basis of a location quotient greater than one for both employment and number of establishments in the sector.
2 Our observations reflect interviews conducted with architects and other creative workers in Toronto.

REFERENCES

Andersen, Kristina, Hogni Kalsø Hansen, Arne Isaksen, and Mike Raunio. 2010. "Nordic city regions in the creative class debate: Putting the creative class theory to a test." *Industry and Innovation* 17 (2): 215–40. http://dx.doi.org/10.1080/13662711003633496.

Andrew, Caroline, David Doloreux, Daniela Defazio, and Cumhur Gülel. 2009. ISRN integrative paper: Ottawa case study. ISRN Integrative Workshop, Toronto, 2–4 November.

Asheim, Bjørn. 2009. "Guest editorial: Introduction to the creative class in European city regions." *Economic Geography* 85 (4): 355–62. http://dx.doi.org/10.1111/j.1944-8287.2009.01046.x.

Asheim, Bjørn, and Hogni Kalsø Hansen. 2009. "Knowledge bases, talents, and contexts: On the usefulness of the creative class approach in Sweden." *Economic Geography* 85 (4): 425–42. http://dx.doi.org/10.1111/j.1944-8287.2009.01051.x.

Barnes, Kendall, Gordon Waitt, Nicholas Gill, and Chris Gibson. 2006. "Community and nostalgia in urban revitalisation: A critique of urban village and creative class strategies as remedies for social 'problems.'" *Australian Geographer* 37 (3): 335–54. http://dx.doi.org/10.1080/00049180600954773.

Barnes, Trevor, and Tom Hutton. 2009. "Situating the new economy: Contingencies of regeneration and dislocation in Vancouver's inner city." *Urban Studies* (Edinburgh, Scotland) 46 (5–6): 1247–69. http://dx.doi.org/10.1177/0042098009103863.

Bartel, Ann P. 1979. "The migration decision: What role does job mobility play?" *American Economic Review* 69: 775–86.

Bathelt, Harald, Andrew Munro, Jen Nelles, Tara Vinodrai, and David Wolfe. 2009. ISRN integrative paper: Kitchener-Waterloo case study. ISRN Integrative Workshop, Toronto, 2–4 November.

Beckstead, Desmond, W. Mark Brown, and Guy Gellatly. 2008. "The left brain of North American cities: Scientists and engineers and urban growth." *International Regional Science Review* 31 (3): 304–38. http://dx.doi.org/10.1177/0160017608318521.

Beckstead, Desmond, and W. Mark Brown. 2003. *From Labrador City to Toronto: The industrial diversity of Canadian cities 1992–2002.* http://dsp-psd.pwgsc.gc.ca/Collection/Statcan/11-624-M/11-624-MIE2003003.pdf.

Berry, Christopher R., and Edward L. Glaeser. 2005. "The divergence of human capital levels across cities." *Regional Science* 84 (3): 407–44.

Blanchard, Olivier, and Lawrence Katz. 1992. "Regional evolutions." *Brookings Papers on Economic Activity* 1992 (1): 1–75. http://dx.doi.org/10.2307/2534556.

Boschma, Ron, and Michael Fritsch. 2009. "Creative class and regional growth: Empirical evidence from seven European countries." *Economic Geography* 85 (4): 391–423. http://dx.doi.org/10.1111/j.1944-8287.2009.01048.x.

Bourgeois, Yves. 2009. ISRN integrative paper: Moncton case study. ISRN Integrative Workshop, Toronto, 2–4 November.

Bradford, Neil. 2009. ISRN integrative paper: London case study. ISRN Integrative Workshop, Toronto, 2–4 November.

Bradford, Neil, and Kadie Ward. 2009. "Social foundations of talent attraction and retention in London." Presented at the ISRN annual meeting, Halifax, 29 April–1 May. http://www.utoronto.ca/isrn/publications/NatMeeting /NatSlides/Nat09/slides/Bradford_Ward%20Tal_Attraction_Retention_ London.pdf.

Bramwell, Alison, Jen Nelles, and David Wolfe. 2008. "Knowledge, innovation and institutions: Global and local dimensions of the ICT cluster in Waterloo, Canada." *Regional Studies* 42 (1): 101–16. http://dx.doi.org/10.1080 /00343400701543231.

Carlino, Gerald, and Edwin Mills. 1987. "The determinants of county growth." *Journal of Regional Science* 27 (1): 39–54. http://dx.doi. org/10.1111/j.1467-9787.1987.tb01143.x. Medline:12268789.

Clark, Terry N., Richard Lloyd, Kenneth K. Wong, and Pushpam Jain. 2002. "Amenities drive urban growth." *Journal of Urban Affairs* 24 (5): 493–515. http://dx.doi.org/10.1111/1467-9906.00134.

Clifton, Nick. 2008. "The 'creative class' in the UK: An initial analysis." *Geografiska Annaler. Series B, Human Geography* 90 (1): 63–82. http://dx.doi.org /10.1111/j.1468-0467.2008.00276.x.

Cooke, Phillip. 2005. "Regional innovation, entrepreneurship and talent systems." *International Journal of Entrepreneurship and Innovation* 7 (2–5): 117–39.

Currid, Elizabeth. 2007. *The Warhol economy: How fashion, art and music drive New York City.* Princeton, Oxford: Princeton University Press.

Delisle, Françoise, and Richard Shearmur. 2010. "Where does all the talent flow? Migration of young graduates and nongraduates, Canada 1996–2001." *Canadian Geographer* 54 (3): 305–23. http://dx.doi.org/10.1111/j.1541-0064 .2009.00276.x.

Donald, Betsy, and Douglas Morrow. 2003. *Competing for talent: Implications for social and cultural policy in Canadian city-regions.* Ottawa: Strategic Research and Analysis, Canadian Heritage.

Donegan, Mary, and Nichola Lowe. 2008. "Inequality in the creative city: Is there still a place for 'old-fashioned' institutions?" *Economic Development Quarterly* 22 (1): 46–62. http://dx.doi.org/10.1177/0891242407310722.

Florida, Richard. 2002a. "Bohemia and economic geography." *Journal of Economic Geography* 2 (1): 55–71. http://dx.doi.org/10.1093/jeg/2.1.55.

Florida, Richard. 2002b. "The economic geography of talent." *Annals of the Association of American Geographers* 92 (4): 743–55. http://dx.doi.org/10.1111/1467 -8306.00314.

Florida, Richard. 2002c. *The rise of the creative class.* New York: Basic Books.

Florida, Richard, and Gary Gates. 2003. "Technology and tolerance: The importance of diversity to high-technology growth." In *The city as an entertainment machine: Research in urban policy*, vol. 9, ed. T.N. Clark, 199–219. Oxford: Elsevier. http://dx.doi.org/10.1016/S1479-3520(03)09007-X.

Florida, Richard, Gary Gates, Brian Knudsen, and Kevin Stolarick. 2006. *The university and the creative economy.* http://www.creativeclass.com/creative _class/2006/11/27/university-and-the-creative-economy/.

Florida, Richard, Charlotta Mellander, and Kevin Stolarick. 2008. "Inside the black box of regional development – human capital, the creative class and tolerance." *Journal of Economic Geography* 8 (5): 615–49. http://dx.doi.org /10.1093/jeg/lbn023.

Florida, Richard, Charlotta Mellander, and Kevin Stolarick. 2010. "Talent, technology and tolerance in Canadian regional development." *Canadian Geographer* 54 (3): 277–304. http://dx.doi.org/10.1111/j.1541-0064.2009.00293.x.

Gertler, Meric S. 2001. "Urban economy and society in Canada: Flows of people, capital and ideas." *Canadian Journal of Policy Research* 2: 119–30.

Gertler, Meric S., Richard Florida, Gary Gates, and Tara Vinodrai. 2002. *Competing on creativity: Placing Ontario's cities in continental context.* Toronto: Institute for Competitiveness and Prosperity, and the Ontario Ministry of Enterprise, Opportunity and Innovation.

Gertler, Meric S., and Kate Geddie. 2008. "Architectural knowledge: Reflective dynamics between place and design." Paper presented at the annual meeting of the Association of American Geographers, 18 April, San Francisco, USA.

Gertler, Meric S., and Tara Vinodrai. 2005. "Anchors of creativity: How do public universities create competitive and cohesive communities?" In *Taking public universities seriously*, ed. F. Iacobucci and C. Tuohy, 293–315. Toronto: University of Toronto Press.

Gertler, Meric S., Tara Vinodrai, and Josephine V. Rekers. 2008. "Innovation and learning in Toronto's biomedical sector: Local and global knowledge dynamics." Paper presented at the annual meeting of the Innovation Systems Research Network, 1 May, Halifax, Canada.

Glaeser, Edward L. 2000. "The new economics of urban and regional growth." In *The Oxford handbook of economic geography*, ed. G. Clark, M. Gertler, and M. Feldman, 83–98. Oxford, UK: Oxford University Press.

Glaeser, Edward L. 2005a. "Review of Richard Florida's 'The rise of the creative class.'" *Regional Science and Urban Economics* 35 (5): 593–6. http://dx.doi.org /10.1016/j.regsciurbeco.2005.01.005.

Glaeser, Edward L. 2005b. *Smart growth: Education, skilled workers and the future of cold-weather cities.* Cambridge, MA: Kennedy School, Harvard University.

Glaeser, Edward L., and Joshua D. Gottlieb. 2006. "Urban resurgence and the consumer city." *Urban Studies* (Edinburgh, Scotland) 43 (8): 1275–99. http://dx.doi.org/10.1080/00420980600775683.

Grant, Jill L. 2009. ISRN integrative paper: Halifax case study. ISRN Integrative Workshop, Toronto, 2–4 November. http://theoryandpractice.planning.dal.ca/pdf/creative_halifax/isrn/social_dynamics.pdf.

Grant, Jill L., and Karin Kronstal. 2010. "The social dynamics of attracting talent in Halifax." *Canadian Geographer* 54 (3): 347–65. http://dx.doi.org/10.1111/j.1541-0064.2010.00310.x.

Greenwood, Robert. 2009. ISRN integrative paper: Saint John case study. ISRN Integrative Workshop, Toronto, 2–4 November.

Hall, Heather, and Betsy Donald. 2009. ISRN integrative paper: Kingston case study. ISRN Integrative Workshop, Toronto, 2–4 November.

Hansen, Hogni K., and Thomas Niedomysl. 2009. "Migration of the creative class: Evidence from Sweden." *Journal of Economic Geography* 9 (2): 191–206. http://dx.doi.org/10.1093/jeg/lbn046.

Houston, Donald, Allen Findlay, Richard Harrison, and Colin Mason. 2008. "Will attracting the 'creative class' boost economic growth in old industrial regions? A case study of Scotland." *Geografiska Annaler. Series B, Human Geography* 90 (2): 133–49. http://dx.doi.org/10.1111/j.1468-0467.2008.00283.x.

Inglehart, Ronald, and Pippa Norris. 2003. *Rising tide.* New York and Cambridge, MA: Cambridge University Press. http://dx.doi.org/10.1017/CBO9780511550362.

Inglehart, Ronald, and Chris Welzel. 2005. *Modernization, cultural change and democracy.* New York and Cambridge, MA: Cambridge University Press.

Jacobs, Jane. 1961. *The death and life of great American cities.* New York: Random House.

Jacobs, Jane. 1970. *The economy of cities.* New York: Random House.

Leslie, Deborah, and Shauna Brail. 2009. "The case of fashion talent in Toronto: A re-evaluation of amenities-based theories." Presented at the ISRN annual meeting, Halifax, 29 April–1 May. http://www.utoronto.ca/isrn/publications/NatMeeting/NatSlides/Nat09/slides/Leslie_Brail%20Fashion_Toronto09.pdf.

Lloyd, Richard, and Terry N. Clark. 2001. "The city as an entertainment machine." In *Research in urban sociology 6: Critical perspectives on urban redevelopment,* ed. F.K. Gatham, 357–78. Oxford, UK: JAI/Elsevier. http://dx.doi.org/10.1016/S1047-0042(01)80014-3.

Lucas, Robert, Jr. 1988. "On the mechanics of economic development." *Journal of Monetary Economics* 22 (1): 3–42. http://dx.doi.org/10.1016/0304-3932(88)90168-7.

Markusen, Ann. 2006. "Urban development and the politics of a creative class: Evidence from a study of artists." *Environment & Planning A* 38 (10): 1921–40. http://dx.doi.org/10.1068/a38179.

Markusen, Ann, and Greg Schrock. 2006. "The artistic dividend: Urban artistic specialisation and economic development implications." *Urban Studies* (Edinburgh, Scotland) 43 (10): 1661–86. http://dx.doi.org/10.1080 /00420980600888478.

Marshall, Alfred. 1890. *Principles of economics*. London: Macmillan and Co.

Maskell, Peter, and Anders Malmberg. 1999. "Localised learning and industrial competitiveness." *Cambridge Journal of Economics* 23 (2): 167–85. http://dx.doi.org/10.1093/cje/23.2.167.

McCann, Eugene J. 2007. "Inequality and politics in the creative city region: Questions of livability and state strategy." *International Journal of Urban and Regional Research* 31 (1): 188–96. http://dx.doi.org/10.1111/j.1468-2427 .2007.00713.x.

Mellander, Charlotta, and Richard Florida. 2011. "Creativity, talent, and regional wages in Sweden." *Annals of Regional Science* 46 (3): 637–60. http://dx.doi.org/10.1007/s00168-009-0354-z.

Noland, Marcus. 2005. "Popular attitudes, globalization and risk." *International Finance* 8 (2): 199–229. http://dx.doi.org/10.1111/j.1468-2362.2005.00157.x.

Ottaviano, Gianmarco I.P., and Giovanni Peri. 2005. "Cities and culture." *Journal of Urban Economics* 58 (2): 304–37. http://dx.doi.org/10.1016/j.jue.2005 .06.004.

Peck, Jamie. 2005. "Struggling with the creative class." *International Journal of Urban and Regional Research* 29 (4): 740–70. http://dx.doi.org/10.1111 /j.1468-2427.2005.00620.x.

Phillips, Peter, and Graeme Webb. Forthcoming. "Saskatoon: From small town to global hub." In the series Innovation, creativity, and governance in Canadian city-regions, volume 4, ed. D.A. Wolfe and M.S. Gertler. Toronto: University of Toronto Press.

Phillips, Peter, Graeme Webb, and Michael Kunz. 2009. "If I had a hammer … The role of infrastructure in creative, innovative clusters and the community in Saskatoon." Presented at the ISRN annual meeting, Halifax, 29 April– 1 May. http://www.utoronto.ca/isrn/publications/NatMeeting/NatSlides /Nat09/slides/PhillipP_Role_Infrastructure_Saskatoon09.pdf.

Polèse, Mario, and Richard Shearmur. 2006. "Why some regions will decline: A Canadian case study with thoughts on local development strategies." *Regional Science* 85: 23–46.

Rantisi, Norma M. 2009. "The geography of marketing design for Montréal fashion: Exploring the role of cultural intermediaries." In *Industrial design, competition and globalization*, ed. Grete Rusten and John R. Bryson, 93–116. Hampshire, UK: Palgrave Macmillan.

Rantisi, Norma M., and Deborah Leslie. 2006. "Branding the design metropole: The case of Montreal, Canada." *Area* 38 (4): 364–76. http://dx.doi.org /10.1111/j.1475-4762.2006.00705.x.

Rantisi, Norma M., and Deborah Leslie. 2008. "The social and material foundations of creativity in Montreal." Presented at the ISRN annual meeting, Montreal, 30 April–2 May. http://www.utoronto.ca/isrn/publications /NatMeeting/NatSlides/Nat08/slides/RantisiN_LeslieD_Foundations _Creativity.pdf.

Roback, Jennifer. 1982. "Wages, rents, and the quality of life." *Journal of Political Economy* 90 (6): 1257–78. http://dx.doi.org/10.1086/261120.

Saxenian, AnnaLee. 2002. *Local and global networks of immigrant professionals in Silicon Valley*. San Francisco: Public Policy Institute of California.

Scott, Allen J. 2006. "Creative cities: Conceptual issues and policy questions." *Journal of Urban Affairs* 28 (1): 1–17. http://dx.doi.org/10.1111/j.0735-2166.2006.00256.x.

Shapiro, Jesse M. 2006. "Smart cities: Quality of life, productivity, and the growth effects of human capital." *Review of Economics and Statistics* 88 (2): 324–35. http://dx.doi.org/10.1162/rest.88.2.324.

Shearmur, Richard. 2007. "The new knowledge aristocracy: The creative class, mobility and urban growth." *Work Organisation, Labour and Globalisation* 1 (1): 31–47.

Shearmur, Richard. 2010. "Space, place and innovation: A distance-based approach." *Canadian Geographer / Géographe canadien* 54 (1): 46–67. http:// dx.doi.org/10.1111/j.1541-0064.2009.00302.x.

Slack, Enid, Larry Bourne, and Meric S. Gertler. 2003. *Vibrant cities and city-regions: Responding to emerging challenges*. The panel on the role of government. http://www.law-lib.utoronto.ca/investing/reports/rp17.pdf.

Storper, Michael, and Michael Manville. 2006. "Behaviour, preferences and cities: Urban theory and urban resurgence." *Urban Studies* (Edinburgh, Scotland) 43 (8): 1247–74. http://dx.doi.org/10.1080/00420980600775642.

Storper, Michael, and Allen J. Scott. 2009. "Rethinking human capital, creativity and urban growth." *Journal of Economic Geography* 9 (2): 147–68. http:// dx.doi.org/10.1093/jeg/lbn052.

Thomas, June M., and Julia Darnton. 2006. "Social diversity and economic development in the metropolis." *Journal of Planning Literature* 21 (2): 153–69. http://dx.doi.org/10.1177/0885412206292259.

Trépanier, Michel, Pierre-Marc Gosselin, and Rosemarie Dallaire. 2009. ISRN integrative paper: Trois-Rivières case study. ISRN Integrative Workshop, Toronto, 2–4 November.

Wojan, Tim R., Dayton M. Lambert, and David A. McGranahan. 2007. "Emoting with their feet: Bohemian attraction to creative milieu." *Journal of Economic Geography* 7 (6): 711–36. http://dx.doi.org/10.1093/jeg/lbm029.

Wolfe, David A., and Meric S. Gertler. 2004. "Clusters from the inside and out: Local dynamics and global linkages." *Urban Studies* (Edinburgh, Scotland) 41 (5–6): 1071–93. http://dx.doi.org/10.1080/00420980410001675832.

2 Attracting and Retaining Talent in Canadian Cities: Towards a Holistic View?

TARA VINODRAI

Introduction: Talent, Cities, and Economic Development

In the contemporary global economy, knowledge and human capital (or talent) are viewed as paramount for economic competitiveness and success. However, the geography of talent is highly variegated and scholars have suggested that cities tend to be places where human capital accumulates and concentrates (Glaeser and Mare 2001; Florida 2002c; Scott 2008; Storper and Scott 2009). Emerging from this line of thought is the notion that the capacity of city-regions to attract and retain highly qualified and skilled personnel is therefore critical to securing the future prosperity of local and national economies. Such thinking has been rapidly translated into public policy across advanced economies. The interest in human capital or talent as a key determinant of economic development has generated lively discussions regarding the role that quality of place and amenities play in attracting and retaining highly skilled labour.

Perhaps the most widely acknowledged and contentious viewpoint emerging from the debate is Richard Florida's (2002c) creative class thesis. His explanations of regional economic development are grounded in talent, technology, and tolerance: "the 3Ts" (Florida 2002a, 2002b; Florida et al. 2008, 2010). An alternative view appears in the national and regional innovation systems literature. While also underscoring the importance of skills and highly educated workers, the literature emphasizes the role of institutions of higher education, access to career buzz, and the overall quality of the regional innovation system as critical to economic development. However, the debate about talent attraction and retention, quality of place, and economic development is nearly silent on issues related to sustainability and the environment, despite a substantial literature examining these issues across city-regions. One recent exception appears in the work of Lewis and Donald (2010): they argue that viewing the creative class thesis through the lens of sustainability and liveability can offer a viable alternative pathway to economic development, especially for smaller urban centres.

In Canada, early findings suggested that similar trends existed between the key variables identified by Florida (Gertler et al. 2002); however, as Gertler (2010) pointed out, the theory, model, and supporting evidence derive disproportionately from the United States. The Innovation Systems Research Network's (ISRN) comprehensive, multi-year study addresses questions about how universal these claims are within the Canadian urban context, particularly as expressed in city-regions of different sizes and across groups of creative workers with distinctive occupational identities. One of the key objectives of the ISRN study was to explore the hypothesis that highly educated, creative individuals are attracted to places that offer an abundance of work opportunities, exhibit openness and tolerance, have a critical mass of cultural activity, and have high levels of social diversity. The study addressed local talent attraction and retention dynamics in Canadian cities through in-depth case studies, as well as complementary quantitative analyses. Evidence from the study overwhelmingly points to the multi-faceted and multidimensional nature of talent attraction and retention dynamics (Wolfe 2009; Grant and Kronstal 2010; Lepawsky et al. 2010; Lewis and Donald 2010; see chapters this volume). Thus, the overall motivation of this chapter is to revisit the quantitative models suggested in the literature armed with new evidence derived from the findings of the ISRN study.

The chapter proceeds by briefly outlining three perspectives on talent attraction and retention related to creativity, innovation systems, and sustainability in city-regions. The third section describes the data and variables used in the analysis. The fourth section provides some key descriptive statistics. The penultimate section presents the results of a series of regression analyses that examine the differences among occupational groups and city-regions of different sizes. A distinction is made between existing local concentrations of talent, as well as domestic and international talent flows. The final section offers a summary of the key findings and the implications for public policy in Canada and elsewhere.

Creativity, Innovation, Sustainability, and the Urban Economy

With myriad ways to view the interest in human capital and urban economies, three perspectives are germane here. First, growing interest in the creative and cultural economy of cities has been articulated in academic and policy circles under the guise of the creative class and the creative city (Landry 2000; Florida 2002c; Scott 2006). This literature views human capital as central to urban economic development: debate has focused on the quality of place characteristics that attract talent. The core argument of most well-known work on the creative class suggests that the most successful urban regions are those that develop tolerant and welcoming attitudes towards social diversity and offer a critical mass of cultural activity (Florida 2002c; Florida et al. 2008). However, scholars have raised issues related to its applicability in smaller cities and rural regions (McGranahan and Wojan 2007; Sands and Reese 2008), the lack of attention paid to mobility patterns (Deslisle and Shearmur 2010; Niedomysl and Hansen 2010), and the absence of differentiation among creative workers (Markusen 2006; Asheim and Hansen 2009). Scholars have raised fundamental questions related to inequality (Peck 2005, 2009; Donegan and Lowe 2008) and causality (Shearmur 2007; Storper and Scott 2009). Collectively, critics raise questions about the creative class thesis on the basis of theory, method, ideology, and evidence.

Second, the literature on innovation identifies urban economies as necessary for generating new ideas. Due to the potential diversity, density, and volume of interactions between economic actors, cities are seen to provide an important platform for knowledge circulation and exchange within and between industrial sectors (Duranton and Puga 2000; Audretsch 2002; Storper and Venables 2004; see also Wolfe and Bramwell 2008). Human capital plays a critical role in innovation and knowledge creation processes due to workers' mobility between projects, firms, and places, which facilitates the transfer of knowledge (Christopherson 2002; Saxenian 2006). Moreover, the innovation process itself is often shaped by the knowledge base that dominates the firm or sector (Asheim and Gertler 2005; Asheim et al. 2007). Authors identify three types of knowledge bases: symbolic, synthetic, and analytical. Each knowledge base is associated with distinct learning dynamics, organizational practices, and geographies. For example, in industries based on symbolic knowledge (e.g., advertising, music), location in or access to particular scenes is critical for success. This provides access to social networks, career buzz, and work opportunities, thereby facilitating local learning, innovation, and knowledge exchange (Grabher 2002; Hauge and Hracs 2010). In science-based industries (e.g., pharmaceuticals), where analytical knowledge predominates, global learning and knowledge flows are more prevalent (Gertler 2008; Moodysson et al. 2008). This work concludes that firms and workers require different conditions to facilitate knowledge exchange and learning and that the place characteristics that matter most depend on the predominant knowledge base.

The national and regional innovation systems literatures also emphasize the role of universities, viewing them as central to learning, innovation, and knowledge-creation processes through providing knowledge and research infrastructure (Lundvall 1992; Nelson 1993; Asheim and Gertler 2005). While the university has many roles including creating, patenting, and licensing intellectual property, several authors argue that the university's largest role may be producing the regional talent base and acting as a local magnet, attracting highly skilled workers, leading-edge firms, and investment (Power and Malmberg 2008). Moreover, this may be especially true in smaller and mid-sized cities (Goldstein and Drucker 2006).

Finally, a growing interest in sustainability and liveability highlights concerns for environmental and social justice, as well as the long-term health and well-being of places. This literature examines a range of issues related to sustainability and governance in city-regions, including transportation, smart growth, energy consumption, waste management, and local food systems (Newman and Kenworthy 1999; Morgan 2004; Krueger and Gibbs 2007). However, within this literature, sustainability is often interpreted narrowly as an environmental concern. As Jonas and While (2007) observe, this overlooks "the less tangible social dimensions of urban sustainability ... [including] social inclusion, cultural diversity, health, nutrition, accessibility, transport, mobility, housing and community development." This wider definition of sustainability resonates with the arguments of Gertler (2001) and Bradford (2004), who suggest that the ability of cities to attract and produce talent may depend on the ability of places to provide affordable, liveable space; strong, socially cohesive neighbourhoods; access to employment and social services; access to childcare; and other amenities (see also OECD 2006). Rather than casting quality of life in terms of the narrow interests of elites, as is the case in much of the creative cities literature (McCann 2007), this perspective calls for a broad-based view of liveability. Indeed, Lewis and

Donald (2010) argue that the creative city discourse can be fruitfully re-framed in terms of liveability and sustainability, providing a different starting point for understanding urban economic development dynamics that would eliminate bias towards larger cities.

Several explanations have emerged to provide a foundation for understanding talent attraction and retention dynamics. A model that uses indicators emphasizing creativity, innovation, and environmental and social sustainability may help explain these dynamics. Such a model should provide a broader and holistic understanding of these dynamics in city-regions. The next sections present a model that attempts a systematic, quantitative analysis of Canadian city-regions.

Data Sources and Variables

Building on previous work on cluster dynamics in Canada (Wolfe and Gertler 2004; Spencer et al. 2010), and to support the research on the social dynamics of economic and creativity performance, ISRN developed a unique database of economic activity in Canadian city-regions. The database includes variables that capture employment and labour market status, migration, industrial and occupational structure, income levels, educational attainment, and other socio-economic and demographic characteristics often used to describe and measure urban economies. The database draws upon data from the 2001 and 2006 Canadian Census of Population, the US Patent and Trademark Office (USPTO), and other sources.

Given the ISRN study's focus on urban-centred regional economies, the core unit of analysis is the city-region. Statistics Canada defines city-regions using employment catchment areas; the geographical reach reflects commuting flows between municipalities around a core urban area. Census Metropolitan Areas (CMAs) have a core urban population of 100,000 or more; Census Agglomerations (CAs) have a core urban population of 10,000 or more. In 2001, Canada had 27 CMAs and 113 CAs; only 134 city-regions are included in the analysis.[1]

Variables for the analysis capture the emerging theoretical and empirical accounts of talent attraction and retention based on creativity, innovation, and sustainability. Three variables measure the presence and mobility patterns of highly educated and creative workers. To reflect Florida's (2002b) original work, and subsequent studies in other national contexts (Gertler et al. 2002, Boschma and Fritsch 2009, Andersen et al. 2010), the first dependent variable measures the local talent pool, calculated as the percentage of the city-region's labour force in creative occupations. To distinguish between local concentrations of talent and the actual flow and movement of talent between places through international and interregional migration, two additional dependent variables are derived. Local talent flows are calculated as the percentage of the local labour force employed in creative occupations that had resided outside the city-region, but within Canada, in 2001. Similarly, global talent flows are the percentage of the local labour force employed in creative occupations that resided outside of Canada in 2001.

The ISRN's qualitative work points to the role of different place characteristics: some emphasize the original creative class discourse, while others highlight the quality of the local or regional innovation systems, or the liveability and sustainability of the urban economy (see Gertler et al. this volume). The variables included reflect these empirical and theoretical observations. First, building directly on the hypotheses posited by Florida (2002c), explanatory variables that reflect the original creative class analysis were calculated for each city-region (see also Gertler et al. 2002; Florida et al. 2008, 2010). These include the percentage of the labour force in artistic occupations (bohemian index), the percentage of the population in same-sex couples (gay index), and the percentage of the population that is foreign born (mosaic/melting pot index). Second, to capture the quality of the regional innovation system, three variables were constructed: the presence of a university, patenting rates, and economic diversity, which takes into account the number of industries in a city-region and how employment is distributed among them (Beckstead and Brown 2003). Third, a group of variables capture the sustainability and liveability of city-regions: the variables explicitly replicate Lewis and Donald's (2010) study of small Canadian cities. Measures of housing quality and affordability capture liveability and social sustainability. The prevalence of bicycling and public transit for daily commuting measures environmental sustainability, due to the assumed reduction in regional carbon emissions and pollution levels.[2] Control variables for distance from other major centres, population size, and borders were also included, since these traditional, structural factors continue to shape mobility patterns (Shearmur, 2007; Deslisle and Shearmur 2010). Table 2.1 provides a brief description of each variable.

Understanding the Geography of Talent in Canadian Cities

The geography of talent is highly uneven across Canadian cities (Gertler et al. 2002). Figure 2.1 shows differences across the twenty-seven largest

Table 2.1 Description of key variables

Variable	Description	Year(s)
Local talent pool	% Creative occupations	2006
Local talent flow	% Creative occupations (2006) living elsewhere in Canada (2001)	2001–6
Global talent flow	% Creative occupations (2006) living outside of Canada (2001)	2001–6
Mosaic/Melting pot index	% Foreign born	2001
Bohemian index	% Bohemians	2001
Gay index	% Same-sex couples	2001
Universities	Presence of a university	2001
Patenting	Patents per capita	2000–3
Economic diversity	Numbers equivalent entropy	2001
Liveability	% Housing not in need of repair	2001
Affordability	% Households spending < 30% income on housing	2001
Sustainability	% Commuting to work by bike or public transit	2001

city-regions in Canada. Canada's largest cities have highly educated workforces. Some smaller centres such as St John's, Victoria, and Halifax also score highly on this measure, perhaps reflecting their role as key administrative centres and hubs of commercial activity within their regional economies. While talent concentrates in particular locations, it also flows between places. Spencer and Vinodrai (2008) demonstrate that, within Canada, domestic mobility patterns are differentiated by region. They find that city-regions in central Canada are strongly linked to the dominant city in each province (Toronto, Ontario; Montreal, Quebec). Moreover, cities in Quebec are rarely connected to other cities in the Canadian urban system due to language and other historical factors (Deslisle and Shearmur 2010). Among the western provinces, three large cities (Calgary, Edmonton, and Vancouver) are most connected to other cities in the region, but none emerges as a dominant hub. Finally, flows of talent in Atlantic Canada's cities are more often connected to places elsewhere in Canada. Lepawsky et al. (2010) note this pattern in Newfoundland: St John's is a staging ground for interprovincial migration as workers seek economic opportunities elsewhere in the country.

Figure 2.1 The geography of talent, 2006

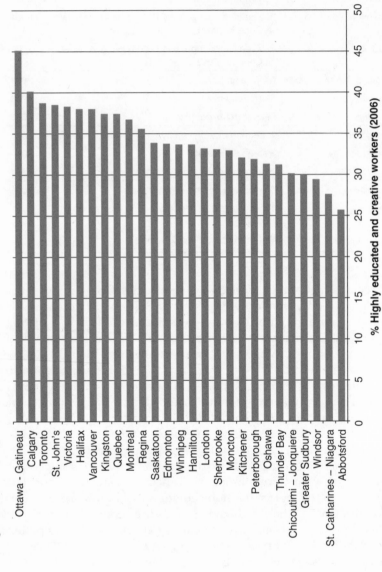

% **Highly educated and creative workers (2006)**

Source: Statistics Canada, 2006 [Author's calculations]

Equally important to understanding the geography of talent is the role that immigration plays in bringing newcomers to Canada. While multiculturalism is viewed as a central tenet of Canadian society and the proportion of the population that is foreign born is higher in Canada than most other countries in the world, an underlying and uneven geography is again associated with this dynamic. Toronto and Vancouver play a key role as gateway cities where a high proportion of newcomers first arrive to Canada. The immigration dynamic shapes outcomes associated with measures such as the melting pot index, used to gauge levels of tolerance and openness (Florida 2002b, 2002c). Figure 2.2 shows the proportion of the population that is foreign born across the twenty-seven largest Canadian cities. It confirms the dominance of Toronto and Vancouver, where more than a third of the urban population was born outside Canada. In general, small and mid-sized urban centres (such as St John's, Halifax, Sudbury, and Saskatoon) have smaller proportions of immigrants.

Florida's (2002a) work emphasizes artists as a signal of tolerance and underlying creativity capacity; he captures this using the bohemian index. Indicators that measure the presence of artists, designers, or other cultural occupations tend to favour large urban centres (Vinodrai 2010). As figure 2.3 demonstrates, this is certainly the case across Canadian cities. The cities with the highest proportion of individuals working in strictly artistic occupations include Vancouver, Victoria, Toronto, and Montreal, followed closely by Calgary, Halifax, Ottawa, and Winnipeg.

Variations in the geography of innovation also appear in Canada. As figure 2.4 shows, patenting rates vary across city-regions. Ottawa has the highest rate of patenting, attributed to its role as the national capital region, the presence of federal research laboratories, and a relatively dynamic ICT cluster (Lucas et al. 2009; Wolfe 2009). Kitchener also has a high rate of patenting, which reflects the technology-focused University of Waterloo and global ICT companies such as OpenText and BlackBerry (Bramwell and Wolfe 2008). Kingston and Saskatoon, two smaller urban centres, also have notable patenting rates. While patenting provides only a limited measure of innovation, it indicates where knowledge-intensive science and technology activities are most prevalent in Canada's economy. A local environment that offers a dynamic science and technology base may be more appealing to star scientists and other workers trained in these fields compared to other creative workers (Asheim and Hansen 2009; Gertler et al. this volume).

Figure 2.2 Gateway cities and the geography of immigration

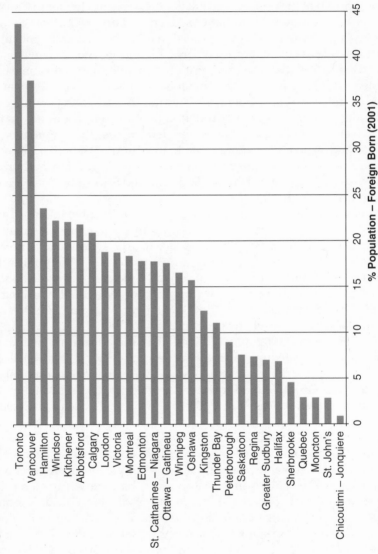

% Population – Foreign Born (2001)

Source: Statistics Canada, 2001 [Author's calculations]

Figure 2.3 Bohemian cities: The geography of the creative and cultural economy

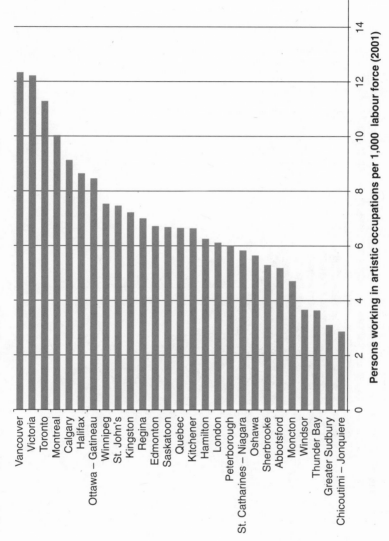

Persons working in artistic occupations per 1,000 labour force (2001)

Source: Statistics Canada, 2001 [Author's calculations]

Figure 2.4 Science cities: The geography of innovation

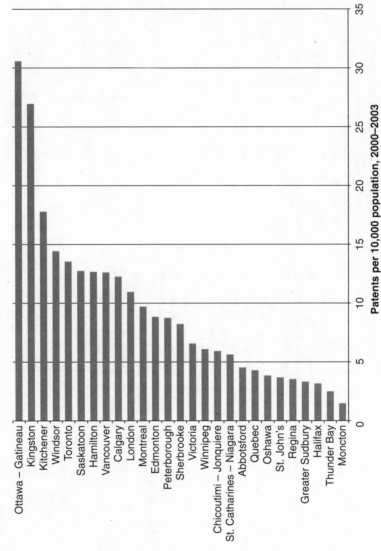

Patents per 10,000 population, 2000–2003

Source: Koegler, 2010 [Author's calculations]

Figure 2.5 shows one measure of social sustainability in Canadian city-regions based on the proportion of households who spend less than 30 per cent of household income on housing: a standard measure of housing affordability. Markusen and Schrock (2006) argue that issues related to affordability are important among some creative workers, namely, artists who may not be able to afford the high rents in cosmopolitan metropolises. Lewis and Donald (2010) and others argue that evaluating places on affordability promotes a just and inclusive vision of economic development that does not privilege large cities. Canadian city-regions with the highest levels of affordability include Winnipeg, Regina, Ottawa, Moncton, and Kitchener. Two of Canada's largest cities, Toronto and Vancouver, have the lowest levels of affordability amongst the twenty-seven city-regions in the chart.

Creativity, Innovation, and Sustainability

The indicators presented above reveal highly differentiated and uneven geographies associated with the variables capturing creativity, innovation, and sustainability that do not neatly align with population size. Moreover, unanswered questions remain about differences between occupational groups. This section examines these issues systematically through a series of ordinary least-squares (OLS) regression models.

Are There Differences between Occupations?

Evidence from the ISRN case studies presented in this volume suggests that different types of talent value different quality-of-place characteristics. A series of OLS regressions focus attention on whether differences exist between types of professionals (arts and culture, natural and applied science); these groups were chosen because they draw upon different knowledge bases and have varying organizational norms, work practices, and labour market mobility patterns. Table 2.2 shows the regression analysis results comparing overall patterns for workers in creative occupations to those in the two subgroups. The overall model, which considers the local concentration of highly creative and educated workers, is statistically significant with an R^2 value of 0.670, meaning that the model explains a high proportion of the variability in the dependent variable. Independent variables associated with each of the three perspectives (creativity, innovation, and sustainability) are significant: the bohemian index, sustainability, the presence of a university,

Figure 2.5 Sustainable and liveable cities: Housing affordability

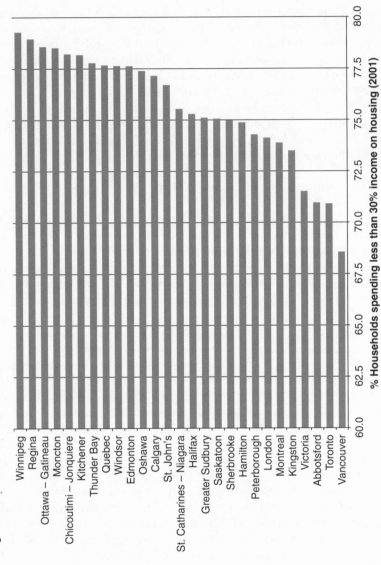

% Households spending less than 30% income on housing (2001)

Source: Statistics Canada, 2001 [Author's calculations]

Table 2.2 Does occupation matter?

Local talent pools	All creative workers			Art & culture professionals			Natural & applied science professionals		
	β	t		β	t		β	t	
Gay index	0.121	1.868	*	0.118	1.748	*	0.006	0.115	
Bohemian index	0.327	4.599	***	0.420	5.668	***	0.037	0.613	
Mosaic/melting pot index	−0.086	−0.666		−0.122	−0.906		0.064	0.576	
Affordability	0.050	0.788		0.015	0.232		0.244	4.453	***
Liveability	0.021	0.287		0.014	0.182		0.114	1.796	*
Sustainability	0.335	3.287	***	0.454	4.279	***	0.719	8.220	***
Universities	0.186	2.476	**	0.158	2.023	**	0.152	2.352	**
Patenting	0.085	1.275		0.058	0.840		0.218	3.803	***
Economic diversity	0.178	2.196	**	−0.092	−1.085		0.068	0.985	
Adj. R-squared	0.670			0.643			0.757		
N	133			133			133		

Note: *** $\alpha = 0.01$; ** $\alpha = 0.05$; * $\alpha = 0.1$

economic diversity, and the gay index, although the latter only at a 90 per cent confidence level. Overall, the findings suggest the necessity for a more holistic view of talent attraction and retention, since a model including openness and diversity, the quality of the regional innovation system, sustainability, and liveability results in a stronger explanation for the presence of a creative labour force within a city-region.

The models for art and culture professionals ($R^2 = 0.643$) and natural and applied science professionals ($R^2 = 0.757$) are both significant and explain a high proportion of the variability in the dependent variable. Unlike the overall model, the bohemian and gay indices are not significant for natural and science professionals; these variables are significant for art and culture professionals. Although patent rates are not significant in predicting overall concentrations of talent or art and culture professionals, this variable is highly significant for the science-based occupations; affordability is also significant for these professionals. Statistically significant for both groups are the variables for sustainability and universities. In other words, arts and cultural professionals demonstrate preferences related to a vibrant arts and culture scene, whereas natural and applied scientists select location based on the quality of the innovation system. This confirms findings of the ISRN case studies, further underscoring key differences between artists (Grant et al., and Hracs and Stolarick this volume) and science-based professionals (Phillips and Webb this volume). While these results are hardly surprising, some characteristics of place quality are important regardless of occupation.

Does City Size Matter?

A key question guiding the ISRN study of talent attraction and retention asked whether different quality-of-place characteristics matter to attracting and retaining talent in large cities compared to their small and mid-sized counterparts? For example, the emphasis on the importance of cosmopolitanism and diversity in large cities like Toronto (Leslie et al. this volume), stand in stark contrast to the issues confronted in smaller cities such as Moncton, St John's, and Kingston (Bourgeois this volume; Lepawsky et al. this volume). This issue is addressed by dividing cities into groups according to size. The size categories reflect the design of the national study: small cities have fewer than 250,000 inhabitants; medium-sized cities have populations between 250,000 and 500,000 people; and large cities have populations of 500,000 or more.[3] Table 2.3 shows the regression results using the three dependent variables that capture the size of the local talent pool, as well as local and global talent flows. First, with respect to local talent pools, the results are relatively consistent regardless of city size. The magnitude and direction of the relationships, as reflected in the size and sign of the beta coefficients, do not change when considering only smaller and mid-sized city-regions. This proves similar to other quantitative studies that use the relative size of the local talent pool as the dependent variable (cf. Gertler et al. 2002; Florida et al. 2008). While Lewis and Donald (2010, 34) argue that "the creative capital model – when quantified – seems to rely on the power of [Canada's] seven or eight largest cities," the evidence suggests that this is not the case. Even though the explanatory power of the model decreases, the same variables – universities, sustainability, economic diversity, and bohemians – are significant in all cases. One exception is the gay index, which is only significant in the model including city-regions of all sizes; this indicator of tolerance and openness may only apply to securing talent in larger urban centres.

The results do not reveal consistency by city-size in local talent flows. First, the gay index is the only variable significant regardless of city-size.

Table 2.3 Does city-region size matter?

Local talent pools	All city-regions		Small and mid-size city-regions		Small city-regions	
	β	t	β	t	β	t
Gay index	0.121	1.868 *	0.112	1.595	0.116	1.567
Bohemian index	0.327	4.599 ***	0.355	4.656 ***	0.367	4.590 ***
Mosaic/melting pot index	−0.086	−0.666	−0.086	−0.597	−0.088	−0.604
Affordability	0.050	0.788	0.060	0.792	0.059	0.709
Liveability	0.021	0.287	0.004	0.042	0.015	0.149
Sustainability	0.335	3.287 ***	0.184	2.242 **	0.149	1.785 *
Universities	0.186	2.476 **	0.199	2.233 **	0.207	2.110 **
Patenting	0.085	1.275	0.021	0.267	0.012	0.138
Economic diversity	0.178	2.196 **	0.246	2.432 **	0.252	2.103 **
Adj. R-squared	0.670		0.549		0.486	
N	133		124		117	

Local talent flows	All city-regions		Small and mid-size city-regions		Small city-regions	
	β	t	β	t	β	t
Gay index	0.215	2.299 **	0.200	2.288 **	0.217	2.592 **
Bohemian index	0.130	1.265	0.098	0.987	0.081	0.861
Mosaic/melting pot index	−0.396	−2.125 **	−0.182	−1.028	−0.218	−1.328
Affordability	0.163	1.780 *	0.185	1.989 **	0.143	1.532
Liveability	0.186	1.744 *	0.154	1.373	0.172	1.523
Sustainability	0.037	0.250	0.158	1.432	0.210	2.186 **
Universities	−0.119	−1.098	−0.074	−0.678	−0.074	−0.656
Patenting	−0.131	−1.321	−0.079	−0.829	−0.052	−0.540
Economic diversity	−0.302	−2.477 **	−0.195	−1.536	−0.211	−1.567
Critical mass	−0.727	−0.737	−0.144	−0.265	0.486	1.135
Adj. R-squared	0.317		0.322		0.355	
N	133		124		117	

(continued)

Table 2.3 Does city-region size matter?

Local talent pools	All city-regions		Small and mid-size city-regions		Small city-regions	
	β	t	β	t	β	t
Gay index	0.030	0.429	0.041	0.531	0.073	0.978
Bohemian index	0.031	0.400	0.011	0.131	0.042	0.494
Mosaic/melting pot index	0.587	4.258 ***	0.462	3.052 ***	0.312	2.222 ***
Affordability	−0.019	−0.272	0.021	0.257	−0.010	−0.125
Liveability	−0.080	−0.982	−0.109	−1.097	−0.080	−0.796
Sustainability	0.394	3.547 ***	0.435	4.548 ***	0.551	6.569 ***
Universities	0.057	0.692	0.074	0.776	0.033	0.334
Patenting	0.173	2.315 **	0.269	3.202 ***	0.270	3.170 ***
Economic diversity	−0.110	−1.177	−0.170	−1.488	−0.116	−0.950
Critical mass	−0.538	−0.721	−0.112	−0.233	0.496	1.319
Adj. R-squared	0.632		0.507		0.527	
N	126		117		110	

Note: *** $\alpha = 0.01$; ** $\alpha = 0.05$; * $\alpha = 0.1$

Second, the melting pot/mosaic index and economic diversity variables are significant, but only when the largest cities are included in the analysis. Moreover, the sign of the beta co-efficient is negative, suggesting that domestic talent is moving to places that are not as economically or socially diverse. Taken together, these findings suggest that careful, nuanced investigation into the role of openness, tolerance, and diversity is needed. Finally, in the regression results that consider local talent flows in small cities, the sustainability variable is positive and significant at the 95 per cent confidence level. In other words, talented people residing elsewhere in Canada are attracted to smaller cities due to factors related to sustainability. This provides quantitative evidence in support of Lewis and Donald's (2010, 29) argument that using liveability and sustainability indicators provides a more "optimistic and empowering picture of creative potential in smaller Canadian cities."

While revealing little consistency in the determinants of local talent flows by city-region size, the models for global talent flows show consistent results. The patenting and sustainability variables are positive and significant across city-size categories. In other words, places with high-quality innovation systems that offer opportunities for sustainable living may be better positioned to attract foreign talent. This confirms the observations of Phillips and Webb (this volume), who describe highly skilled talent as attracted to places like Saskatoon because of a flourishing science-based community engaged in leading-edge research. The melting pot/mosaic index variable is positive and significant, which suggests that a pre-existing immigrant community acts to draw further immigrant talent. This supports Florida's original hypothesis that highly qualified personnel will be attracted to city-regions that are open and welcome diversity, but adds a caveat regarding sensitivity to the geographic origins of the workers. Overall, the findings reveal that the different quality of place characteristics related to creativity, innovation, and sustainability matter to talent retention and attraction dynamics and that the latter vary substantially by city-size (Gertler et al. this volume).

Towards a Holistic Perspective on Talent Attraction and Retention in Canadian Cities

A model that uses indicators emphasizing creativity, innovation, and environmental and social sustainability may improve our understanding of the dynamics of talent attraction and retention in city-regions. Informed by the respective literatures on these topics, this chapter presented a statistical model that demonstrates that, in addition to the variables identified in the creative class discourse, variables capturing the quality of the regional innovation system, sustainability, and liveability also prove significant. In other words, these variables must be accounted for in explanations of the role that attracting and retaining talent plays in urban and regional economic development. Evidence reveals the differences that emerge in refined analyses which account for city size or which more narrowly consider particular occupational specializations, rather than treating highly educated, creative workers as a homogeneous group. While place characteristics (such as the presence of a university and environmental sustainability) are important to attracting and retaining talent regardless of occupation, clear differences emerge between art and culture professionals and natural and applied-science professionals (with the latter drawn to places with a high-quality local innovation system and the former attracted to places that demonstrate openness and diversity). This affirms that sensitivity to difference according to occupational status or identity is a necessary additional layer or lens through which to understand talent attraction and retention. Moreover, analysts must attend to issues related to city-region size. Most notably, the evidence validates Lewis and Donald's (2010) argument that sustainability and liveability are of utmost importance in theorizing and analysing talent attraction in smaller urban centres. Overall, the findings reinforce the argument that a holistic and nuanced view of the dynamics of talent attraction and retention is necessary.

While this chapter has established the case for taking a balanced perspective on talent attraction and retention that accounts for variation by occupation and city size, several avenues for future research remain. First, the quantitative models suggest that issues around diversity – social and economic – are far more complex than can be captured in this analysis. These issues related to diversity require further exploration. Second, more attention needs to be paid to local and global talent flows, the relationship between these migratory patterns, and the networks and flows of ideas and people that result. Third, there is ample opportunity to improve the variables used to capture social and environmental sustainability; such endeavours will undoubtedly be challenging due to data limitations. Finally, the growing academic, policy, and media attention being paid to sustainability, the green economy, and the environment (cf. Cooke 2009; Chapple et al. 2011) suggests that the intersections between creativity, innovation, and sustainability in urban and regional economic development need to be investigated more fully and explicitly through in-depth case studies and other forms of analysis.

Cities and regions across Canada and elsewhere seem intent on adopting creative city policies as a foundation for urban and regional economic development. Evidence presented here, however, suggests that public policymakers, as well as urban planning and economic development practitioners, should proceed with caution, paying close attention to the local and regional context. Policymakers must remain sensitive to the existing occupational mix and composition of the labour market within the city-region, while remaining aware of its relative size and location in the urban system. A wide range of place characteristics and local assets need addressing under the rubric of talent-based economic development. Overall, the findings presented support a broad-based vision of urban liveability and a need for holistic economic development strategies that consider both talent attraction *and* retention, with sensitivity to the opportunities, challenges, and limitations that accompany such strategies.

ACKNOWLEDGMENTS

This research was funded by the Social Sciences and Humanities Research Council of Canada (SSHRC) grant no. 412-2005-1001. The author acknowledges the editorial assistance provided by Jill Grant, as well as the valuable comments and insights provided by David Wolfe, Meric Gertler, Greg Spencer, and the other members of the Innovation Systems Research Network (ISRN). Dieter Kogler and Scott Pennington provided some of the data used in this analysis.

NOTES

1 In 2003, Statistics Canada altered the definition of a CMA. To ensure consistency in the analysis, which covers the period between 2001 and 2006, several city-regions were excluded from the analysis.
2 While other measures of environmental sustainability (e.g., ecological or carbon footprints, greenhouse-gas emissions levels, energy and water consumption rates) are desirable, challenges limit the availability of comprehensive indicators at the appropriate geographic scale (Federation of Canadian Municipalities 2005; Pembina Institute 2007)
3 Sensitivity analysis was performed to ensure that the results were not influenced by changes at the margins.

REFERENCES

Andersen, Kristina K., Høgne Kalsø Hansen, Arne Isaksen, and Mika Raunio. 2010. "Nordic city regions in the creative class debate: Putting the creative class thesis to a test." *Industry and Innovation* 17 (2): 215–40. http://dx.doi .org/10.1080/13662711003633496.
Asheim, Bjørn, Lars Coenen, and Jan Vang. 2007. "Face-to-face, buzz, and knowledge bases: Sociospatial implications for learning, innovation, and innovation policy." *Environment and Planning. C, Government & Policy* 25 (5): 655–70. http://dx.doi.org/10.1068/c0648.
Asheim, Bjørn, and Meric S. Gertler. 2005. "The geography of innovation: Regional innovation systems." In *The Oxford handbook of innovation*, ed. Jan Fagerberg, David C. Mowery, and Richard R. Nelson, 291–317. Oxford: Oxford University Press.
Asheim, Bjørn, and Høgne Kalsø Hansen. 2009. "Knowledge bases, talents, and contexts: On the usefulness of the creative class approach in Sweden."

Economic Geography 85 (4): 425–42. http://dx.doi.org/10.1111/j.1944-8287 .2009.01051.x.

Audretsch, David. 2002. "The innovative advantage of US cities." *European Planning Studies* 10 (2): 165–76. http://dx.doi.org/10.1080/09654310120114472.

Beckstead, Desmond, and Mark Brown. 2003. "From Labrador City to Toronto: The industrial diversity of Canadian cities, 1992–2002." *Insights on the Canadian economy*, Catalogue no. 11-624-MIE2003003. Ottawa: Analytical Studies Branch, Statistics Canada.

Boschma, Ron, and Michael Fritsch. 2009. "Creative class and regional growth: Empirical evidence from eight European countries." *Economic Geography* 85 (4): 391–423. http://dx.doi.org/10.1111/j.1944-8287.2009.01048.x.

Bradford, Neil. 2004. *Creative cities: Structured policy dialogue report.* Ottawa: Canadian Policy Research Networks. http://cprn.org/documents/31340_en.pdf.

Bramwell, Alison, and David A. Wolfe. 2008. "Universities and regional economic development: The entrepreneurial University of Waterloo." *Research Policy* 37 (8): 1175–87. http://dx.doi.org/10.1016/j.respol.2008.04.016.

Chapple, Karen, Cynthia Kroll, T. William Lester, and Sergo Montero. 2011. "Innovation in the green economy: An extension of the regional innovation system model?" *Economic Development Quarterly* 25 (1): 5–25. http://dx.doi .org/10.1177/0891242410386219.

Christopherson, Susan. 2002. "Why do national labor market practices continue to diverge in the global economy? The 'missing link' of investment rules." *Economic Geography* 78 (1): 1–20. http://dx.doi.org/10.2307/4140821.

Cooke, Philip. 2009. "Transition regions: Green innovation and economic development." Paper presented at the DRUID Summer Conference, Copenhagen, Denmark, 17–19 June. http://www2.druid.dk/conferences/ viewpaper.php?id=5348&cf=32.

Deslisle, Françoise, and Richard Shearmur. 2010. "Where does all the talent flow? Migration of young graduates and nongraduates, Canada 1996–2001." *Canadian Geographer* 54 (3): 305–23.

Donegan, Mary, and Nichola Lowe. 2008. "Inequality in the creative city: Is there still a place for 'old-fashioned' institutions?" *Economic Development Quarterly* 22 (1): 46–62. http://dx.doi.org/10.1177/0891242407310722.

Duranton, Gilles, and Diego Puga. 2000. "Diversity and specialization in cities: Why, where and when does it matter." *Urban Studies* (Edinburgh, Scotland) 37 (3): 533–55. http://dx.doi.org/10.1080/0042098002104.

Federation of Canadian Municipalities. 2005. *Quality of life reporting system: Growth, the economy and the urban environment.* Ottawa: Federation of Canadian Municipalities. http://www.fcm.ca/Documents/reports/Growth _the_Economy_and_the_Urban_Environment_EN.pdf.

Florida, Richard. 2002a. "Bohemia and economic geography." *Journal of Economic Geography* 2 (1): 55–71. http://dx.doi.org/10.1093/jeg/2.1.55.

Florida, Richard. 2002b. "The economic geography of talent." *Annals of the Association of American Geographers* 92 (4): 743–55. http://dx.doi.org/10.1111/1467-8306.00314.

Florida, Richard. 2002c. *The rise of the creative class.* New York: Basic Books.

Florida, Richard, Charlotta Mellander, and Kevin Stolarick. 2008. "Inside the black box of regional development: Human capital, the creative class and tolerance." *Journal of Economic Geography* 8 (5): 615–49. http://dx.doi.org/10.1093/jeg/lbn023.

Florida, Richard, Charlotta Mellander, and Kevin Stolarick. 2010. "Talent, technology and tolerance in Canadian regional development." *Canadian Geographer* 54 (3): 277–304. http://dx.doi.org/10.1111/j.1541-0064.2009.00293.x.

Gertler, Meric S. 2001. "Urban economy and society in Canada: Flows of people, capital and ideas." *ISUMA: Canadian Journal of Policy Research* 2 (3): 1–29.

Gertler, Meric S. 2008. "Buzz without being there? Communities of practice in context." In *Community, economic creativity and organization*, ed. Ash Amin and Joanne Roberts, 203–26. Oxford: Oxford University Press. http://dx.doi.org/10.1093/acprof:oso/9780199545490.003.0009.

Gertler, Meric S. 2010. "Rules of the game: The place of institutions in regional economic change." *Regional Studies* 44 (1): 1–15. http://dx.doi.org/10.1080/00343400903389979.

Gertler, Meric S., Richard Florida, Gary Gates, and Tara Vinodrai. 2002. *Competing on creativity: Ontario cities in North American context.* Toronto: Institute for Competitiveness and Prosperity, and Ontario Ministry of Enterprise, Opportunity and Innovation. http://www.urban.org/publications/410889.html.

Glaeser, Edward L., and David C. Mare. 2001. "Cities and skills." *Journal of Labor Economics* 19 (2): 316–42. http://dx.doi.org/10.1086/319563.

Goldstein, Harvey, and Joshua Drucker. 2006. "The economic development impacts of universities on regions: Do size and distance matter?" *Economic Development Quarterly* 20 (1): 22–43. http://dx.doi.org/10.1177/0891242405283387.

Grabher, Gernot. 2002. "The project ecology of advertising: Talents, tasks, and teams." *Regional Studies* 36 (3): 245–62. http://dx.doi.org/10.1080/00343400220122052.

Grant, Jill L., and Karin Kronstal. 2010. "The social dynamics of attracting talent in Halifax." *Canadian Geographer* 54 (3): 347–65. http://dx.doi.org/10.1111/j.1541-0064.2010.00310.x.

Hauge, Atle, and Brian Hracs. 2010. "See the sound, hear the style: Collaborative linkages between indie musicians and fashion designers in local scenes." *Industry and Innovation* 17 (1): 113–29. http://dx.doi.org/10.1080/13662710903573893.

Jonas, Andrew E.G., and Aidan While. 2007. "Greening the entrepreneurial city? Looking for spaces of sustainability politics in the competitive city." In *The sustainable development paradox: Urban political economy in the United States and Europe*, ed. Rob Krueger and David Gibbs, 123–59. New York: Guilford.

Koegler, Dieter Franz. 2010. *Canadian patent database (PATDAT), 1983–2007*. Toronto: University of Toronto.

Krueger, Rob, and David Gibbs, eds. 2007. *The sustainable development paradox: Urban political economy in the United States and Europe*. New York: Guilford.

Landry, Charles. 2000. *The creative city: A toolkit for urban innovators*. London: Earthscan.

Lepawsky, Josh, Chrystal Phan, and Rob Greenwood. 2010. "Metropolis on the margins: Talent attraction and retention to the St. John's city-region." *Canadian Geographer* 54 (3): 324–46. http://dx.doi.org/10.1111/j.1541-0064.2010.00315.x.

Lewis, Nathaniel M., and Betsy Donald. 2010. "A new rubric for creative city potential in Canada's smaller cities." *Urban Studies* (Edinburgh, Scotland) 47 (1): 29–54. http://dx.doi.org/10.1177/0042098009346867.

Lucas, Matthew, Anita Sands, and David A. Wolfe. 2009. "Regional clusters in a global industry: ICT clusters in Canada." *European Planning Studies* 17 (2): 189–209. http://dx.doi.org/10.1080/09654310802553415.

Lundvall, Bengt-Åke, ed. 1992. *National systems of innovation: Towards a theory of innovation and interactive learning*. London: Pinter.

Markusen, Ann. 2006. "Urban development and the politics of a creative class: Evidence from the study of artists." *Environment & Planning A* 38 (10): 1921–40. http://dx.doi.org/10.1068/a38179.

Markusen, Ann, and Greg Schrock. 2006. "The artistic dividend: Urban artistic specialization and economic development implications." *Urban Studies* (Edinburgh, Scotland) 43 (10): 1661–86. http://dx.doi.org/10.1080/00420980600888478.

McCann, Eugene. 2007. "Inequality and politics in the creative city-region: Questions of livability and state strategy." *International Journal of Urban and Regional Research* 31 (1): 188–96. http://dx.doi.org/10.1111/j.1468-2427.2007.00713.x.

McGranahan, David A., and Timothy R. Wojan. 2007. "Recasting the creative class to examine growth processes in rural and urban counties." *Regional Studies* 41 (2): 197–216. http://dx.doi.org/10.1080/00343400600928285.

Moodysson, Jerker, Lars Coenen, and Bjørn Asheim. 2008. "Explaining spatial patterns of innovation: Analytical and synthetic modes of knowledge creation in the Medicon Valley life science cluster." *Environment & Planning A* 40 (5): 1040–56. http://dx.doi.org/10.1068/a39110.

Morgan, Kevin. 2004. "Sustainable regions: Governance, innovation and scale." *European Planning Studies* 12 (6): 871–89. http://dx.doi.org/10.1080/0965431042000251909.

Nelson, Richard R., ed. 1993. *National innovation systems: A comparative study.* Oxford: Oxford University Press.

Newman, Peter, and Jeffery Kenworthy. 1999. *Sustainability and cities: Overcoming automobile dependence.* Washington: Island Press.

Niedomysl, Thomas, and Høgne Kalsø Hansen. 2010. "What matters more for the decision to move: Jobs versus amenities." *Environment & Planning A* 42 (7): 1636–49. http://dx.doi.org/10.1068/a42432.

OECD (Organization for Economic Cooperation and Development). 2006. *OECD territorial reviews: Competitive cities in the global economy.* Paris: OECD.

Peck, Jamie. 2005. "Struggling with the creative class." *International Journal of Urban and Regional Research* 29 (4): 740–70. http://dx.doi.org/10.1111/j.1468-2427.2005.00620.x.

Peck, Jamie. 2009. "The cult of urban creativity." In *Leviathan undone? Towards a political economy of scale*, ed. Roger Kiel and Rianne Mahon, 159–76. Vancouver: UBC Press.

Pembina Institute. 2007. *Ontario community sustainability report.* Drayton Valley, AB: Pembina Institute.

Power, Dominic, and Anders Malmberg. 2008. "The contribution of universities to innovation and economic development: In what sense a regional problem? *Cambridge Journal of Regions.*" *Economy and Society* 1 (2): 233–45.

Sands, Gary, and Laura A. Reese. 2008. "Cultivating the creative class: And what about Nanaimo?" *Economic Development Quarterly* 22 (1): 8–23. http://dx.doi.org/10.1177/0891242407309822.

Saxenian, AnnaLee. 2006. *The new Argonauts: Regional advantage in a global economy.* Boston: Harvard University Press.

Scott, Allen J. 2006. "Creative cities: Conceptual issues and policy problems." *Journal of Urban Affairs* 28 (1): 1–17. http://dx.doi.org/10.1111/j.0735-2166.2006.00256.x.

Scott, Allen J. 2008. *Social economy of the metropolis: Cognitive-cultural capitalism and the global resurgence of cities.* Oxford: Oxford University Press. http://dx.doi.org/10.1093/acprof:oso/9780199549306.001.0001.

Shearmur, Richard. 2007. "The new knowledge aristocracy: The creative class, mobility and urban growth." *Work Organisation, Labour, and Globalisation* 1 (1): 31–47.

·Spencer, Gregory M., and Tara Vinodrai. 2008. "Where have all the cowboys gone? Assessing talent flows between Canadian cities." Paper presented at the annual meetings of the Innovation Systems Research Network, Montreal, Quebec, 30 April–2 May. http://www.utoronto.ca/isrn/publications /NatMeeting/NatSlides/Nat08/slides/Spencer_Cowboys.pdf.

Spencer, Gregory, Tara Vinodrai, Meric S. Gertler, and David A. Wolfe. 2010. "Do clusters make a difference? Defining and assessing their economic performance." *Regional Studies* 44 (6): 697–715. http://dx.doi.org/10.1080 /00343400903107736.

Statistics Canada. 2001. *Occupation – 2001 National Occupational Classification for Statistics (720A), Selected Labour Force, Demographic, Cultural, Educational and Income Characteristics (258) and Sex (3) for Population 15 Years and Over, for Canada, Provinces, Territories, Census Metropolitan Areas and Census Agglomerations.* Catalogue no. 97-F0012-XCB01050. Ottawa: Statistics Canada.

Statistics Canada. 2006. *Occupation – National Occupational Classification for Statistics 2006 (720C), Sex (3) and Selected Demographic, Cultural, Labour Force, Educational and Income Characteristics (273) for the Population 15 Years and Over of Canada, Provinces, Territories, Census Metropolitan Areas and Census Agglomerations.* Catalogue no. 97-564-XCB2006005. Ottawa: Statistics Canada.

Storper, Michael, and Allen J. Scott. 2009. "Rethinking human capital, creativity and urban growth." *Journal of Economic Geography* 9 (2): 1–21.

Storper, Michael, and Anthony J. Venables. 2004. "Buzz: Face-to-face contact and the urban economy." *Journal of Economic Geography* 4 (4): 351–70.

Vinodrai, Tara. 2010. "The dynamics of economic change in Canadian cities: Innovation, culture and the emergence of a knowledge based economy." In *Canadian cities in transition*, 4th ed., ed. Trudi Bunting, Pierre Filion, and Ryan Walker, 87–109. London: Oxford.

Wolfe, David A. 2009. *21st century cities in Canada: The geography of innovation.* Ottawa: Conference Board of Canada.

Wolfe, David A., and Alison Bramwell. 2008. "Innovation, creativity and governance: Social dynamics of economic performance in city-regions." *Innovation: Management, Policy and Practice* 10 (2–3): 170–82. http://dx.doi.org /10.5172/impp.453.10.2-3.170.

Wolfe, David A., and Meric S. Gertler. 2004. "Clusters from the inside and out: Local dynamics and global linkages." *Urban Studies* (Edinburgh, Scotland) 41 (5–6): 1071–93. http://dx.doi.org/10.1080/00420980410001675832.

PART II

Attracting Creative Sector Workers

3 Cosmopolitanism, Cultural Diversity, and Inclusion: Attracting and Retaining Artistic Talent in Toronto

DEBORAH LESLIE, MIA A. HUNT, AND SHAUNA BRAIL

Introduction – Visual Artists in Toronto: Cultural Diversity, Social Exclusion, and Tolerance

In recent years, there has been growing recognition that the economic performance of a city-region is related to quality-of-place characteristics. While production networks and employment opportunities are of critical importance in attracting and retaining talent, Florida (2002) suggests that workers are also attracted to cities offering a range of amenities. In this paper we examine the role of cultural diversity, social inclusion, and tolerance in attracting and retaining artists. We consider the extent to which members of disadvantaged social groups are able to participate fully in the city's creative economy, and the role that institutions, policies, and practices play in integrating talented newcomers into a city's artistic networks.

Within Canada, Toronto has the largest concentration of artists. Hill Strategies Research (2010) estimates that 22,300 artists practise in the city, and that Toronto had the fastest-growing arts sector in Canada throughout the 1990s.[1] The city also boasts the highest median earnings in art among Canada's major centres (ibid.). Like other Canadian cities, however, Toronto loses artists to major international art centres, including New York, Berlin, and London. Contributing factors include the relative scarcity of buyers and more competitive international residencies (Miller 2008).

Given that Toronto is not a major international art centre, we examine aspects of the local milieu that keep artists rooted in the city. We argue that the city's multicultural diversity helps retain artists. This cosmopolitanism provides an array of consumption choices and contributes positively to overall quality of life. Diversity is also a source of creative inspiration, contributing to a rich and multifaceted local artistic ecology. Toronto is welcoming of newcomers; several art-related institutions facilitate the integration of newcomers. However, a key finding of our research is that Toronto's diversity does not always translate into meaningful tolerance and inclusion.

Our analysis draws upon fifty-seven semi-structured interviews with artists and representatives of arts institutions. Interviews were conducted between 2007 and 2010, and ranged between one and two hours in length. We identified initial participants through reviewing trade publications and media coverage. Arts organizations and festivals also provided potential contacts. We interviewed visual artists working in different realms, including painting, photography, and sculpture. Our interviewees were diverse in age, gender, profile, and stage of career. They also varied in race, ethnicity, nationality, and immigration status. Of the forty-nine artists interviewed, sixteen were visible minorities, and fourteen had immigrated to Canada from other countries.[2] Our participants thus present a range of perspectives. Interviews were digitally recorded, transcribed, and coded according to theme. The quotations used reflect the prevalence of particular themes in the interviews.

The chapter contains three sections. First we review the literature on cultural diversity and creativity to examine how creative city policies in Toronto support cultural diversity. In the second section we identify how cultural diversity attracts and retains artistic talent in the city. In the final section, we discuss exclusion within the city's artistic networks, arguing that Toronto's ability to retain artists is contingent upon incorporating artists in more meaningful ways.

Cultural Diversity and Creativity

In *The rise of the creative class*, Florida (2002) argues that rather than simply following jobs, the creative class is attracted to the quality-of-life characteristics of an urban region (see also Clark et al. 2002; Glaeser 2005). Quality of place is a broad concept, encompassing various amenities such as a vibrant music scene, restaurants, and art galleries, as well as authentic neighbourhoods, outdoor spaces, and heritage architecture. Of particular importance to Florida's conception of quality of place is the notion of tolerance, which is seen as indicative of the low entry barriers to human capital crucial to facilitating the acceptance of new ideas (Florida 2002, 256).

According to Florida, key indicators of tolerance include the size of a city's gay and immigrant communities. The use of the Gay Index as a measure of tolerance stems from the premise that gay people are subjected to particularly high levels of discrimination, and that "a place that welcomes the gay community welcomes all kinds of people" (Florida 2002, 256). Florida also develops a Melting Pot Index, which measures the relative percentage of an urban region's population that is foreign born. He argues that "those who choose to leave their countries are predisposed to risk and can be thought of as 'innovative outsiders'" (ibid., 253). A region that attracts such outsiders will be characterized by a high level of entrepreneurship that attracts other talent and sparks a spiral of cumulative growth.

Stolarick and Florida (2006) suggest that in addition to furnishing a plethora of consumption choices (including cuisines, music genres, and festivals), cultural diversity provides a wealth of creative influences. A variety of aesthetic styles, materials, genres, and colour palettes, emanating from different parts of the world, can lead to the formation of hybrid art forms. A culturally diverse local market can be an asset in testing new products or concepts. Products that meet the needs of diverse consumers have greater potential for success in global markets (Stolarick and Florida 2006).

Policy agendas inspired by Florida's theory of the creative class recognize the connections between creativity and cultural diversity. In Toronto, for example, the 2003 *Culture Plan for the Creative City* recommends support for artistic projects which celebrate Toronto's multicultural diversity (City of Toronto 2003, 19; see also Catungal and Leslie 2009). The City has allocated funding to the Caribana festival and Pride Toronto. Another aim of the culture plan is to increase accessibility to the arts for low-income and ethnic-minority populations (City of Toronto 2003).

The creative city agenda dovetails with official discourses of multiculturalism in Canada. Canadian identity has long been defined by a fear of being absorbed into American culture (Mitchell 1993). As a result, Canada has avoided the use of American symbols, such as the melting pot. Through the discourse of multiculturalism, the state has attempted to promote a unique Canadian identity that fosters the acceptance of immigrant communities into the nation and constructs a "national framework of 'unity within diversity'" (Mahtani 2002, 70). The notion of multiculturalism is premised on equal access for all Canadians to economic, social, cultural, and political resources.

There are, however, problems with the discourse of multiculturalism, problems which are also evident in the creative city agenda. Donald and

Morrow (2003, 13), for example, argue that creative city discourses tend to assume that a diverse city is harmonious when the reality for immigrants and people of colour often suggests otherwise. Superficial celebrations of diversity often mask labour market exclusion, deskilling, and discrimination. Ethno-racialized and immigrant populations are frequently subject to poverty and residential segregation (Hulchanski 2007). They do not generally benefit from creative class policies. On the contrary, they are often displaced by gentrification related to the construction of creative districts (Catungal et al. 2009). Studies indicate that creative class cities are often the most racially segregated cities (Thomas and Darnton 2006, 162), a trend that Florida (2005) has acknowledged.

Another problem with the conceptualization of diversity encoded within the creative city discourse is that it relies on an instrumental understanding of difference, whereby difference is mainly valued for its economic contribution. Such an understanding can lead to a narrow view that commodifies difference (Donald and Morrow 2003). This logic views cultural diversity as an amenity that can be used to attract talented workers and tourists. As Goonewardena and Kipfer (2005) point out, this represents a neoliberalization of difference (see also Catungal and Leslie 2009).

Part of the problem is that Florida equates the presence of immigrants with tolerance and inclusion. He fails to unpack differences among immigrants, and to examine issues of exclusion within creative networks. Creative occupations are often highly racialized and characterized by high levels of inequality and discrimination (Anthony 2001; Christopherson 2008; Gill and Pratt 2008). In the following sections, we explore the role that diversity plays in attracting and retaining visual artists and the extent to which diversity translates into meaningful equality.

Attracting and Retaining Artistic Talent in Toronto: The Role of Cultural Diversity

Various considerations – including employment prospects and quality of life – shape artists' decisions to come to Toronto. Many artists interviewed referred to traditional big-city reasons for living in Toronto. Toronto is widely considered the centre of the Canadian art world, despite its second-tier status internationally. For many artists, having the largest absolute population means that Toronto has the best prospective art market. An artist of Chinese descent noted: "Toronto is the biggest city in Canada, so I guess they're open to more experimental work, and because they have a larger audience, it attracts different events and different artists that have an opportunity to experiment, to showcase their work."

Toronto is home to renowned galleries and museums, such as the Art Gallery of Ontario (AGO), and numerous publicly funded, artist-run centres. These centres perform multiple functions, serving as sites of arts promotion, meeting places, exhibition spaces, and educational facilities. The city is also home to the Ontario College of Art and Design (OCAD). Both the quality of instruction and the cost of education in Toronto present competitive advantages for artists. One American artist indicated that she and her partner chose to relocate to Toronto specifically for study: "[Despite being American, studying in the States] wasn't so much an option because ... we were able to go to school so much cheaper here and the cost of living was more affordable to both of us being students and we were both still able to live comfortably. OCAD, it was internationally known and so it was important for me to go to a school that was known."

Artists also spoke of specialized services, including hard-to-find supplies, unusual or expensive tools, and local expertise. The clustering of artists and services in the city enables artists to practise and learn within a specialized environment.

Many artists cited the presence of varied cultural venues and festivals from which they derive inspiration. These events and facilities have received increased funding and support in recent years as part of Toronto's creative city agenda. As one artist noted, the investment resulted in local creative buzz: "In the last couple of years, especially with the events of Nuit Blanche and Luminato coming, and these great pieces of infrastructure, like OCAD, the AGO, and the ROM [Royal Ontario Museum], it's a great city to be in terms of arts and culture." Through art institutions and events, Toronto offers artists opportunities to network, helping them gain access to specialized suppliers, galleries, and job opportunities.

Quality-of-place considerations shape artists' decisions to practise in Toronto. For both Canadian and foreign-born artists, Toronto's affordability was important, as was the presence of social support structures, including universal health care and high-quality education (see also Gertler et al. and Grant et al. this volume). As one Toronto-born artist put it: "Health care is huge. I'm daunted by the idea of living in the States ... I think if you had kids it would be even harder. I can't imagine living with that kind of stress ... I hate to make generalizations but artists are usually in the lower income bracket ... So, for me, I find that health care policies here are very appealing."

Multicultural diversity is an essential quality-of-life factor for Toronto. Toronto is one of the most culturally diverse cities in the world, with over 51 per cent of residents being foreign-born (City of Toronto 2003, 10; Price and Benton-Short 2007). Forty-seven per cent of residents identify as visible minorities (City of Toronto 2010). A majority of interviewees were attracted to the city because of this diversity, and benefited from it once here (see also Davis et al. this volume). This is true both for white artists and for artists of colour, for those born in Canada and those from abroad. As one artist of Chinese descent told us, "I think artists come to Toronto from other countries because there are so many different ethnic areas. It's easy for them to start a new life, and also to slowly mix with mainstream Canadian [culture]. I have met a fair number of artists from different countries. I think that's the major reason to come to Toronto."

It is not only the presence of other immigrants that attracts newcomers. Toronto has an international reputation as a relatively harmonious city. A Japanese artist who lived in New York City before coming to Toronto told us, "I've heard a lot about Toronto ... It was quite different than New York [where] Germans, Europeans, Italians, Chinese, Koreans all live separately ... I had heard Toronto was different."

Artists arriving in Toronto see it as tolerant. One artist who came from Mexico told us, "Since the first day I arrived here I felt accepted. I guess that's multiculturalism. No one looked at me like I'm a foreigner for the way I look, for what I wear, anything. It was very fast acceptance." Another artist recounted: "Originally I was born in Malta and we ... immigrated to Canada when I was seven and we settled in Windsor. Now, all of us are living in Toronto. We should have come here in the beginning ... Toronto is definitely much more open. And if anything is going to attract an artist it is the openness and the versatility ... There is just a range of cultures. It's a perfect place to come as an artist." Such sentiments accord with the experience of musicians in the city, who also value the openness and diversity of Toronto (Hracs and Stolarick this volume).

Freedom of expression is important to artists, who often challenge hegemonic understandings of the world. As one artist indicated:

> Diversity – now that is a Canadian ideology ... In other places ... there would be a lot more adversity in terms of social and political restraints on the artists' expression in varying degrees, where an artist simply cannot

express themselves at all. So the fact that people can do and say what they want and have a platform to express themselves as an artist, whether that be a positive or negative message, in the end I think that contributes quite a bit to the dynamics and success of this particular art market, as well as the lack of censorship. I think it is fairly open.

Toronto's diversity is appreciated for the consumption experiences it offers. As one white, Toronto-born photographer told us, "I love Toronto. I love the diversity. I love ... being able to go for breakfast in Kensington Market, go for lunch in Little India, go for dinner in Little Portugal, and then go have dessert over at Chinatown."

The multiculturalism of Toronto also provides a diverse local market. One artist noted: "Your average person on the subway is used to seeing a lot of different things and I think that just percolates down into people's attitudes towards the arts and attitudes towards ... everything." Another artist spoke of "more different people, more different tastes, more of a chance of ... somebody liking your stuff."

In addition to enhancing local vibrancy and markets, and creating a sense of tolerance – aspects benefiting all Torontonians – diversity offers artists creative inspiration and exposure to culturally specific art practices. Our informants discussed how diversity inspires them and how their art mixes different cultural languages. One Chinese-Canadian noted:

> I use certain colours that are not considered traditional for certain cultural backgrounds ... I have lots of Italian friends. They like really bright colours. Somehow it influences me when I paint ... Lots of my recent inspiration from my work is from what I've seen every day in Toronto. Lots are based on the immigrant experience ... I call it a combination of eastern and western technique.

Canadian-born white artists also enjoy playing with Toronto's diverse visual languages. One multimedia artist explained:

> I use a lot of Asian characters, like Japanese text and Chinese text so I have no idea what they mean, and just mixing cultures and mixing times and different styles. I have lived in this city for about five years now, and it's really been an influence. You go to Chinatown and they have a certain look to their packaging, and the different design of their clothing, and what they wear and just taking all that in and amalgamating it into this one idea.

In Toronto, artists can learn specialized, culturally specific techniques without travelling abroad. A Toronto-born metal artist of European origin indicated, "A lot of my work uses a technique called Makumagane. It's a Japanese technique of layering metal. I would love to go to Japan and learn, but there's a lot of Japanese people here, so it's not something that's lost ... It might be without so many people from Asia."

Cultural diversity attracts Canadian and foreign-born artists to Toronto and helps retain them. Cultural diversity creates a source of inspiration and specialized skill sets. It provides a diverse local market which increases the chance of selling art. Canada's official multiculturalism policies are seen to foster an open environment that accepts different cultures and traditions. While the city has demonstrated an ability to attract creative people by building on its multicultural assets, in the next section we argue that Toronto's artistic communities may be failing to engage artistic newcomers in meaningful ways.

Artistic Retention and Meaningful Inclusion: Sources of Exclusion within Toronto's Artistic Networks

The literature on innovation often assumes that creative networks operate positively, connecting actors to sources of knowledge and facilitating innovation (Christopherson 2008). In addition, the literature emphasizes the role of networks in mediating risks and uncertainties associated with creative work. Networks are seen as an integral component of career advancement in creative industries. More recently, however, we find growing recognition that creative industry networks are often exclusionary, particularly along the lines of race and gender. Christopherson (2008), for example, illustrates how women and ethnic minorities are ghettoized within the film industry and left out of an old boys' network (see also Gill and Pratt 2008). Davis et al. (this volume) similarly report that middle-aged white anglophone males dominate screenwriting networks in Toronto.

We found that immigrant artists, First Nations artists, and artists of colour often described themselves as outside of established artistic networks. Most interviewees noted a lack of diversity in their artistic fields. When asked if Toronto's reputation as a multicultural city attracts creative people, a white artist noted: "It attracts a lot of white people ... like me. I came here to replicate ... a fantasyland of a multicultural kind of New York *happening* place with lots of mixing and stuff like that. Unfortunately it just doesn't pan out that way. The art community that I'm involved with – and it's a big community – is pretty much all white."

Artistic networks can be exclusionary, particularly in terms of language and social codes, the lack of mentorship and family support, and financial constraints that limit opportunities to show work. Many artists confront these challenges, irrespective of cultural background; not all artists of colour and immigrant artists face these difficulties. However, we found that issues of language, style, and support were more often considered sources of exclusion for culturally diverse artists.

Language and social codes are essential for networking, preparing grant applications, and discussing artistic work. Language skills relate both to artists' ability to speak English and to their ability to communicate the meaning of their art through appropriate codes and terminology (see also Bauder 2003). As one artist of South American descent said, "A lot of people think the art should speak for itself, but in this [Canadian] culture, it is not like that. You have to articulate what you are trying to express, contextualize it. Those are huge barriers, cultural barriers too, which is difficult for Latin American artists." A community arts organizer similarly noted, "There is a kind of snobbery and exclusiveness to the club … Certain codes you have to figure out, and if you don't, you're not allowed to be in." These codes are learned within artistic institutions.

Understanding what is expected provides artists with credibility and access to opportunities. A First Nations artist described the value of understanding unwritten rules of communicating in order to achieve commercial success: "It's like getting street cred. If you can carry on a discussion in certain realms, doors will open … It depends where you want to go. As an arts and culture organization, culturally I don't necessarily see it as mandatory in order for your career, but if you want to go into fine art, into the nicer galleries, you have to be prepared."

The ability to work as an artist in Toronto is tied to the ability to develop networks and understand unwritten rules. Without access to institutional and cultural capital, outsiders remain outside, and are challenged to secure shows, build collaborations, and gain recognition (Bourdieu 1993).

One means of learning these cues is through mentorships, which Davis et al. (this volume) also found important in screenwriting. Mentorships are especially valuable for artists from minority ethnic groups or those new to Canada. Like social networks, mentorships are often out of reach for immigrant and minority artists. Mentorships are often tied to formal institutions and difficult to establish informally in a competitive culture. As one artist of South Asian descent argued, "Not having mentorship, not knowing the ins and outs of the industry and learning as you go, are partly the barriers. I think those are shared by all, but especially immigrants. There's always a feeling that you're outside looking in." Although she wanted to pursue art, without artistic confidence, she first entered advertising and design. Like many artists from immigrant families, her career path reflected her parents' expectations: "This is something that I think is very important in immigrant communities, [that] we have business degrees or [become] a lawyer. We're still not sure if being an artist is something viable." Due to economic difficulties and expectations, many artists of colour and immigrant artists lack family support.

Concern by immigrant parents is understandable in light of the low earning potential of artists overall. A career in art is prohibitive without social and economic support (see also Bourdieu 1993). When asked to explain why Toronto's art scene lacks diversity, an artist from India, pursuing her MFA in Toronto noted, "One of the main reasons ... is poverty ... I would say most of us who are in the arts come from a certain ... amount of privilege." Indeed, notwithstanding exceptional circumstances, an art career requires investment. Materials and studio space are expensive. Many galleries charge fees to show work. In addition, arts education is a source of validation that is inaccessible to many artists. One figurative painter lamented: "How are you going to get to that school to get that name to get to the [opportunities] if you don't have money to go to the school to begin with? And a lot of people need that school. [Galleries and granting agencies] want to know where you went. They want to know what university you've gone to, before you can be accepted."

Exclusion of immigrant and minority artists was also attributed to their style of artistic production, which is often construed as foreign and exotic. Art embodies personal experience and history. Although Toronto's diversity results in varied artistic expression, some work can be marginalized. When asked why she stopped trying to show work in Toronto, one Polish artist told us: "My painting just wasn't a sell in Toronto. It's too colourful. It's too emotional. Being Polish ... I'm a passionate person, I'm a colourful person, and no matter how beige I tried to get it, it never worked out ... And it's almost like something takes over when I paint and I stopped trying to control it. And I realized I have to make money elsewhere."

The artist's frustrations are echoed in the comments of others, including a Mexican artist living in Toronto for five years. He noted: "Latin art ... is hard for [an] audience here to understand ... I don't know if the art we do is complex. The history … We have social issues. We have all that frustration … Everyone's an immigrant and Europeans have history, but somehow here, the art seems to be more light … There's the other art and the Canadian art and it's more accepted."

Like many respondents, the artist was uncomfortable attributing his lack of commercial success to the themes of his work alone, but he suspected that they might be a contributing factor: "Sometimes I feel like, why people don't understand what I'm doing? All artists struggle. I'm sure everyone feels like, why am I not that successful?"

Many immigrant and minority artists address culturally specific themes in their work, including issues of exclusion. As one First Nations artist noted, "There's a certain amount of social justice issues that come into our art just because of who we are, just because of what we carry … Certainly in my own practice, that's what I care about. So my work isn't particularly commercially viable. I've been fortunate not having to depend on that." Instead, like many others, this artist depends on Ontario Arts Council grants and shows in subsidized artist-run centres, both of which support less commercially viable work.

While some marginalized artists are able to support themselves through grants, and others find success in contemporary commercial galleries, some are only able to sell their work as ethnic art. Their work is understood within an Orientalist frame, constructed as exotic or primitive, as "other" within the context of mainstream art inspired by Western traditions (Said 1979). Framing art in this way may give artists exhibition opportunities, especially in conjunction with certain City-supported cultural festivals, but marginalizes this work in the process.

Similarly, when culturally specific work is shown, it may be presented through the lens of cultural heritage, not of artistic merit. An artist of Chinese origin explained:

> Not being born in Canada, you always feel like an outsider. If I travelled outside Canada, I'll always be first a Canadian artist. But if I'm in Canada, I always have a hyphen: Chinese-Canadian artist. That's a thing I find a little bit uncomfortable. Why can't I just be a Canadian artist in Canada? Why do I have to have a hyphen? … It doesn't have to do with what I do in art. It has more to do with my skin colour or how I look.

Participants described some expectation that artists from minority backgrounds will produce culturally specific work. One photographer revealed that he was asked to leave a gallery when his work began to lack aboriginality. He said, "I used to do portraits of Native people. I was told [by the gallery owner], 'You are known for a certain style, I don't mean you have to take pictures of people in feathers, but it would be nice.'" Other artists of colour noted a tokenistic approach to multiculturalism within the arts community. For example, an artist of African descent admitted, "Unfortunately the busiest time of the year for me is Black History Month."

Many galleries and public institutions have mandates to show diverse work. However, instead of encouraging meaningful inclusion, one artist described the practice as a "tokenistic box ticking exercise [that] will get [arts institutions] more funding." Awareness of this approach puts some artists in an awkward position. They may want to explore their cultural identities, but also want to avoid being pigeonholed. Some artists react by refusing to participate in culturally specific shows, while others navigate the terrain carefully. Reflecting on her decision to participate in a show of Chinese-Canadian painters, one artist noted:

> I do want to tell people what I think from this perspective and that's always the thing. Are you pigeonholing yourself as an Asian arts show, or is it solidarity and like "yeah, we have these unique perspectives." That goes back to that issue of community or identity. To show off what you are and to be proud, at the same time thinking about that within the larger context of all the larger clichés and the stereotypes that exist.

Such challenges keep marginalized artists from accessing institutions that provide resources. Some arts associations, galleries, and schools create additional barriers. The limitations of the commercial arts scene produce intense competition for funding. An advocate of community arts programs admitted: "There's a bit of protectionism going on and the pots are limited and there's competition in the way that our funding is designed and delivered in Canada. There are powerful lobby groups and advocates that represent a lot of the traditional art forms. For marginalized or excluded communities, they don't have the same access." The same interviewee discussed the lack of diversity among art policymakers:

> If you go to Ottawa and see the senior policy people, I would say 90 per cent of them are white. Ninety per cent of them are above 45. Obviously those aren't accurate statistics but the vast majority are not from [poor] communities. Most are from upper-middle-class backgrounds. I don't

think their policy staff reflects diversity and I also think they're out of touch with what's happening on the ground.

The perception of limited diversity among arts officials ultimately affects the city's ability to support and retain artists from minority backgrounds.

Granting agencies have been increasingly supportive of artists from different cultural backgrounds. Still, some marginalized artists are unable to access resources. An artist of Caribbean descent suggested that marginalized artists receive less funding because they are unfamiliar to the councils: "There's an unknown. There's not enough knowledge about that culture, or that specific art form, and then not knowing [the artists] at all." Many art institutions demand community connectedness for entry. As such, they provide excellent networking opportunities for some artists, and represent conservative bastions for others as an old boys' network.

Like other institutions, art schools were discussed as sometimes unsupportive of culturally specific art. For example, a First Nations MFA student described how a professor said her "politics [were] becoming cliché." A Caribbean artist who attended a private art school relayed her disappointment on how her work was received by instructors: "Some of the people that are maybe older and established in the career, they don't understand [when] an artist of colour brings something forth … Maybe it's also a painful topic. It might not be something they want to deal with … It feels like you're being told that something that's relevant to you is not something that is aesthetically pleasing or something of merit."

While institutional barriers exist, it is clear that newcomers benefit from the presence of specific institutions, which help integrate artists from diverse cultural backgrounds. For example, artist-run centres funded by arts councils are unique to Canada. These centres pay artists Canadian Artists' Representation rates to present their work in environments that are not market-driven. This provides opportunities for artists whose work is too political, conceptual, or interactive for commercial galleries. Many artists show their work exclusively in such venues.

Toronto is home to various artist-run centres, many of which have mandates to show diverse work. SAVAC – the South Asian Visual Arts Centre – is Toronto's only culturally specific artist-run centre for visual arts, although other culturally specific arts organizations operate in Toronto under different public funding structures. For newcomers, these organizations represent important points of entry into the city's arts scene. As one artist of South Asian descent told us: "The point about organizations like SAVAC or any other organization, why they're so important, is that they provide those opportunities to learn those skills and be part of that system, because there is a system ... They develop the knowledge and they develop the networking. That is important. They develop the access to resources." ·

Artist-run centres also support visible minorities and First Nations artists who describe feeling left out by commercial galleries: "Artist-run centres are essential. The commercial galleries are only interested ... in work they can sell. The more discursive work, installation work, for example, that isn't just a picture you can frame and hang on your wall and sell for $300 ... So the only opportunity to show that kind of discursive or polemical work is in an artist-run centre. They are essential."

Some artists argue that despite their value, culturally specific institutions can create enclaves isolated according to ethnicity or heritage. As a result, many arts organizations have developed mandates to collaborate across cultural groups. SAVAC, for example, which does not have gallery space, collaborates to integrate South Asian artists into other Toronto communities. In a similar approach, each year the Latino Canadian Cultural Association includes different cultural groups in their festivals. In 2009, they celebrated the Latin-Afro-First Nations Festival, and in 2010 organized a Latin-Afro-South Asian Festival. While some cultural arts communities become insular, other efforts bring diverse work to a greater public and avoid cultural isolation.

We found that many local artists, irrespective of colour or immigration history, believed Toronto's concept of diversity is problematic in reality, especially in the arts community. One community arts advocate noted: "[Diversity] is only celebrated in a certain framework, where it is economically and politically beneficial. Especially if we're talking about art, because ... a lot of art is political and a lot of art is revolutionary in a lot of ways. It's a statement on our culture and it's a statement on injustice in a lot of cases and it can make people uncomfortable."

Many of our interviewees suggested that Toronto's diversity is not reflected in local artistic circles. Our participants could only speculate about how their race, ethnicity, and nationality factored into their experience. Some immigrant or minority artists try to avoid self-disclosing their identities in artistic circles, while others have had success exploring issues of identity in their art, so long as they do so within a language of contemporary art. Issues of communication, mentorship, financial security, and cultural respect are faced by all artists, but seem particularly difficult for artists of colour and recent immigrants. This perception is important because it affects artists' decisions about whether to remain in Toronto. Retaining artists and creating a thriving inclusive arts community requires meaningful equality on the part of Toronto's artist communities and institutions. It requires an openness to ask questions and create dialogue.

The Discourse of Cultural Diversity: Inclusive Policy for an Inclusive City

In this chapter we have explored factors that bring artists to a city, with a specific focus on the role that cultural diversity plays in attracting and retaining artistic talent. We find that the city's rich cultural diversity provides a range of opportunities for artists, inspiring experimentation and creativity. Many artists perceive Toronto as not only a culturally diverse and cosmopolitan city, but also a fairly open and tolerant place that is accepting of newcomers and new ways of thinking. These features of the local environment are particularly appealing to artists who traffic in unconventional ideas, often challenging established orthodoxies, both aesthetic and political. As Gertler et al. (this volume) suggest, quality-of-place considerations, such as diversity and tolerance, may be more important to those in creative industries than in science or engineering (see Phillips and Webb this volume).

Despite seeing Toronto as a tolerant city, newcomers often feel excluded from the city's artistic networks. In particular, the city's art institutions may not reflect the city's broader cultural diversity. Language barriers are significant sources of exclusion. Immigrant artists and First Nations artists frequently find their work subject to Orientalist interpretations that construct it as exotic and "other." Some artists are ghettoized in ethnic-based artistic communities.

The City of Toronto employs the discourse of cultural diversity as an asset to attract innovative workers and tourists, who bring capital to local economies. As such, diversity is used as a tool for economic growth. Diversity makes Toronto attractive to outsiders and provides inspiration for creative people, but it must not be taken for granted or treated as spectacle. A diverse arts community demands equal access to public institutions, respect for artists beyond the frame of ethnicity, and support for individual voices and new ideas. It requires support on the ground for the same innovation and diversity espoused by creative city discourses.

Initiating change in the art world could involve more proactive attempts to ensure representation of artists from diverse backgrounds on arts councils and special granting programs to fund work exploring issues of identity, colonialism, migration, or mobility. Policies could ensure that galleries and museums show a broad spectrum of work, as well as creating internship and mentorship programs for new immigrants. Public institutions and their curators need to be encouraged to take risks. Support for culturally specific arts organizations and artist-run centres are excellent examples of public arts investment that is reaching diverse artists. Further support for inter-cultural collaborative initiatives will ensure that culturally specific arts are not ghettoized.

While Toronto's rich cultural diversity is a strong asset in attracting and retaining artists from across Canada and around the world, in the long run, the ability to keep artists in Toronto will depend on addressing some of these sources of exclusion through policy initiatives, in order to create more meaningful equality and inclusion in artistic circles.

ACKNOWLEDGMENTS

The authors thank Meric Gertler and David Wolfe for guiding the intellectual development of this project. We also thank the other ISRN participants, who presented their findings at the annual conferences, and Jill Grant for her suggestions. Thanks also to the participants who shared their experiences of practising art in Toronto.

NOTES

1 In absolute numbers Toronto has about 9000 more artists than Montreal and about 14,000 more than Vancouver (Hill Strategies Research Inc. 2010).
2 Many participants self-identified either as white or as a visible minority.

REFERENCES

Anthony, Kathryn H. 2001. *Designing for diversity: Gender, race, and ethnicity in the architectural profession.* Champaign: University of Illinois Press.
Bauder, Harald. 2003. "'Brain abuse,' or the devaluation of immigrant labour in Canada." *Antipode* 35 (4): 699–717. http://dx.doi.org/10.1046/j.1467-8330.2003.00346.x.

Bourdieu, Pierre. 1993. *The field of cultural production*. New York: Columbia University Press.

Catungal, Jean-Paul, and Deborah Leslie. 2009. "Contesting the creative city: Race, nation, and multiculturalism." *Geoforum* 40 (5): 701–4. http://dx.doi .org/10.1016/j.geoforum.2009.05.005.

Catungal, Jean-Paul, Deborah Leslie, and Yvonne Hii. 2009. "Geographies of displacement in the creative city: The case of Liberty Village, Toronto." *Urban Studies* (Edinburgh, Scotland) 46 (5–6): 1095–114. http://dx.doi.org /10.1177/0042098009103856.

Christopherson, Susan. 2008. "Beyond the self-expressive creative worker: An industry perspective on entertainment media." *Theory, Culture & Society* 25 (7–8): 73–95. http://dx.doi.org/10.1177/0263276408097797.

City of Toronto. 2003. *Culture plan for the creative city*. http://www.toronto.ca /culture/brochures/2003_cultureplan.pdf.

City of Toronto. 2010. *Toronto's racial diversity*. http://www.toronto.ca/toronto _facts/diversity.htm.

Clark, Terry Nichols, Richard Lloyd, Kenneth K. Wong, and Pushpam Jain. 2002. "Amenities drive urban growth." *Journal of Urban Affairs* 24 (5): 493–515. http://dx.doi.org/10.1111/1467-9906.00134.

Donald, Betsy, and Doug Morrow. 2003. *Competing for Talent: Implications for social and cultural policy in Canadian city-regions*. Hull: Report prepared for the Strategic Planning and Policy Coordination Department of Canadian Heritage.

Florida, Richard. 2002. *The rise of the creative class: And how it's transforming work, leisure, community and everyday life*. New York: Basic Books.

Florida, Richard. 2005. *Cities and the creative class*. New York: Routledge.

Gill, Rosalind, and Andy Pratt. 2008. "In the social factory? Immaterial labour, precariousness and cultural work." *Theory, Culture & Society* 25 (7–8): 1–30. http://dx.doi.org/10.1177/0263276408097794.

Glaeser, Edward L. 2005. *Smart growth: Education, skilled workers, and the future of cold-weather cities*. Cambridge, MA: Harvard University Kennedy School policy brief PB-2005-1. http://www.hks.harvard.edu/var/ezp_site/ storage/fckeditor/file/pdfs/centers-programs/centers/taubman/ skilledcities.pdf.

Goonewardena, Kanishka, and Stefan Kipfer. 2005. "Spaces of difference: Reflections from Toronto on multiculturalism, bourgeois urbanism, and the possibilities for radical urban politics." *International Journal of Urban and Regional Research* 29 (3): 670–8. http://dx.doi.org/10.1111/j.1468-2427.2005 .00611.x.

Hill Strategies Research Inc. 2010. *Mapping artists and cultural workers in Canada's large cities*. Study prepared for the City of Vancouver, the City of

Calgary, the City of Toronto, the City of Ottawa, and the Ville de Montréal based on 2006 census data. http://www.hillstrategies.com/content/mapping-artists-and-cultural-workers-canada%E2%80%99s-large-cities.

Hulchanski, David. 2007. *The three cities within Toronto: Income polarization among Toronto's neighbourhoods, 1970–2000*. Centre for Urban and Community Studies, Research bulletin 41. http://www.urbancentre.utoronto.ca/pdfs/researchbulletins/CUCSRB41_Hulchanski_Three_Cities_Toronto.pdf.

Mahtani, Minelle. 2002. "Interrogating the hyphen-nation: Canadian multicultural policy and mixed race identities." *Social Identities* 8 (1): 67–90. http://dx.doi.org/10.1080/13504630220132026.

Miller, Earl. 2008. "Global Canadians: As Earl Miller notes, leaving the country is something of a tradition for Canadian artists." *C Magazine: International Contemporary Art*: 99.

Mitchell, Katharyne. 1993. "Multiculturalism, or the united colours of capitalism?" *Antipode* 25 (4): 263–94. http://dx.doi.org/10.1111/j.1467-8330.1993.tb00220.x.

Price, Marie, and Lisa Benton-Short. 2007. "Immigrants and world cities: From the hyper-diverse to the bypassed." *GeoJournal* 68 (2–3): 103–17. http://dx.doi.org/10.1007/s10708-007-9076-x.

Said, Edward. 1979. *Orientalism*. New York: Vintage.

Stolarick, Kevin, and Richard Florida. 2006. "Creativity, connections and innovation: A study of linkages in the Montréal Region." *Environment & Planning A* 38 (10): 1799–817. http://dx.doi.org/10.1068/a3874.

Thomas, June Manning, and Julie Darnton. 2006. "Social diversity and economic development in the metropolis." *Journal of Planning Literature* 21 (2): 153–68. http://dx.doi.org/10.1177/0885412206292259.

4 Screenwriters in Toronto: Centre, Periphery, and Exclusionary Networks in Canadian Screen Storytelling

CHARLES H. DAVIS, JEREMY SHTERN,
MICHAEL COUTANCHE, AND ELIZABETH GODO

Introduction: Creative Work Requires More than Talent

A narrative across several scholarly literatures casts post-industrial creative workers as highly footloose, enjoying wide freedom to earn a living through self-expression, with abundant opportunities for lucrative short-term employment in various attractive metropolitan centres. This narrative is expressed notably in creative class theory (Florida 2002), creative city theory (Montgomery 2007), and in the strands of creative economy theory that foreground creative labour's self-expressive, self-managed, and self-creative attributes (Leadbeater 1999).

Screenwriters conform to the generic portrait of the creative worker in the sense that they are mainly well-educated individuals who are drawn to large, culturally important urban centres to earn their living through immaterial labour. Screenwriting, however, does not conform in important respects to prevailing views of footloose creative activity. Notably, in the screenwriter profession, talent shortage per se is not an issue because, as is true in many other cultural occupations, the supply of talented hopefuls far exceeds the number of available opportunities to earn a living.

The social dynamics of innovation in screenwriting revolve instead around selection and social sorting mechanisms *other than talent* at work in the screen industry. Screenwriting is steeply stratified, with relatively few highly visible and well remunerated individuals at the centre, and many part-time or economically inactive screenwriters on the margins. As we explain below, in English-speaking Canada the screenwriting occupation is defined by exclusionary networks dominated by white middle-aged anglophone males. The social process of selection has important implications for innovation in the Canadian screen industry, which in Canada revolves mainly around television. The television industry in Canada is required by law to produce and disseminate Canadian content, and Canadian governments devote considerable attention and public subsidies to this purpose (Le Goff et al. 2011). Public support for Canadian screen content production is motivated by concerns about nation building and national cultural expression. It also has recently come to be regarded as a means to spur development of promising "cognitive-cultural" metropolitan economic activities (Davis 2011; Davis and Mills forthcoming).

Toronto plays a key role as the central hub of Canada's English-language screen industry. Toronto's gravitational pull attracts many aspiring screenwriters to the city. At the same time, Toronto occupies a secondary position in the international division of cultural labour. The screen industry is highly concentrated in a small number of cities, especially in North America, where Hollywood and New York City eclipse Toronto in terms of size, prestige, and the financial rewards they can offer to successful screenwriters. These factors constrain Toronto in the scale and variety of cultural outputs it can produce, as well as in the range and quality of opportunities it can offer to screenwriters.

In this chapter, we draw on results of research on Canadian English-language screenwriters undertaken in connection with the ISRN Innovation and Creativity in City-Regions project. We show that the social dynamics of economic innovation in the screen industry affect Toronto screenwriters in three key ways: Toronto's secondary position in the international division of cultural labour (Miller 2011); exclusionary networks in the market for screenwriting talent; and the challenges experienced by the indigenous film and television industry in meeting its cultural and economic objectives, which evidently are related to the characteristics of the screen products it delivers to Canadian audiences.

Screenwriters and the Work of Screenwriting

Screenwriters are key contributors to the success of film and television, providing the script or screenplay without which many types of screen productions cannot take place. Analysis of the critical success factors of thousands of feature films points to the quality of the screenplay and quality of the direction as the two most important factors (Simonton 2002).

As a form of creative labour, screenwriting has *exemplary* and *idiosyncratic* features (Conor 2010a, 2010b). Screenwriting exemplifies post-Fordist creative labour in terms of its economic insecurity, freelancing, multitasking, perpetual networking, inequitable collaboration, complex subjectivity, portfolio careers, and self-performing work behaviour (ibid.). Screen production is a project-based industry, and screenwriters (like many other production workers in this industry) are employed on a "life-of-project" basis (Bielby and Bielby 1999). Screenwriting work offers no guarantee that efforts will be culturally or financially successful. Agents, producers, or other industrial gatekeepers read only a small fraction of the thousands of screenplays offered to them, and only 1 or 2 per cent among these reach production (Macdonald 2003). Thus, most screenwriters do not live from their writing activity: only 5 per cent of the members of the Writers Guild of America earn their living from writing screenplays (Elbert 1998, xiii). A major occupational challenge for screenwriters is to generate income from multiple sources. As one Canadian writer/director told us, "We do whatever we can between writing contracts … We teach, we story edit, we work at other jobs … whatever it takes to fill the gap."

Screenwriting also has *idiosyncratic* features of an institutional, sociological, and national cultural/political-economic nature that shape the social dynamics of screenwriting as much as generic creative-labour features do (Kaye and Davis 2010). Institutional features refer to industrial and organizational practices in the film and television industry. For example, the screen industry in Canada revolves around television, not feature films. This has several implications for the demand for screenwriting talent in Canada. Television differs from feature film in terms of storytelling formats, conventions, and aesthetics, and also in terms of the dynamics of the labour market, offering larger volumes of smaller contracts for freelancers than feature films do, as well as relatively stable employment for some writers for television series. Because television writers often work collaboratively in "writing rooms," they are more dependent on co-location with production firms or broadcasters than are film writers. Furthermore, in the television industry a hybrid writer-producer role called showrunning is becoming more prevalent. As the term implies, showrunners are writers who are responsible for running the show on a television series by managing the creative content and its execution over many episodes, for which they receive executive producer credit (Nadler and Davis 2012). Showrunning is a high-status role without a close equivalent in the feature film industry. The role emerged first in the United States and only recently appeared in Canada, where the screen industry is believed to suffer from a show-runner deficit.

Screenwriting has ambiguous status as a creative activity. In the highly collectivized and industrialized film and television production process, product conception is separated from execution. Writers may be commissioned to write one or more elements of a script under development: proposal, treatment, outline, story, drafts, rewrite, or polish. The script delivered by the screenwriter is only an approximation of what eventually ends up on the screen; the screenwriting function is eclipsed by the work of producers, directors, and actors, diminishing the authorial status of the screenwriter (Maras 2009; Price 2010). The screenplay itself, the product of the writer's labours, has neither economic nor cultural value on its own: "The script may be the blueprint for the film, [but] it is rarely admired in itself; the screenplay has been understood as part of an industrial process and thus viewed as a craft rather than a creative act, part of an industry which is driven by profit. This has resulted in the screenplay being generally considered a lesser form than playwriting or prose" (Nelmes 2007, 108).

Apart from some hobbyists and collectors, the general public does not purchase screenplays or teleplays and only a few specialty stores stock them for sale, usually for other screenwriters or academics to purchase. Screenwriting's relative marginality leaves it a largely invisible occupation in the public's eye, in scholarly research, and in the film and television industry itself. As Mehring (1990, 1) writes, "The screenwriter has always been and continues to be the low person on the totem pole," suffering from relative anonymity in a creative occupation in which nobody knows his or her name (Prover 1994). This invisibility affects screenwriter occupational culture and the individual motivation of screenwriters. Screenwriters must expect to undergo emotional roller-coaster rides, anxiety from "being scared out of their wits by stress, pressure, and the premonition that it all may end very soon," and suffer from "pain, disappointment, rejection, critics, and executives" says Elbert in *Why We Write* (1998). Signalling psychological resilience in the face of structural marginalization is an important feature of the occupational culture of screenwriting, and the invisibility of screenwriters and the ambiguous literary status of the screenplay are unavoidable topics in the scholarly literature on the theory and practice of screenwriting (Kaye and Davis 2010).

By differentially shaping access to screenwriting work and employment opportunities according to ethnicity, gender, and age, sociological factors within network-based reputational labour markets make screenwriting in Canada an extraordinarily homogeneous occupation. Well-documented exclusionary networks differentially allocate work opportunities to white males, and pigeonhole or deflect females, ethnic/cultural minorities, and older writers (Bielby 2009; Christopherson 2009). In the United States, screenwriting is dominated by middle-aged white males despite decades of efforts to call attention to the problem and induce greater diversity in the occupation (cf. WGA West 2007, 2009).

National cultural and political factors also exert influences on the screenwriter occupation in Canada, giving it idiosyncratic attributes. Film and television are highly capital-intensive industries requiring considerable domestic business and policy infrastructure and capabilities. The indigenous English-language screen industry is centred in Toronto largely as an outcome of government policies and programs intended to support advanced cultural production for purposes of affirming and strengthening Canadian national identity and cultural sovereignty (Davis 2011).

In spite of the many obstacles to economic and psychological fulfilment, screenwriting exercises an enormous power of attraction over many creative individuals, inducing thousands to prepare screenplays, pitch ideas, and work on the margins of the industry until the big break occurs. More than money alone, expressive freedom and gratification from telling stories that appear on screen, and the cultural capital that many associate with professional screenwriting credits, are considered the screenwriter's true compensation for the trials and tribulations along the way. Said one Toronto-based screenwriter we interviewed, "People pay you to dream" – a rarity in English-speaking Canada, a society that sources most of its screen-based dreams in California.

Toronto as Centre

Screen industries are highly geographically clustered, usually in major metropolitan regions (Picard, 2009; 2008). Toronto is the only "second-tier" media production centre in North America (Krätke 2003) and is the principal creative screen production centre of English-speaking Canada, where decisions to produce Canadian content for English-language film and television are taken (Davis 2011).[1] Canadian content, especially scripted drama, is the principal source of demand for screenwriters in

Canada. In 2007–8, $933 million was spent in Canada on producing Canadian television content in the fiction genre, and $240 million on Canadian-content fiction feature-film production, of which nearly three-quarters was in the English language (CFTPA 2009). Approximately 80 per cent of Ontario's nearly $2 billion in film and television production in 2009 was indigenous (i.e., Canadian or broadcaster in-house production).

Toronto offers many opportunities to writers in addition to screenwriting. It ranks as the third- or fourth-largest North American city for core copyright industries, encompassing film, television, interactive media, book and magazine publishing, live and recorded music (see Hracs and Stolarick this volume), advertising, newspapers, and live theatre (Davis 2011). English-speaking Canada's major book, magazine, music, and newspaper publishers are headquartered in Toronto. The city is home to many of the country's major screen production houses, its principal English-language public broadcasters, and many of its private broadcasters. Four of the major Canadian media conglomerates are headquartered in Toronto. The Toronto region hosts Canada's largest population of independent screen-content producers, specialty broadcasters, and suppliers of specialized services and inputs (ibid.). Toronto's screen industry is unlike Vancouver's, which is based mainly on foreign-location or "runaway" productions from California. Foreign-location production engages mainly below-the-line labour and does not offer opportunities to Canadian screenwriters (Davis and Kaye 2010).

In order to draw the first-ever portrait of English-speaking screenwriters in Canada, in 2010 we conducted an online survey of the members of the Writers Guild of Canada.[2] Of the nearly 2000 WGC members, 266 completed our survey, for a response rate of around 13 per cent. Although a screenwriter is not required to belong to the Writers Guild, we assume that most established English-language screenwriters (i.e., those who have been produced or who have screen credits) in Canada are members. The geographical distribution of respondents did not differ much from that of the WGC population: 49.4 per cent of respondents call the Toronto region their home, with 15.1 per cent living in Vancouver, 10.6 per cent in Los Angeles and 7.9 per cent in Montreal.[3]

Some Toronto-based writers described the Toronto region's urban (and suburban) environments as inspirations for their work, or described how urban centres inspire creativity due to close contact with various cultures and youth populations. "It's the most multicultural, heterogeneous city in Canada" pointed out one respondent, before continuing: "My writing reflects the (now) urban sensibility of most

Canadians, and the increasing demographic tilt of younger viewers. I am exposed daily to people who live, think, worship, believe, and exist with different values, beliefs, and life and economic circumstances – and those interactions enrich and widen my worldview. It makes my writing less provincial."

But the fact that Canadian screen stories are seldom set in Toronto or Vancouver was underlined as a creative challenge for many writers who are forced to write in general about "who you know" and "how you live" rather than "where you live." Most suggestions that Toronto inspired writers creatively came from screenwriters discussing the ability to connect, meet, and develop relationships with other writers, not from the aesthetic, cultural, or larger social characteristics of the city itself.

The prevailing view, however, was that a writer's location in Toronto is important because of proximity to broadcasters, agents, production companies, and the other gatekeepers and decision-makers in the English-Canadian screen industry. In general, numbers support this logic. Nationally, 53 per cent of Canadian screenwriters report earning less than $40,000 per year from screenwriting (table 4.1). This figure drops to 43 per cent for Toronto-based screenwriters. For those who aspire to a middle-class income based on screenwriting work, Toronto is the place to be.

At the same time, nearly half of those who make less than $10,000 per year from screenwriting are Toronto residents, suggesting that the city attracts the highest and lowest earners in the field. The economic advantages to screenwriters' location in Toronto stem primarily from the Canadian screen industry's geographic centralization, as well as the country's implicit cultural policy that brought the Toronto media-production cluster to predominance.

Toronto provides opportunities unavailable elsewhere in Canada for screenwriters to move more easily into senior positions in the industry. Of the writers who listed "Story Editor of a TV Show" as their most common contracted writing task, 61 per cent are based in Toronto. The same concentration in Toronto is seen among those who listed "Show Concept Creator–Story Bible Writer" (55 per cent), and especially "Showrunner/ Writer Producer" (74 per cent). Of all respondents reporting showrunning experience, 63 per cent identified Toronto as their primary place of residence. In comparison, writers listing "feature film screenplay" as their most common job were severely underrepresented in Toronto (29 per cent), an indication that Toronto's importance as a television production centre is not equalled in film.

Table 4.1 Screenwriters' income from screenwriting

Income from screenwriting	National (%)	Toronto (%)
< $40,000	53	43
$40K–$60K	10	12
$60K–$80K	9	13
$80K–$100K	9	12
$100K–$150K	7	8
$150K+	9	12

It might be expected that one of Toronto's advantages in attracting and retaining screenwriters would be its status as a creative city where a professional writer could find other ways to capitalize on creative talent outside of the screen production sector. Yet evidence from our survey suggests that this is not the case. The half of Canadian screenwriters based in Toronto accounted for 35 per cent of all Canadian screenwriters who are also journalists; 40 per cent of novelists; 38 percent of short-story writers; half of poets; half of those writing for advertising firms; 40 per cent of those doing corporate technical writing; 49 per cent of theatrical script writers; and half of Internet writers. Toronto writers reported earning income from such activities with no greater frequency than their counterparts across Canada, and with less frequency in many categories. In other words, despite being based in a major creative metropole where opportunities for professional work in various other creative industries abound, Toronto-based screenwriters are slightly less likely to work at other forms of writing than their screenwriter counterparts elsewhere in Canada.

This might be explained by the fact that Toronto-based screenwriters are busier working on screen production than colleagues across Canada. Toronto hosts a disproportionately large share of screenwriters in each of the three highest ranges of screen credits. Conversely, despite playing port-of-arrival for many novices aiming to break into the industry, Toronto has a disproportionately low share of screenwriters in the lower brackets of screen credits.

Toronto attracts screenwriters from the Canadian hinterland, playing the role of national centre for English-speaking Canada. This tendency is reflected through the myriad screenwriters who move from elsewhere in Canada to Toronto, and also through the high percentage of non-Toronto-based screenwriters who occasionally travel to Toronto to work. Toronto exerts a strong gravitational pull on young Canadian screenwriters looking to get their start. Screenwriters living in Toronto tend to be only slightly younger than average, but Toronto attracts a disproportionately large share of young screenwriters; of the eleven WGC members in their twenties who responded to our survey, only one was based outside of Toronto. This difference is reflected in the number of years Toronto-based screenwriters have been in the industry. While 36.6 per cent of Canadian screenwriters have been writing for less than ten years, 48.9 per cent of screenwriters in Toronto have less than ten years' experience. Similarly, 58.8 per cent of Canadian screenwriters have worked between eleven and thirty-five years, while less than half of the writers in Toronto fall into the same category. Clearly, Toronto is regarded as the port-of-entry for those wishing to enter the Canadian English-language screenwriting labour market.

Toronto offers two major advantages to persons seeking to enter screenwriting: an elite training centre – the Canadian Film Centre – and widespread opportunities for mentoring and networking.

Founded by Canadian director and Hollywood icon Norman Jewison, the Canadian Film Centre (CFC) is "committed to promoting and investing in Canada's diverse talent; providing exhibition, financial, and distribution opportunities for top creative content leaders from coast to coast" (http://www.cfccreates.com). The CFC offers a range of training programs and master classes, often drawing on prominent local media practitioners as resident instructors. Many of Toronto's production community elite are among the CFC's network of alumni, benefactors, and party crashers, making CFC training a door-opener for many and a fast-track for some. The CFC proclaims itself "Canada's leading institution for advanced training in film, television and new media": more than 1300 media professionals have passed through its training programs since 1988.

Many screenwriters receive formal training in the craft. Overall, the percentage of screenwriters who have taken some form of formal training program or professional workshop was relatively constant in (27 per cent) and outside (26 per cent) Toronto. Thus, providing access to screenwriter training does not distinguish Toronto from other places. In their comments, certain respondents insisted that training was irrelevant to learning the craft, since professional screenwriting could only be learned "on the job," by doing.

However, the CFC training programs offer an advantage to Toronto-based screenwriters. CFC training contributes to the "stickiness" of the Toronto labour market, since 80 per cent of CFC graduates surveyed described their primary place of residence as the Toronto area. Thirteen per cent of survey respondents had participated in training programs offered by the CFC, but while 20 per cent of Toronto-based screenwriters have attended the CFC, only 5 per cent of Canadian screenwriters based outside the Toronto area had done so.

CFC training directly correlates with financial success among English-language Canadian screenwriters. While 53 per cent of screenwriters earn less than $40,000 per year from screenwriting alone, only 30 per cent of CFC graduates fail to earn that much from screenwriting. This income advantage may reflect the quality of the instruction of the CFC programs relative to comparable programs offered elsewhere; it may also reflect the role the CFC plays in helping screenwriters get into the Toronto screenwriting network by establishing mentoring relationships.

Mentorship is crucial to honing the craft of professional screenwriting, to helping individuals develop, market, and transfer their skills to work on the ideas and projects of others. In a freelance business in which success and opportunity depend on reputation and professional contacts, mentorship plays a crucial networking function, connecting workers with employers, ideas with funding, and skills with projects. This is particularly true given the extent to which respondents made it clear that personal contacts are absolutely crucial to success in the Canadian screenwriting industry, a claim corroborated by scholarship on the importance of personal relationships in breaking into elite project–based work networks in Hollywood (Lee 2011; Skilton 2008).

Strong evidence suggests that a culture of mentorship and networking operates among screenwriters in Toronto, providing a unique social mechanism for those entering the Canadian screenwriting occupation. Mentorship relationships among screenwriters are a more common practice in Toronto than elsewhere in Canada: 56 per cent of Toronto-based respondents report having had mentors, as opposed to only 34 per cent of Canadian screenwriters living elsewhere. The mentorship gap between Toronto-based screenwriters and those from other parts of Canada is not a simple case of an urban-rural divide, since Toronto's rate significantly exceeds that of Vancouver (38 per cent) and Montreal (19 per cent). Among urban centres with significant populations of respondents, only Los Angeles–based WGC members reported similar levels of mentorship (57 per cent). In other words, Canadian screenwriters are as likely to find mentors in Toronto as in the global centre of the screen production industry.

The CFC and other formal mentorship organizations and institutions might help to explain Toronto's advantage. The critical mass of talent located in the Greater Toronto Area provides more options to both mentors and apprentices for finding individuals with complementary personalities and career ambitions. The sheer volume of screen production in the Toronto area might lead well-connected, successful screenwriters to feel that opportunities abound and thus to be more cooperative and less competitive with their younger colleagues than screenwriters working in centres where opportunities are scarcer.

Toronto as Periphery

While Toronto is the principal screenwriting centre for English-speaking Canada, it is also a periphery, losing some of its talent to Hollywood. Many Canadian screenwriters believe that the brightest talent moves to Los Angeles. When asked for a general word of advice to young aspiring Canadian screenwriters, many of our respondents replied simply: "Move to LA."

The American and Canadian markets for screen products are asymmetrical. Hollywood screen products circulate easily in Canada, but Canadian English-language screen products make little impact in American markets. The reality is that Canadian English-language screen products – especially indigenous drama – struggle for audience attention and distributor shelf space even in Canada. In 2006–7 Canadian English-language television drama captured only 14 per cent of peak-period viewing of drama programming on Canadian television, and Canadian feature films captured only 1.1 per cent of the English-language box office (CFTPA 2009). Recognizably Canadian fare is not valued in the United States, requiring aspiring Canadian exporters of film and television to align production to American aesthetic standards and to efface cultural markers that identify their product as Canadian (Davis and Nadler 2009).

The low domestic market share of indigenous English-language Canadian scripted screen products reflects the ongoing marginalization of the scripted-content segments of the Canadian industry, a situation suffered to varying extents in other small English-language countries (Grant 2008). The problematic status of indigenous screen-based culture in English Canada magnifies the attraction of Hollywood, where the inherent occupational risks of screenwriting are similar, but the rewards are greater, and where a few Canadian screenwriters, such as superstars Paul Haggis and David Shore, have earned fame and fortune (Kaye and Davis 2010).

According to survey respondents, the main advantage of locating in Los Angeles is the competition to meet the most demanding standards. "LA is a very creative, happening place," according to one WGC member located in California, "and I get a lot done here because the bar is so high." This view is echoed by another writer who observes: "Living in Los Angeles affects my writing as I am in the big time and what I write goes against the best." Reputational success in Los Angeles has undeniable financial benefits, since California-based WGC members make up almost a third of respondents reporting screenwriting income of more than $150,000 per year (although LA-based WGC screenwriters account for only 11 per cent of responses). Among the obstacles to success that make Los Angeles intrinsically appealing for Canadian screenwriters are: frustration with the complexities and uncertainties of Canadian production funding models, a (perhaps naive) view that screenwriters are more likely to get ahead based on merit rather than connections in Los Angeles than they are in Canada, frustration with working anonymously in Canada on productions that have little traction with audiences, and a sense that the occupational dynamics of the screenwriting industry in Canada lead to creative stagnation. In the words of one respondent, in Canada the system often leads "to the best of the worst rising to the top rather than what is truly good writing." Said one Toronto-based Canadian writer who has had success in Canada but is still pitching in Los Angeles, "Sadly, I'm th e best we've got."

Toronto as Centre of Periphery

To qualify Toronto's position as the centre of the periphery is to describe not only the centripetal and centrifugal forces that affect screenwriting talent movements into and out of the city, but also the ways in which Toronto's concurrent centrality and peripherality influence the creative process of Toronto-based screenwriters. The city serves primarily as a creative production centre for the Canadian hinterland. Screen stories developed or produced in Toronto are infrequently set in Toronto. Consequently, Toronto rarely tells stories about itself to Toronto audiences. Often working with a "will it play in Moose Jaw" rule-of-thumb, many Canadian productions intended for the domestic market consciously avoid urban settings and, in particular, distinctly Toronto sensibilities, in favour of generic Canada-scapes or specific regional flavours like those of the Prairies or Newfoundland. Many Toronto screen productions are service productions for Hollywood studios: Toronto vigorously markets itself to stand in for more expensive American centres, especially New York, Chicago, and Washington (Davis and Kaye 2010). This versatility is good for Toronto's service production business, but does not contribute to Canadian identity or to a Toronto urban cultural aesthetic, a key differentiator among metropolitan regions competing in the cognitive-cultural economy (Davis 2011; Davis and Mills forthcoming).

This reality is reflected in the comments posted by Toronto-based screenwriters. One screenwriter who also works as a novelist lamented: "In my books, the GTA is my backdrop. In my TV writing, I try to think American." For another screenwriter used to working towards stories that will play in Moose Jaw, Toronto is "perhaps too urban for the audience we are mostly reaching" to be creatively inspiring as a location. Generally, survey responses contained variations of the theme that, for Toronto-based screenwriters, "Where the story is set has a greater influence on my writing than where I live."

Toronto and Exclusionary Networks

In an industry that requires strong networking behaviour and has a high attrition rate, Toronto's attraction for screenwriters lies in the opportunity to join a select group of writers able to leverage their proximity to the main production centre of anglophone Canada to remain aware of writing opportunities, mainly defined by broadcasters. This advantage is reinforced through gate-keeping institutions, formal and informal mentorships, and a professional culture that uses reputation and personal networks as currency.

Proximity to opportunities is not merely spatial but also *cultural*. Breaking into the Toronto screen industry syndicate can open up a rewarding career path for a screenwriter, but many individuals are sooner or later excluded on the basis of race, age, gender, and class, including those who are not able to attend the CFC, who do not have contacts with the right people, or who do not conform to the image of "Canadianness" required to produce screen culture for the Canadian hinterland.

Professional screenwriting is difficult for young people to break into. Only 4 per cent of survey respondents were in their twenties. In addition to workable raw ideas for stories, novices require contacts to get projects off the ground, and mentorship and experience in order to refine ideas and polish scripts appropriate for professional production environments. Getting that first professional credit and opening the door to

Guild membership requires prolonged networking, professionalization, idea refining, and perseverance that can take years. For example, when asked to give advice to younger screenwriters, one responded opined: "Count on ten years of getting nowhere, but eventually a break will come your way."

Breaking into the screenwriter fraternity apparently requires paying one's dues: this often means working for free, at a discount, or under dubious arrangements. In their responses to our survey, many screenwriters expressed frustration with the challenges associated with being compensated in a fair and timely fashion. In the words of one respondent, "Many deceitful, dishonest producers [are] in the business for the wrong reason. I have been screwed so many times by well-known companies." Certain respondents expressed frustration with the extent to which gatekeepers are able to leverage freelancers' dependence on reputation and contacts for getting future work to renege on agreed working arrangements with screenwriters, knowing that writers are unlikely to risk being blackballed by mounting a serious protest. An oft-cited example was the tendency for screenwriters to find themselves working "on spec" or at dramatically unfair wages for prolonged periods of time and on an indeterminate basis on projects "under development" that were ultimately never funded for production. In such cases, screenwriters often had neither credit nor fair pay to show for serious investments of time, energy, and creativity. The difficulty of being paid in a fair and timely fashion is far worse in Toronto than elsewhere in Canada. Only Los Angeles is comparable, suggesting that such practices are common in larger production centres with a standing reserve of surplus talent.

Reflecting the problematic nature of an industry in which personal connections and social networks are crucial determinants of creative and economic opportunities, and everyone is considered personally responsible for personal success or failure, responses to questions about the industry's effectiveness at fostering, mentoring, or apprenticing new writing talent were decidedly bifurcated.

Evidence suggests that membership in the club is exclusive; getting in depends on circumstance and luck, favouritism, preferential treatment, and avoiding exclusionary practices. Some screenwriters told positive personal stories of relatively friction-free initiations into the Canadian screenwriting industry. One respondent described how "I developed as a writer and producer because of the excellent mentorship I've received from seasoned writers/producers in the industry";

another was "very lucky to have a mentor who pushed me to write all the time." Recognizing that "it's difficult to break into the industry," and that not many are given the same kind of chance, one respondent described how a big break came when "I was fortunate in that I worked on a non-scripted show with a mentor who taught at the CFC and thought I had potential as a writer. When the opportunity arose for a scripted show, he gave me a chance."

Many assessments of new talent development in the Canadian screen-writing industry were positive, putting the onus to break through on the individual. Typical of this view were statements such as "The industry is good, but the young screenwriter has to go and seek out the mentor-ship – sometimes meeting 10, 20, or even 30 people before you find someone who can give you a break" and "The industry has ample op-portunities for fostering new talent and opportunities to develop screen-writing skills if new writers seek them out."

Clearly this recipe for success depends on having access to thirty important people in the industry more than on drive, gumption, or the willingness to hustle. Many personal anecdotes of how individuals eventually got their big break seem to hinge on being in the right place at the right time, or on patronage or extraordinary support from estab-lished industry insiders. The "self-made success" theme was also re-peated in certain personal narratives such as "I had the good fortune to get a script coordinator job and I don't credit the Canadian industry for that" or the more direct response that "I've had to do everything myself."

Other respondents – those who likely struggled to get appointments with thirty industry insiders – feel stonewalled by entry barriers. For example, only 15 per cent of respondents gave the industry a score of 4 or above on a 5-point scale (where 5 was excellent) on the question about how well the industry develops new talent. Comments ranged from criticism of the competitive nature of the screenwriting business to frank assessments about the prospects for sustainable careers to ex-pressions of frustration and even puzzlement with the seeming impen-etrability of the system.

Exclusionary networks affect older writers: age defines an individual professional screenwriter's career prospects. Nearly 80 per cent of Canadian screenwriters are between the ages of thirty and fifty-nine. Screenwriting is a professional occupation requiring constant novel-ty in a context of rapidly changing technologies, tastes, and styles.

Table 4.2 Demographic characteristics of English-language Canadian and
Toronto-based screenwriters

	Toronto – general (2006 Canada census data)[1]	Canada – screenwriters	Toronto-based screenwriters
% female	52%	35%	35%
% university degree	37%	70%	71%
% visible minority	47%	3%	4%
% born outside Canada	50%	26%	21%
% mother tongue other than English	47%	5%	3%

1 Source: 2006 census backgrounder: http://www.toronto.ca/demographics/reports.htm.

Broadcasters, film studios, and advertisers like to appeal to young audiences with hip content. Many participants expressed profound frustration with structural ageism that pushes all but the most successful screenwriters into other facets of screen production or out of the industry altogether. Overall, 26 per cent of respondents reported being the victim of age-based discrimination. Some described writers being sidelined because producers felt they were too far removed from the themes and characters in youth-oriented shows to write in an appropriate voice. Older female writers are especially vulnerable to ageism.

Given the general difficulty experienced by individuals trying to break in and remain screenwriters, the extra degree of challenge that this highly networked profession presents to women and minorities can readily be imagined. Although Toronto is one of the most culturally diverse cities in the world, the screenwriting profession is overwhelmingly white, male, and native English-speaking.

Table 4.2 illustrates the effects of exclusionary networks in the screenwriting profession and points to the predominance of culturally elite perspectives in Canadian storytelling, even when the screen industry is located in Canada's most diverse city. The exceptional cultural diversity found in Toronto and Canada as a whole is not reflected in the extremely homogeneous group of Canadians working as screenwriters. In fact, Toronto-based screenwriters are not much different from the national population of English-language screenwriters. While Toronto does not struggle to recruit and retain screenwriters from other parts of Canada, few individuals from Toronto's culturally diverse population make screenwriting their career.

Screenwriters and the Stories Told

Our investigation of the social dynamics of screenwriting in the Greater Toronto Area raises three major questions that require further research. First, some of the conceptual models developed within the cultural-labour, creative economy, and creative cities literature do not apply in the case of screenwriters, or require considerable nuance. Industry-specific practices and nation-specific institutions, more than abstractions about creativity and mobility, explain the social dynamics of screenwriting in Canada, which, as we have seen, have very strong parallels with screenwriting in the United States. Such industry-specific and national-specific practices need to be factored into research on the geography of creative labour.

Second, unlike the cases of artists or musicians (see Leslie et al., Hracs and Stolarik, and Grant et al. this volume), opportunities to earn a living through screenwriting are highly localized in a small number of cities in North America, obviating the need to market or brand these cities for purposes of attracting screenwriting talent, and making marketing or branding campaigns largely irrelevant in other locations. Similarly, considerations regarding the attractiveness of local cultural scenes, the perceived degree of authenticity of a city, or preferences that culture producers may have for particular cultural styles assume that creative workers have multiple geographic options in the market for employment. In the case of screenwriting, however, the range of options is relatively narrow, and the career implications of each option are not difficult to imagine. Further, screen production is a capital-intensive, highly institutionalized industry, and while these factors may not determine which screenplays a writer may choose to write, they certainly affect the selection of screenplays that are produced.

Third, our study underscores the need for research into how the social dynamics of creative professions affect the cultural products offered to consumers. Other chapters in this volume (Leslie et al., Grant et al.) emphasize how social processes of selection and sorting in the market for talent affect cultural outcomes through exclusion or inclusion. Unlike with artists or musicians, however, screenwriting is affected by regulatory measures in an industry, broadcasting, which has received an explicit mandate and public subsidies to fulfil multicultural policy goals

through its programming and the employment opportunities arising out of its operations, [to] serve the needs and interests, and reflect the circumstances and aspirations, of Canadian men, women and children, including

equal rights, the linguistic duality and multicultural and multiracial nature of Canadian society and the special place of aboriginal peoples within
that society. (Broadcasting Act, S.C. 1991, c. 11)

Exclusionary networks in screenwriting affect the kinds of stories that
show up on Canadian film and television screens. Despite exceptions to
the general rule, English-Canadian film and television products do not
attract large audiences or animate popular culture. They function mainly to fill content quotas and round out screening schedules (Beatty and
Sullivan 2006). The exclusionary attributes of the screenwriter profession in English-speaking Canada are entirely consistent with what is
known about the social dynamics of labour in elite project–based cultural industries, of which Hollywood is the exemplar (Skilton 2008). The
difference between Hollywood and Toronto is that the screen industry
in Canada is more of a national cultural project than an economically
viable industry, a situation that reflects the much smaller size of the domestic market, competition from Hollywood, the cost of screen production, and the chicken-and-egg problem of generally low public interest
in Canadian screen products.

The City of Toronto's motto is "Diversity Our Strength." If Canada's
screenwriting population better represented the Canadian people, perhaps their stories would resonate with Canadian audiences (Raboy and
Shtern 2010), who live mainly in urban regions. Indeed, if Canadian
screen offerings reflected greater diversity in storytelling voices, the
results might be more attractive in creative as well as in commercial
terms, domestically as well as internationally. This is why Canadians
need to ask the same question the Writers Guild of America asked in
2007: "Whose stories are we telling?"

ACKNOWLEDGMENTS

The Writers Guild of Canada facilitated our access to Canadian screenwriters
by communicating our survey invitation to its members and encouraging them
to participate. The research reported here was supported by a grant from the
Social Sciences and Humanities Research Council on Innovation and Creativity in City Regions, and by internal research awards from Ryerson University.
While a post-doctoral research fellow at Ryerson University, Janice Kaye provided valuable assistance in developing and launching the screenwriter survey.

We are grateful to each of the above-mentioned for the support they provided. Also thanks to Laurie Channer, Bridget Conor, and Jill Grant for helpful comments on earlier drafts.

NOTES

1 For a film to qualify as a "Canadian" screen production by the Canadian Audio-Visual Certification Office (CAVCO), the director or screenwriter must be Canadian, and points are awarded for the Canadian nationality of the top creative talent. Certification as Canadian has important implications for tax-credit eligibility. An analogous system certifies Canadian content requirements for broadcasters. For an overview of "Canadian Content" policies in broadcasting, see House of Commons 2003 (chap. 5) and Raboy and Shtern 2010 (chaps. 4 and 9).
2 The WGC is the principal professional association for Canadian English-language writers for film, television, radio, and digital media (see http://www.writersguildofcanada.com/).
3 Approximately 43% of the 1885 WGC members (in 2008) live in the GTA. The other principal locations of English-language Canadian screenwriters are Quebec (9%), British Columbia (13%), and California (17%) – predominantly in the Montreal, Vancouver, and Los Angeles metropolitan regions, respectively.

REFERENCES

Beatty, Bart, and Rebecca Sullivan. 2006. *Canadian television today*. Calgary: University of Calgary Press.

Bielby, Denise D. 2009. "Gender inequality in culture industries: Women and men writers in film and television." *Sociologie du Travail* 51 (2): 237–52. http://dx.doi.org/10.1016/j.soctra.2009.03.006.

Bielby, William T., and Denise D. Bielby. 1999. "Organizational mediation of project-based labor markets: Talent agencies and the careers of screenwriters." *American Sociological Review* 64 (1): 64–85. http://dx.doi.org/10.2307/2657278.

CFTPA. 2009. *09 Profile. An economic report on the Canadian film and television production industry*. Ottawa: Canadian Film and Television Production Association.

Christopherson, Susan. 2009. "Working in the creative economy: Risk, adaptation, and the persistence of exclusionary networks." In *Creative labour: Working in the creative industries*, ed. Alan McKinlay and Chris Smith, 72–90. Basingstoke, UK: Palgrave Macmillan.

Conor, Bridget. 2010a. "Everybody's a writer: Theorizing screenwriting as creative labour." *Journal of Screenwriting* 1 (1): 27–43. http://dx.doi.org/10.1386 /josc.1.1.27/1.

Conor, Bridget. 2010b. *Screenwriting as creative labour: Pedagogies, practices and livelihoods in the new cultural economy*. London: Goldsmiths College, University of London, doctoral dissertation.

Davis, Charles H. 2011. "The Toronto media cluster: Between culture and commerce." In *Media clusters across the globe: Developing, expanding, and reinvigorating content capabilities*, ed. Charlie Karlsson and Robert Picard, 223–50. Cheltenham, UK: Edward Elgar.

Davis, Charles H., and Janice Kaye. 2010. "International production outsourcing and the development of indigenous film and television capabilities – the case of Canada." In *Locating migrating media*, ed. G. Elmer, C. Davis, J. Marchessault, and J. McCullough, 57–78. Lanham, MD: Rowman and Littlefield.

Davis, Charles H., and Nicholas Mills. Forthcoming. "Innovation and Toronto's cognitive-cultural economy." In *Innovating in urban economies*, ed. David Wolfe. Toronto: University of Toronto Press.

Davis, Charles H., and James Nadler. 2009. "International television co-productions and the cultural discount: The case of *Family Biz*, a comedy." In *Uddevalla Symposium: The geography of innovation and entrepreneurship*, ed. Irene Bernhard, 359–78. Trollhattan, Sweden: University West, Research Reports.

Elbert, Lorian Tamara. 1998. *Why we write. Personal statements and photographic portraits of 25 top screenwriters*. Los Angeles: Silman-James Press.

Florida, Richard. 2002. *The rise of the creative class and how it's transforming work, leisure, community and everyday life*. New York: Basic Books.

Grant, Peter S. 2008. *Stories under stress: The challenge for indigenous television drama in English-language broadcast markets*. Report prepared for the International Affiliation of Writers Guilds, December. http://www.mccarthy.ca /pubs/iawg_drama_report_final.pdf.

House of Commons (Standing Committee on Canadian Heritage). 2003. *Our cultural sovereignty: The second century of Canadian broadcasting*. Ottawa: Communication Canada.

Kaye, Janice, and Charles H. Davis. 2010. "'If it ain't on the page, it ain't on the stage': Screenwriting, national specificity and the English-Canadian feature film." *Journal of Screenwriting* 2 (1): 62–83.

Krätke, Stefan. 2003. "Global media cities in a world-wide urban network." *European Planning Studies* 11 (6): 605–28. http://dx.doi.org/10.1080 /0965431032000108350.

Leadbeater, Charles. 1999. *Living on thin air: The new economy.* London, UK: Viking.

Lee, David. 2011. "Networks, cultural capital and creative labour in the British independent television industry." *Media Culture & Society* 33 (4): 549–65. http://dx.doi.org/10.1177/0163443711398693.

Le Goff, Jean-Pierre, Johanne Brunet, Charles H. Davis, Daniel Giroux, and Florian Sauvageau. 2011. *La production audiovisuelle canadienne indépendante: Aides financières, diffusion et écoute.* Sainte-Foy, QC: Centre d'études sur les médias, Université Laval.

Macdonald, Ian W. 2003. "Finding the needle: How readers see screen ideas." *Journal of Media Practice* 4 (1): 27–40. http://dx.doi.org/10.1386/jmpr.4.1 .27/0.

Maras, Steven. 2009. *Screenwriting: History, theory and practice.* London: Wallflower Press.

Mehring, Margaret. 1990. *The screenplay: A blend of film form and content.* Boston: Focal Press.

Miller, Toby. 2011. "The new international division of cultural labor." In *Managing media work,* ed. Mark Deuze, 87–99. Thousand Oaks, CA: Sage.

Montgomery, John. 2007. *The new wealth of cities: City dynamics and the fifth wave.* Aldershot, UK: Ashgate Publishing.

Nadler, James, and Charles H. Davis. 2012. "The Showrunner: Creative, economic, and transmedia coordination of project-based production in the North American television industry." Paper presented at the International Symposium on Media Innovations, Oslo, April.

Nelmes, Jill. 2007. "Some thoughts on analyzing the screenplay, the process of screenplay writing and the balance between craft and creativity." *Journal of Media Practice* 8 (2): 107–13. http://dx.doi.org/10.1386/jmpr.8.2.107_1.

Picard, Robert G. 2008. *Media clusters: Local agglomeration in an industry developing networked virtual clusters.* Jönköping: Jönköping International Business School Working Paper series 2008-3, 16 pp. http://center.hj.se/download/18. 6be93ddc12f544239c38000909/1302875871219/WP-2008-3+Picard-Publ.pdf.

Picard, Robert G. 2009. "Media clusters and regional development: Reflections on the significance of location in media production." In *Uddevalla Symposium: The geography of innovation and entrepreneurship,* ed. Irene Bernhard. 877–85. Trollhattan, Sweden: University West, Research Reports.

Price, Steven. 2010. *The screenplay: Authorship, theory and criticism.* Basingstoke: Palgrave Macmillan.

Prover, Jorja. 1994. *No one knows their names: Screenwriters in Hollywood*. Madison: University of Wisconsin Press.

Raboy, Marc, and Jeremy Shtern. 2010. *Media divides: Communication rights and the right to communicate in Canada*. Vancouver: UBC Press.

Simonton, Dean K. 2002. "Collaboration aesthetics in the feature film: Cinematic components predicting the differential impact of 2,323 Oscar-nominated movies." *Empirical Studies of the Arts* 20 (2): 115–25. http://dx.doi.org /10.2190/RHQ2-9UC3-6T32-HR66.

Skilton, Paul F. 2008. "Similarity, familiarity and access to elite work in Hollywood: Employer and employee characteristics in breakthrough employment." *Human Relations* 61 (12): 1743–73. http://dx.doi.org/10.1177 /0018726708098084.

WGA West. 2007. *Whose stories are we telling? The 2007 Hollywood writers report*. Report prepared by D.M. Hunt for the Writers Guild of America, West. Los Angeles, UCLA. http://www.wga.org/uploadedFiles/who_we_are /HWR07.pdf.

WGA West. 2009. *Rewriting an all-too-familiar story? The 2009 Hollywood writers report*. Report prepared by D.M. Hunt for the Writers Guild of America, West. Los Angeles, UCLA. http://www.wga.org/subpage_whoweare .aspx?id=922.

5 Satisfaction Guaranteed? Individual Preferences, Experiences, and Mobility

BRIAN J. HRACS AND KEVIN STOLARICK

> Individualization of life situations and processes thus means that biographies become *self-reflexive*; socially prescribed biography is transformed into biography that is self-produced and continues to be produced. Decisions on education, profession, job, place of residence, spouse, number of children and so forth, with all the secondary decisions implied, no longer can be, they must be made.
>
> (Beck 1992, 135)

As individuals become responsible for constructing their own biographies and decision making becomes more complex, social scientists endeavour to understand the factors that motivate specific choices. In geography as a discipline, the last decade has witnessed a growing fascination with the locational choices of individuals with high levels of human capital and mobility. Identifying the factors that attract and retain talent has become an important research agenda and one that has produced a robust yet contradictory body of literature. Two camps have emerged. On the one hand, Storper and Scott (2009) argue that good-quality jobs must be present before talent will migrate. On the other hand, many say that talent is attracted to locations that offer a rich mix of amenities: Florida (2002) examines the importance of tolerance, Glaeser et al. (2001) point to the availability of consumption opportunities, and Clark et al. (2002) argue that talent is drawn to leisure activities and entertainment amenities (see Gertler et al. this volume for a more detailed review).

The link between jobs and amenities does not provide sufficient nuance to explain choices. It fails to reflect the evolving nature of what constitutes a job and the degree to which the preferences of talent are differentiated by factors including occupation, gender, ethnicity, life cycle, and past experience. As Leslie et al., Davis et al., and Grant et al. demonstrate in this volume, freelance creative workers and entrepreneurs do not migrate for specific firm-based jobs, but rather for thick labour markets that offer opportunities for paid employment. Moreover, specific amenities such as culture, climate, low crime levels, good schools, and tolerance matter to varying degrees depending on individual tastes, subjectivities, and life-cycle requirements. The existing literature says little about scale and access (Lepawsky et al. this volume). Recent studies (Hracs 2009; Hracs et al. 2011) demonstrate, for example, that the mere presence of attractive labour markets and amenities does not ensure that incoming talent will be able to access employment opportunities and enjoy a high quality of life. We view this as a "disconnect" between the macro-perception of a location, which is often constructed by city-branding strategies (Rantisi and Leslie 2006), and the reality of lived experience at the scale of the individual. This problem is compounded by the tendency of the literature and development strategies to privilege the attraction stage over the equally important retention stage. Understanding what attracts and ultimately retains talent requires a multi-stage analysis.

In this chapter we draw on fifty-one interviews with musicians in Toronto to explore the factors that motivate individuals to relocate. We combine a conceptual model with sample comments from the interviews to demonstrate that talent retention is based on how well the initial expectations of place are met in reality. We begin by focusing on the initial move and how musicians imagine and select potential destinations. We then explore how the macro-perception of a city matches the lived experience of individuals. In each individual case the variance will produce one of four outcomes. If the expectations have been met, the individual will stay in the current location. If the expectations have not been met the individual will either change expectations, move within the city-region to improve the situation, or leave entirely. By using interviews to explore the decision-making process of one strand of talent, this chapter nuances the existing literature and identifies opportunities for further research.

The Individualized Nature of Locational Choice

To preface the empirical analysis, we acknowledge the rich literature on locational choice: in particular, choice has long been recognized as a highly individualized process. For example, Tiebout (1956) argued that individuals who were dissatisfied in their current location voted with their feet. He argued that individuals move to places that offer the bundle of public goods and services and taxes that best fit their requirements. In this way migration reflects a market-like solution in which people attempt to find their best fit. In other words, every individual creates his or her own calculus by weighing specific factors related to employment and amenities. By extension, Rosen (1979) and Roback (1982) demonstrate that, in some cases, individuals will accept lower wages or higher cost of housing in exchange for an increase in their quality of life. Underpinning our subsequent discussion on intra- and inter-regional migration, Blomquist et al. (1988) indicate that these trade-offs apply for movements both within and across regions.

In the global competition for talent, reconciling broad attraction strategies that tout specific amenities with the subjective preferences of individuals is problematic: the literature offers several cautionary tales. In their analysis of Singapore's Global City of the Arts initiative, for example, Chang and Lee (2003) argue that the results from significant investment aimed at attraction proved marginal at best. Indeed, in this case, low awareness, appreciation, and participation created amenities that did not meet the needs, desires, or expectations of the citizenry. Donald (2001, 269) warns against conflating measures of quality of life with quality of place, and explains that "quality of life is an individualized concept, whereas quality of place suggests a consensus in place regarding how quality of life strategies should be prioritized in terms of an overall development plan." She argues that the *descriptive* analysis of the relationship between amenities and regional growth – put forward by Florida, Clark, and Glaeser – has been translated into *prescriptive* development efforts at the local and regional scale. Donald explains that this translation has resulted in a "focus on marketing the consumption value of gay neighbourhoods and 'funky' bohemian districts. Yet, surface-level 'place' marketing may have the potential of glossing over the essential investments required to maintain and enhance a creative city" (Donald et al. 2003, 11).

Behavioural scientists suggest that the subjective perceptions of potential migrants are an important determinant of location choice. Wolpert (1965) argues that individual-level behavioural traits are critical to understanding migration patterns. He describes three dimensions to understanding migration behaviour. First is the value individuals either gain from staying in their current location or expect to gain from an alternative location. Second are the constraints (spatial and social) on the flow of information about the current and potential locations. Personal characteristics, including age, race, income, marital status, and occupation, constitute the third critical dimension. The ability of individuals to obtain correct, objective information about their current location and alternative locations is limited and filtered by individual perceptions and the availability of information. Evaluation of this information is further complicated by individual traits, expectations, and life-stage characteristics. The result is that the analysis of migration decisions is invariably subjective and is as varied by individual as by location. Wolpert argues that research in migration decision making must account for attitudes and choices being determined by highly personal, individual lived experiences. Using uniform, fixed criteria to determine quality of life within a region without accounting for individual expectations and traits is likely to be difficult and problematic.

Herzog et al. (1986) and Whisler et al. (2008) note that satisfaction with current location affects the decisions of individuals to stay or move. Florida et al. (2010a, 2010b) find that place-based factors, in particular the beauty and physical appeal of the current location and the ability to meet people and make friends, explain more of an individual's desire to stay than does community economic conditions or individual demographic characteristics.

At present the literature on talent attraction and retention displays a tendency to aggregate and generalize. Although recent studies, including Scott (2010) and Niedomysl and Hansen (2010), succeed in reversing this trend, important specificities related to place and occupations are often overlooked. Drawing on the work of Markusen and King (2003) – who call for an occupational approach to talent – our empirical investigation focuses on one strand of talent in one location: independent musicians who are currently living and working in Toronto.

The Case of Independent Musicians in Toronto

To explore the decision-making process in a population with a high degree of mobility, we chose independent musicians. In the reconfigured landscape of digital music production, independent musicians – who are not tied to established music-industry centres such as Los Angeles, New York, or Nashville (Scott 1999) – can essentially live and work anywhere (Hracs 2009; Hracs et al. 2011; Hracs 2012; Grant et al. this volume). Between 2007 and 2008 we conducted fifty-one interviews

with independent musicians. We sought a broad cross-section of experiences and opinions, and so the musicians interviewed varied by age,
gender, level of education, genre, and career stage. Figure 5.1 describes
the research participants.

Although each musician was living and working in Toronto at the
time of the interview, only half of them were born in Toronto. Moreover,
many in the sample had lived and worked in other music centres before
arriving in or returning to Toronto. The diversity of the sample allows
us to explore the perceptions and expectations of musicians who have
different reference points. For example, we can contrast how Toronto is
perceived by musicians with no experience in other larger cities to
those of musicians who have lived and worked in New York, London,
Los Angeles, Berlin, Amsterdam, Halifax, Montreal, and Nashville.

Perceptions, expectations, and satisfaction are relative constructs
shaped by prior experiences. Whereas musicians from small towns
may regard Toronto as a Mecca for opportunity, those with broader
frames of reference may consider Toronto competitive and exclusionary. Artists (Leslie et al. this volume) and screenwriters (Davis et al. this
volume) also perceive Toronto in different ways based on prior experience. To ensure consistent coverage of key issues across the interviews
we used an interview guide. In particular, we probed the spatial history
of each participant, their locational preferences, their perceptions of living and working in Toronto, and whether they intended to stay in
Toronto or relocate in the future. The responses demonstrated the individualized way in which musicians think about place and relocation.
To investigate the process, we developed a multi-stage model (figure 5.2) based on the interview responses. Although we acknowledge
its simplicity, the model is meant to add structure to the discussion. In
the following sections we walk through the stages of the model and
provide illustrative quotes and analysis.

Stage 1: Establishing Expectations

The first stage of the model involves the decision to move. Here we are
interested in the impetus for relocation and how expectations about potential destinations are formed. Highlighting the complexity of the process, our sample included musicians who approached this stage in a
rational way, researching locations and weighing their options according
to criteria found in the literature. Others, however, reported coming to
Toronto because of subjective reasons, including personal relationships

Figure 5.1 Interview sample, Toronto musicians

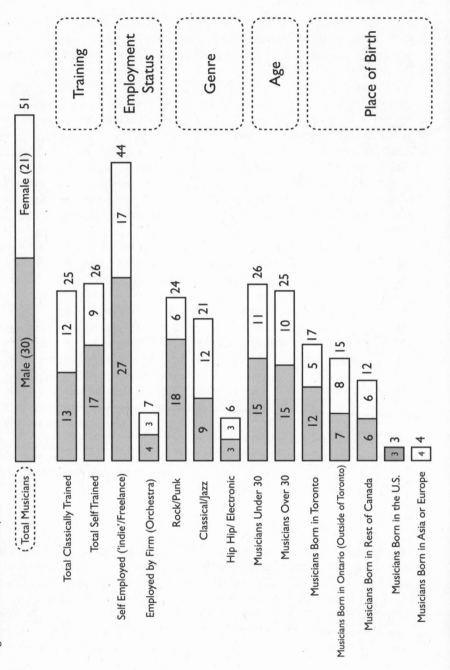

Total Musicians
Male (30) Female (21) 51

Training
Total Classically Trained: 13 | 12 | 25
Total Self Trained: 17 | 9 | 26

Employment Status
Self Employed ('indie'/Freelance): 27 | 17 | 44
Employed by Firm (Orchestra): 4 | 3 | 7

Genre
Rock/Punk: 18 | 6 | 24
Classical/Jazz: 9 | 12 | 21
Hip Hip/ Electronic: 3 | 3 | 6

Age
Musicians Under 30: 15 | 11 | 26
Musicians Over 30: 15 | 10 | 25

Place of Birth
Musicians Born in Toronto: 12 | 5 | 17
Musicians Born in Ontario (Outside of Toronto): 7 | 8 | 15
Musicians Born in Rest of Canada: 6 | 6 | 12
Musicians Born in the U.S.: 3 | 3
Musicians Born in Asia or Europe: 4 | 4

Figure 5.2 A model of locational expectations, satisfaction, and mobility

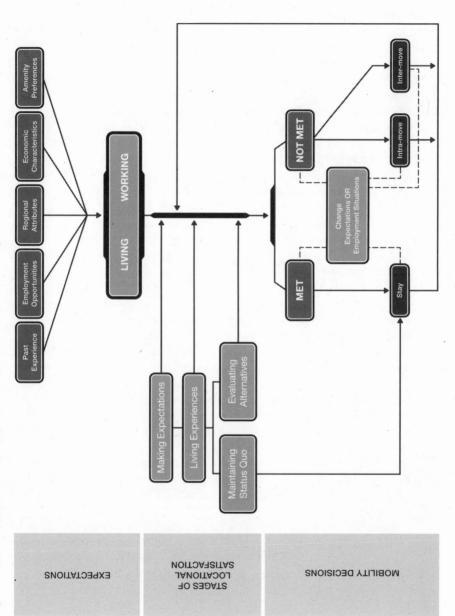

or a feeling that Toronto was the place to be. In some cases, specific employment or educational opportunities served as the primary attraction. As one musician explained, "I was born in Hong Kong and came to Toronto ten years ago. I came here to study with a great violinist who taught at the Conservatory of Music." Or, as another musician put it, "I was born in Orlando, Florida. I came to Toronto for my work here. I was invited to audition for Tafelmusik, which operates here. Prior to that I had never been to Toronto. I knew the orchestra existed up here, but I never seriously contemplated moving here … I agreed to come here and work with the orchestra to see what the city and the orchestra were like."

These two musicians had never worked in or visited Toronto, but simply intended to come for a position to see how things went. This underscores the incompleteness of the decision-making process. In other examples, respondents reported moving to Toronto on the advice of peers. As a musician explained: "I am from a smaller town: Guelph, Ontario. When I was 27 I moved to Toronto. I came for the music. I had been playing local jams and cafes in Guelph, but then you start to play out of town. You get older and everybody you know, one by one, they all just migrate to Toronto and it just seems like the thing to do." Another musician recalled:

> I am from Calgary originally. I spent five years in Europe and I never intended on returning to Canada. I thought I would spend the rest of my life in Europe. I really love it there. I was in London and I was playing so much music there, I felt like I was home. But after three years my visa expired and I had to return to Calgary. I worked at the Banff Centre for Music and fully intended to return to England. Honestly what happened, I met a guy and we moved to Toronto. He wanted to move to Montréal. I knew that there wasn't much happening there musically and I knew I wouldn't be able to work there. But I knew that there would be a lot of work in Toronto. I called a friend and they said please come there is so much work, we need somebody like you. I never thought I would end up in Toronto but I have been here for fourteen years now.

The perception that Toronto, as the national centre, is the logical place for musicians to advance their careers is shared by artists and screenwriters (see Leslie et al. and Davis et al. this volume). Yet the findings presented in this volume clearly demonstrate that a variety of factors can attract talented individuals to specific locations (see Phillips and Webb).

In the next section we consider how individuals determine their locational satisfaction and whether or not they will stay or relocate in the future.

Stage 2: Stages of Locational Satisfaction

Once in Toronto, individuals attempt to realize their expectations of place. People enter the labour market, find a place to live, form networks and social relationships, and begin to explore and use the available amenities. After a period of time, opinions of place can be formed and individuals can compare their lived experience to their expectations. This evaluation process can be triggered by major life-cycle events, bad experiences in traffic, or not at all. In the context of the research, reflexivity was prompted by our interview questions. Although we asked each participant about their experience of living and working in Toronto, respondents were free to discuss any aspects of the city. The range of responses and evaluative criteria highlights the individualized nature of experiences, but for the purposes of analysis here we focus on dominant themes related to diversity, employment, affordability, and amenities. The quotes presented demonstrate that each individual experiences aspects of a place differently and forms unique perceptions and opinions. The personal evaluation of experience ultimately compels individuals to stay or go.

Florida (2002) uses population diversity as a measurable proxy for tolerance and openness. He argues that places that are welcoming and provide low barriers to entering the labour market and trying out new things will attract and retain talent. In Toronto, diversity – in the form of foreign-born residents – is considered a competitive advantage and an indication that the city is easy to plug into. Over 53 per cent of the Toronto region's population are immigrants (Statistics Canada 2006). Our findings suggest that individual perceptions of diversity vary depending on musicians' frames of reference and their experiences living and working in Toronto. One European musician, for example, focused on multiculturalism in Toronto:

> I find Toronto amazingly diverse and tolerant. I am a foreigner myself, but I never feel like a foreigner because everyone else has some kind of accent too. You don't get that anywhere else. For example, I was just in Amsterdam last week and there are a lot of Muslims, but it is not working very well in terms of integration … You see these Muslims sitting in the bus and they're

looking down at the floor. They are uncomfortable: it is not a happy mix ...
So I think Toronto is unique in terms of multiculturalism and it is just really nice. I really like that about the city.

One musician had a different interpretation of tolerance:

My experience totally confirms the idea that Toronto is an open and tolerant city. Compared to the years, for example, that I lived in London,
Ontario, Toronto for me is like heaven. Even for me, coming from Halifax,
[it] made a big difference. I am gay, so Halifax is probably fine for that
now, but when I was a high school student it was pretty tough. So coming
to Toronto was like another world altogether. That is huge for me. For me
that is where diversity matters a lot and Toronto is a great safe and happy
place to be.

Finally, a self-described woman of colour was interested in diversity
within power structures:

The power structures aren't that diverse within the city, especially among
the decision-makers for arts and culture. In one meeting we went around
the room and talked about what makes Toronto great and a lot of people
talk about the whole diversity thing, but there were two non-white people
sitting around a table in this large group. So those are important things to
discuss: the demographics, yes, are diverse, but it is about more than just
being there. It is about who is there at the decision-making table and who's
calling the shots. So diversity hasn't really trickled up to that level yet.

Varying perceptions of tolerance and diversity and the influences of
identity and experience were also noted by Leslie et al. (this volume)
with respect to artists.

For individuals who work in creative occupations, the ability to access employment opportunities and collaborative opportunities is important (Christopherson 2002; Hauge and Hracs 2010). As this access is
often granted via networks, the degree to which places are welcoming
and easy to plug into influences their attractiveness. Once again,
Toronto's music scenes can be perceived in different ways depending
on individual experiences. A classically trained musician from Guelph
found Toronto welcoming and easy to engage: "There is so much going
on and so much creativity and new things all the time. We meet so
many people who are really eager to collaborate and do new things. I

think it is amazing! It is really exciting, constantly exciting. I think it is pretty warm and welcoming too."

An indie rock musician from Ottawa, however, found Toronto exclusionary: "It is a little clique and if they don't like you or the band you're in, you won't be able to get any gigs, or if you don't hang around at the bars that they hang around at. The networks can be exclusionary, just like high school."

In highlighting the range of perceptions towards the openness of Toronto's music scenes, we note that Leslie et al. and Davis et al. (this volume) argue that exclusion is a major factor that limits Toronto's ability to incubate and retain artists and screenwriters.

Although employment opportunities are important to all workers, highly educated and mobile individuals migrate to optimize their employment experiences. In other words, thick and robust labour markets that offer high-quality employment opportunities are attractive (Florida 2002; Storper and Scott 2009). Several musicians illustrated the disconnect between labour markets and specific scenes and highlight the influence of lived experience on individual perceptions. Due to her skill set and network, one musician reported an abundance of satisfying work in Toronto: "Strings are in demand right now, so I can always get work. I have worked on contemporary dance and original compositions. I play in classical groups and indie rock groups, too." Another respondent commented on the broader characteristics of Toronto's labour market that make it attractive:

> There is no other market in the country that has the amount of affluence to support what we do ... As a manager of musicians, as somebody that puts different groups of musicians together for performances, Toronto's standard quality of musicianship and number of musicians is the only way I could actually keep my business going. In Toronto there is a thick labour market that I can draw from.

By contrast, one musician expressed frustration about the lack of quality employment opportunities in the city: "It is hard to make money as a musician. Often you play and at the end of the night you get $20 and that is of course for the whole band. So you think, 'I played for this? I schlepped all my stuff down here and paid for gas and parking for this?'"

Interestingly, Toronto boasts the largest number of musicians and venues in Canada, but the ratio of venues to musicians results in intense competition and downward price pressure on pay for performances. In

Halifax, by contrast, a higher ratio results in more opportunities for paid employment and lower levels of competition and exclusion (Grant et al. this volume; Hracs et al. 2011).

In addition to employment opportunities, creative strands of talent are attracted to places that can support various artistic forms and are open to creative experimentation. In probing perceptions of this openness, we found that individual goals and experiences helped to differentiate the responses. Although some respondents described Toronto as a "great place to experiment or dabble in different styles," others felt their career ambitions constrained by the city's lack of support. In comparison to Niagara Falls, one musician found Toronto open to new styles:

> I consider Toronto as being pretty open, specifically because I am coming from a small town where nothing gets made really there. In Niagara Falls all the bands are cover bands of Pink Floyd or Led Zeppelin and that is as far it goes. So being able to come here and make original music from scratch, music that people will listen to, it is so impressive to me. So Toronto is amazingly open in my experience.

By contrast, another respondent described the difficulty of making it as a metal musician in Toronto: "Toronto is probably the worst city for Metal for getting a following. You would think that because of its size Toronto would be a great place, but there are too many alternatives and things to do. You can't develop a steady fan base. Europe and the States and even South America and Japan are much better. Canada is the worst: you can't make it here."

Although some talent is highly paid, income figures vary by occupation. According to the 2006 Canadian census, musicians in Toronto had average annual incomes of $14,659 (Statistics Canada 2008). Respondents emphasized the importance of finding affordable places to live and work (see also Grant el al. this volume); however, the perception of affordability varied. Musicians who had lived and worked in other global cities such as New York and Paris considered Toronto relatively cheap. As one musician explained:

> New York has huge apartments with large rooms and high ceilings, but nobody in my class can live in a whole house. Musicians in New York have to live in chopped up little apartments. But I can live in Toronto and live in

the equivalent of a rowhouse or brownstone. I think it is fantastic, I can live in this city, I can live in this urban environment. I can live five minutes' walk from the subway and a five-minute walk from shops and restaurants. I can do my food shopping on foot, which I think is a great thing about living in an urban environment. So that to me is the great thing about Toronto, its liveability.

For musicians with expectations of affordability based on their experiences in smaller cities or places like Montreal with strong rent controls, the high cost of living in Toronto was a major concern. As one musician argued, "When your work is not steady and you have a low income, Toronto can be very difficult because it is so expensive here ... In Montreal I was paying $650 for a large place. But here in Toronto I was paying just over $1,500 for a place that is barely big enough to fit my double bed."

Despite the emphasis placed on amenities in the literature on talent attraction (Florida 2002; Clark et al. 2002), few respondents spoke about being attracted to specific amenities. Rather, several respondents indicated that the availability of amenities is a non-issue because they simply do not have the time or money to experience them. Moreover, the perception of affordability varied by respondent. For one established and affluent musician, Toronto offers quality of life at a discount: "I go to probably 50 events a year. I couldn't do that in any other city in Canada and I couldn't have the quality of life and standard of living I have in large cities. I love London, London is fantastic; but you have to be a millionaire to live there. So Toronto has an affordability aspect to it: it is liveable."

For other musicians trying to cope with the demands, uncertainty, and low incomes associated with independent music production, Toronto's quality-of-life amenities seemed expensive and inaccessible: "Of course there is a lot going on in Toronto, but I don't tend to do any of it. This is mainly because I can't afford it, but also because I am too busy trying to make a living."

The location decisions of musicians directly influence the extent to which musical amenities are available for other existing or potentially new residents. The evidence demonstrates the individualized nature of lived experience and how widely the expectations, perceptions, and satisfaction with a place can vary even within one occupational group. In the next section we consider the outcomes of the evaluation process.

Stage 3: Mobility Decisions

Our conceptual model identifies four potential outcomes from the evaluation process. If the expectations of a place are met, the individual is satisfied and will stay in the current location. As one musician put it, "I love living in Toronto, I have never wanted to live anywhere else since I moved here." If, however, the expectations are not met, the individual can recalibrate expectations or change the employment situation. He or she may also decide to relocate either within the existing city-region (intra-city move) or to a new destination (inter-city move). Our findings suggest that the decision reflects the level of dissatisfaction or the discrepancy between expectations and experience. If the discrepancy is minor or moderate, moving to a different neighbourhood that better suits the needs and preferences of the individual might suffice. Hracs (2009) argues that those musicians who were dissatisfied with aspects of living in the downtown core (including the cost of living and labour-market competition) chose to relocate to Toronto's inner and outer suburbs. These musicians still wanted to live and work in Toronto, but tried to optimize their situation by relocating within the region.

In other cases, if an individual does not think satisfaction can be attained by staying in the city-region, the process starts again, with the individual forming expectations about a new range of potential locations. When asked about where they would like to move to and why, each respondent provided a different answer based on their past experiences, current situation, future goals, and preferences. Even when more than one respondent described the same location, the factors they linked to its attractiveness varied. New York, for example, was deemed attractive because of employment and lifestyle considerations by different musicians. As it becomes more difficult to sell recorded music and the emphasis shifts to live performances, the number of venues a location offers represents a strong pull factor (Hauge and Hracs 2010; Hracs et al. 2011). As one musician put it:

> I would move to New York or Los Angeles primarily because there are just so many venues and so much going on there with music. They are both great places to go to get noticed. Toronto is great for Canada and indie rock has been a hotbed lately. But for playing clubs and getting that quality exposure and playing for 300 people on a weeknight, Los Angeles or New York are the places to go. It is the mass and the concentration of

people: they have millions and millions of people. There are three million people in Toronto, but we only have two all-ages venues. I think that is ridiculous. If you go to a place like New York, there is a huge market and endless amounts of venues.

The perception that career advancement requires relocating to the largest cultural centres is common among several occupational groups in the cultural industries. Indeed, Davis et al. (this volume) identify a similar desire among screenwriters in Toronto to pursue greater opportunities in Los Angeles.

For musicians who are dissatisfied with the limited respect they and their music receive from citizens and consumers in Toronto, more supportive scenes such as Halifax or Seattle were reported as potential alternatives (Hracs et al. 2011). As one musician explained:

I would move to Seattle because I visited there once and the main reason why I am playing music is because of the scene that came out of Seattle. I have read a lot about Seattle and a lot about the music bank and what went on there and how much they really respect music up there. You go up there and everybody loves music and nobody treats anybody differently because they are a musician or an artist. There is more support there. Whereas in Toronto sometimes I feel like the general public does not appreciate the amount of hard work and dedication it takes to be a musician and the hardships. I mean they look at us like we are bums ...

Finally, several respondents expressed a desire to take advantage of their mobility to move to smaller, rural, or aesthetically pleasing locales. As one musician put it:

The more I live in Toronto the more I want to go somewhere else. Now that I do the advertising work I don't necessarily have to live in Toronto, because I can work from anywhere. I can upload the files to firms in Los Angeles, Vancouver, or New York ... I see myself outside of the city trying to make a living in a quiet little place somewhere with less action and hassle, in a smaller place. I want to live in a green space with lots of trees. To have the ability to be in one room and have all of this technology and be so hooked up and connected to all these different parts of the world, but then step through another door and just have peace and a rabbit hopping around. So I don't see myself in Toronto. I want to try the online approach to my work.

Implications for Theory and Practice

The ability of a region to attract and retain talent results from a subjective but fully describable iterative process. First, individuals develop expectations about one or more locations to which they could move. Those expectations are limited by available information, restricted search, and personal priorities. Second, based on expectations, a person selects and moves to a region. As the person lives in that region, his/her experiences meet, exceed, or fail to meet the original expectations. However, simply having unsatisfied expectations is not sufficient to impel a person to consider moving. By default, individuals will maintain the status quo and stay put; however, something (which could range from the mundane to a dramatic life-stage event) can trigger the final stage. Then, the individual can either stay by changing expectations or an employment situation or move after developing a new set of expectations about a different neighbourhood within the city or different city altogether.

While somewhat complicated, our model takes into account the limited (satisficing) nature of available information and information-seeking behaviour and the limited cognitive energy most individuals devote to location decisions as revealed in the interviews. It also considers three other important factors. First, regional expectations are subjective and not objective: what is important to one person may not even be considered by someone else. The model does this without resorting to some undefined utility function: it assumes that although the combination and specific values may be individually unique, the factors are identifiable. Second, as individuals' expectations evolve over time, the model dynamically allows expectations to change with life stage or with lived experience. The evolution of expectations, however, does not necessarily imply relocation. Finally, the concept that a trigger brings about the evaluation process is more in line with reported experiences and observed behaviour than with modelling of the move/stay question that uses some kind of continuous evaluation process.

The results of our research contribute to the debate among jobs, amenities, and the fuzzy concept of authenticity. Storper and Scott (2009) investigate the relationship between the impact of amenities and increased production (jobs) on urban growth, which they mistakenly identify as prosperity. While failing to recognize the potential sea change in location decision making that has resulted from the transition from an industrial to a post-industrial knowledge economy, they essentially find that although amenities may play a role, employment opportunities prove the more significant factor to regional growth. Indeed, while the presence of available jobs is a *necessary* component to regional growth, it is no longer *sufficient*. However, in today's post-industrial, creative, or knowledge economy, the same thing is generally true of various regional amenities. In other words, both the right kind of unfilled jobs and the right kind of amenities are needed if a region is to attract new residents and retain its current residents. Regional increases in productivity, with their corresponding increases in regional wages and prosperity, require innovation and creativity generated by talented and skilled individuals who are either retained in or attracted to that region.

Earlier work (Florida 2002) pointed to authenticity as being the most important factor for attracting skilled individuals to a region. However, other than a generally unsatisfying definition as "the opposite of generic" (Florida 2002, 228), authenticity has proved somewhat difficult to nail down. By modelling talent mobility and regional satisfaction using individual expectations, triggers, and evaluation processes we may develop new ways of understanding and measuring authenticity beneficial to future research.

Our model also helps to generate important policy recommendations. The limited nature of available information and the way it is gathered and used (or misused) points to the limitations of regional branding initiatives. Individual expectations affect decisions about whether and where to move. Regions need to be aware of how localities are presented and perceived and need to make sure that those perceptions are accurate. It does a region no good to advertise itself as something that it cannot be. In addition, the limited nature of the search that most people undertake means that migrants put a great deal of weight on rumours, hearsay, and the opinions of colleagues, neighbours, friends, and family. If a region is specifically interested in attracting talented and skilled individuals, the subjective nature of the expectations and the limits on available information will result in people looking to others in their professional networks to find out more about a place. Musicians learn about places from other musicians and creative individuals. Experience suggests that the same holds for computer professionals, MBAs, researchers, and educators. As a result, régions need more than one brand: they need tailored brands for each type of people and families that they would like to attract. In other words, regional talent attraction should not be based on a one-size-fits-all approach to either economic opportunities or amenities.

ACKNOWLEDGMENTS

The authors would like to thank Jill Grant for helpful comments, Michelle Hopgood for the graphic design of figure 5.2, and Joe Minichini for research assistance. We also owe a debt of gratitude to the musicians in Toronto who donated their time and their ideas to the research.

REFERENCES

Beck, Ulrich. 1992. *Risk society: Towards a new modernity*. London: Sage.

Blomquist, Glenn C., Mark C. Berger, and John P. Hoehn. 1988. "New estimates of quality of life in urban areas." *American Economic Review* 78 (1): 89–107.

Chang, Tou Chuang, and Wai Kin Lee. 2003. "Renaissance city Singapore: A study of arts spaces." *Area* 35 (2): 128–41. http://dx.doi.org/10.1111/1475-4762.00155.

Christopherson, Susan. 2002. "Project work in context: Regulatory change and the new geography of media." *Environment & Planning A* 34 (11): 2003–15. http://dx.doi.org/10.1068/a34182.

Clark, Terry N., Richard Lloyd, Kenneth W. Wong, and Pushpam Jain. 2002. "Amenities drive urban growth." *Journal of Urban Affairs* 24 (5): 493–515. http://dx.doi.org/10.1111/1467-9906.00134.

Donald, Betsy. 2001. "Economic competitiveness and quality of life in city regions: Compatible concepts?" *Canadian Journal of Urban Research* 10 (2): 259–74.

Donald, Betsy, Douglas Morrow, and Andrew Athanasiu. 2003. "Competing for talent: Implications for social and cultural policy in Canadian city-regions." A report prepared for Strategic Research and Analysis, Strategic Planning and Policy Coordination, Department of Canadian Heritage. Reference SRA-674. http://geog.queensu.ca/faculty/donald/Donald&Morrow_-_Competing_for_Talent.pdf.

Florida, Richard. 2002. *The rise of the creative class and how it's transforming work, leisure, community and everyday life*. New York: Basic Books.

Florida, Richard, Charlotta Mellander, and Kevin Stolarick. 2010a. "Music scenes to music clusters: The economic geography of music in the US, 1970–2000." *Environment & Planning A* 42 (4): 785–804. http://dx.doi.org/10.1068/a4253.

Florida, Richard, Charlotta Mellander, and Kevin Stolarick. 2010b. "Should I stay or should I go now: The effect of community satisfaction on the decision to stay or move." In *Working Paper Series*, 1–31. Toronto: Martin Prosperity Research. http://www.hrp.org/Site/docs/ResourceLibrary/Should_I_Stay_or_Should_I_Go_Now_2010_Florida_Mellander_Stolarick.pdf.

Glaeser, Edward L., Jed Kolko, and Albert Saiz. 2001. "Consumer city." *Journal of Economic Geography* 1 (1): 27–50. http://dx.doi.org/10.1093/jeg/1.1.27.

Hauge, Atle, and Brian J. Hracs. 2010. "See the sound, hear the style: Collaborative linkages between indie musicians and fashion designers in local scenes." *Industry and Innovation* 17 (1): 113–29. http://dx.doi.org/10.1080/13662710903573893.

Herzog, Henry W., Jr., Alan M. Schlottmann, and Donald L. Johnson. 1986. "High technology jobs and worker mobility." *Journal of Regional Science* 26 (3): 445–59. http://dx.doi.org/10.1111/j.1467-9787.1986.tb01053.x.

Hracs, Brian J. 2009. "Beyond bohemia: Geographies of everyday creativity for musicians in Toronto." In *Spaces of vernacular creativity: Rethinking the cultural economy*, ed. Tim Edensor, Deborah Leslie, Steve Millington, and Norma M. Rantisi, 75–88. London: Routledge.

Hracs, Brian J. 2012. "A creative industry in transition: The rise of digitally-driven independent music production." *Growth and Change* 43 (3): 442–6.

Hracs, Brian J., Jill L. Grant, Jeff Haggett, and Jesse Morton. 2011. "A tale of two scenes: Civic capital and retaining musical talent in Toronto and Halifax." *Canadian Geographer* 55 (3): 365–82. http://dx.doi.org/10.1111/j.1541-0064.2011.00364.x.

Markusen, Ann, and David King. 2003. "The artistic dividend: The arts' hidden contributions to regional development." Humphrey Institute of Public Affairs, University of Minnesota. http://www.hhh.umn.edu/img/assets/6158/artistic_dividend.pdf.

Niedomysl, Thomas, and Hogni K. Hansen. 2010. "What matters more for the decision to move: Jobs versus amenities." *Environment & Planning A* 42 (7): 1636–49. http://dx.doi.org/10.1068/a42432.

Rantisi, Norma M., and Deborah Leslie. 2006. "Branding the design metropole: The case of Montréal, Canada." *Area* 38 (4): 364–76. http://dx.doi.org/10.1111/j.1475-4762.2006.00705.x.

Roback, Jennifer. 1982. "Wages, rents, and the quality of life." *Journal of Political Economy* 90 (6): 1257–78. http://dx.doi.org/10.1086/261120.

Rosen, Sherwin. 1979. "Wage-based indexes of urban quality of life." *Current Issues in Urban Economics* 3: 74–104.

Scott, Allen J. 1999. "The US recorded music industry: On the relations between organization, location; and creativity, in the cultural economy." *Environment & Planning A* 31 (11): 1965–84. http://dx.doi.org/10.1068/a311965.

Scott, Allen J. 2010. "Jobs or amenities? Destination choices of migrant engineers in the USA." *Papers in Regional Science* 89 (1): 43–63. http://dx.doi.org/10.1111/j.1435-5957.2009.00263.x.

Statistics Canada. 2006. Census of Population, Statistics Canada catalogue no. 97-564-XCB2006008 (Toronto).

Statistics Canada. 2008. Census of Canada 2006: Labour force activity, highest certificate, diploma or degree, location of study, age groups and sex. (Topic-based tabulations; 97-564-XCB2006005).

Storper, Michael, and Allen J. Scott. 2009. "Rethinking human capital, creativity and urban growth." *Journal of Economic Geography* 9 (2): 147–67. http://dx.doi.org/10.1093/jeg/lbn052.

Tiebout, Charles M. 1956. "A pure theory of local expenditures." *Journal of Political Economy* 64 (5): 416–24. http://dx.doi.org/10.1086/257839.

Whisler, Ronald L., Brigitte S. Waldorf, Gordon F. Mulligan, and David A. Plane. 2008. "Quality of life and the migration of the college educated: A life course approach." *Growth and Change* 39 (1): 58–94. http://dx.doi.org/10.1111/j.1468-2257.2007.00405.x.

Wolpert, Julian. 1965. "Behavioral aspects of the decision to migrate." *Papers in Regional Science* 15 (1): 159–69. http://dx.doi.org/10.1007/BF01947871.

6 "Those Hermit Artists": Musical Talent on the Edge of the Continent

JILL L. GRANT, JEFFRY HAGGETT, AND JESSE MORTON

Introduction: Where Do Musicians Choose to Live?

Over the last decade, the ideas of Richard Florida (2002c, 2005a, 2005b) have had an immense influence on local development policy across North America. Florida has suggested that in the new economy, growth depends on cities' abilities to attract talented and creative workers. In an economy reliant on high levels of education and knowledge, Florida holds, talented workers can choose where they want to live and work. Florida (2002a) argues that talented and creative workers are attracted by tolerance, as measured by diversity (race, sexual orientation, and ethnicity). He proposes rating places by a coolness index that includes measures for culture, nightlife, and youth of the population. The paradigm suggests that places with large numbers of artists and musicians attract other types of talented workers because they signal openness to creativity and innovation (Florida 2002b; Florida et al. 2008).

Since artists and musicians indicate economic potential and a place's attractiveness, understanding why these creative workers cluster where they do gains traction as a research question. Glaeser and Gottlieb (2006) argue that places with a better climate, less crime, and more amenities have an edge over other cities in attracting migrants. Larger cities have an advantage: as places of entertainment and consumption they provide opportunities for creative workers (Scott 2000, 2007). As Markusen (2006) notes, self-employed artists are relatively footloose: they make reasoned choices about where they go, carefully evaluating local conditions in the process. Lorentzen (2009) found that the experience economy – where people search out particular kinds of experiences – can also favour smaller cities with particular attributes attractive to creative workers.

Based on data from the 2000 US census, Florida and Jackson (2010) argue that musicians cluster in major cities where incomes and diversity are high: they found the greatest concentrations in Chicago, Los Angeles, and New York. Florida and Jackson examined trends from 1970 to 2004 to discover that the geography of music has become more concentrated: music centres like Chicago and Detroit, which played important roles in the mid-twentieth century, have given way to Nashville, which has emerged as the third centre of music production. Music scenes have persisted in some smaller locations with affluent and educated populations and location-specific assets: as Florida and Jackson (2010) note, technological changes within the industry mean that access to fixed production infrastructure no longer constrain musicians' location choices. Florida et al. (2010, 798) demonstrate that musicians have become highly mobile: "where musicians were located in 1970 or even 1990 [did] not appear to affect the location of muscans [sic] in 2000."

Since the 1990s, production processes and consumption practices have dramatically reoriented the music industry (Leyshon 2001, 2009; Jones 2002; Bishop 2005; Burkart 2005). As music consumers turned to downloading music from the Internet instead of purchasing CDs, producers scrambled to find new economic models to realize returns on investments. CD sales plummeted; record labels consolidated; major studios folded (Leyshon 2009). For Canadian musicians trying to make a living from their art, the economic landscape changed dramatically (Hracs 2010). Improved computer hardware and software allowed musicians to produce recordings at home or in local studios for relatively low cost, without support from a major label. Social networking became increasingly important for musicians as they worked to build up their own artist brands (Stein-Sacks 2006). Musicians depending more on buzz environments within which local knowledge flows benefit from face-to-face contacts that generate trust and collaboration (Bathelt et al. 2002; Storper and Venables 2004). The quality of songwriting gained in significance in this new context where musicians could no longer rely on record labels to promote their work, but instead had to demonstrate their competence to the world. While authenticity is an essential rhetorical claim within music scenes generally (Frith 1987; Hracs and Stolarick this volume; Peterson 2005), the crisis in music production has opened new opportunities for musicians to link their creative voices with particular localities far from the production centres that once dominated the industry. Halifax is arguably one such remote location.

Alternative Music Scenes

Music is a social practice that typically involves music producers, consumers, and intermediaries who include promoters, agents, venue operators, managers, and critics (Connell and Gibson 2003). While individuals can make music anywhere, those hoping to make a living through music or seeking to develop their talents by learning from others are often drawn to clusters of music producers and consumers: to a music scene. Straw (1991, 373) describes a music scene as "that cultural space within which a range of musical practices coexist" within a local community. Florida and Jackson (2010, 311) write that "a music scene is a geographically delimited market in a microcosm rooted in location." Large cities often have well-known music scenes, but economic conditions have "intermittently enabled smaller locations with a constellation of talent and commercial interests willing to embrace new forms to gain a strategic advantage" (ibid., 319). In recent decades alternative music scenes have developed in some college towns (H. Kruse 1993; Shank 1994; Currid 2009) or in particular remote locations such as Tasmania (McLeay 1994; Gibson and Connell 2003). By creating shared experiences music contributes to generating shared identities and local definitions of place (Frith 1987; Hibbett 2005). Local music scenes help to brand places as attractive to university students (Brown et al. 2000; Florida and Jackson 2010; Grant and Kronstal 2010) and visitors (Gibson and Connell 2003; Dowdy 2007). At the same time, as Florida and Jackson (2010, 312) note, "place helps to brand music along with other cultural goods." Places with recognized alternative scenes lend credibility and identity to the music produced there.

The history of music shows that innovations in music genres often develop in particular cities or regions and become associated with those places in the public mind. Thus, jazz erupted in New Orleans in a period of diversity and developing connections between African-American, Creole, and white music scenes in the late nineteenth and early twentieth centuries (Carney 2006). Liverpool cemented its place in pop history with the emergence of bands such as the Beatles in the 1960s (R. Kruse 2005). In the 1980s and 1990s cities such as Austin, Texas, and Seattle, Washington, developed recognizable scenes producing innovative musical styles. Austin generated an industry around its progressive music scene (Shank 1994), while the rise of grunge rock bands like Nirvana created a music style that put Seattle on the map (H. Kruse 1993). Nashville, Tennessee, long the home of country music, became a major centre for music writing, recording, and publishing in various musical styles: a destination for ambitious musicians (Florida and Jackson 2010).

While the music industry remains heavily concentrated in major cities like Los Angeles, New York, and London (Scott 2000; Currid 2007), the rise of distinctive scenes in smaller cities has opened opportunities for musicians to consider a wider range of options about where to locate. Restructuring within the music industry in the wake of new technologies that have undermined record sales and given musicians the means to produce their music in local studios on home computers is reordering the spatial dynamics of musicians' choices. Given that most Canadian musicians operate independently of record labels (CIRAA 2010), they had less need to live in major music cities in 2010 than they did in 1980. By contrast with other categories of creative workers, like screenwriters, who need to be close to the centre of the industry (Davis et al. this volume), musicians can live in a range of locations. In the context of the contemporary music industry, living on the edge physically, as they do fiscally, may have become more acceptable to musicians.

Space and Place for Creativity

Artistic work occurs within a particular local social context. As Scott (1999, 809) explains, place-based communities are "vortexes of social reproduction in which critical cultural competencies are generated and circulated." Musicians need space and social networks that help them develop their skills and their collaborative networks. As Drake (2003) notes, places can inspire individuals and generate social and collective processes that contribute to creative production. Of course, because artists look for different things, they find it in different places (see Hracs and Stolaric this volume): some may seek the buzz and intensity of a major city like London, while others want a quiet space to work (Drake 2003). Over time, particular types of products – including musical genres – and communities become associated with particular places from which they are exported to other markets.

In describing the music scene in Dunedin, New Zealand, McLeay (1994) suggests that although music produced there two decades ago was conventional rock music responding to the global industry, the isolation of the local landscape provided an authentic backdrop to performances for videos and record art. Gibson and Connell (2003) describe a distinct local cultural economy around backpacker culture and music in Byron Bay, Australia. Writing about world music, Connell and Gibson (2004, 353) explain: "The credibility of some musical styles and genres arises from their origins, their sites of production, evident in a number of possible ways: small location, places 'off the beaten track,' exclusion from capitalist growth, isolation and remoteness from hearths of industrial production or working-class communities."

An artist Drake (2003, 521) interviewed in Sheffield, England, said that artistic production in London was seen as a hobby for rich kids, while the same activity in Sheffield was taken seriously as art. The reputation of a place can add cachet to a product: remoteness may convey a sense of authenticity seen as lacking in major urban centres. If, as Peterson (2005) argues, authenticity is socially constructed, then for some creatives isolation can help to achieve it.

The Halifax Music Scene

Halifax, Nova Scotia, is a mid-sized city of about 390,000 on the Atlantic coast of Canada. Founded in 1749 as a British army outpost and naval base, it has a long history as a government town. The provincial capital, it has a well-educated population and a cluster of government services. With six universities it attracts students from across Canada and beyond. Although the region has struggled with a relatively weak economy since Canadian confederation (Wynn 1998), in recent years Halifax has experienced reasonably robust growth and has attracted talented and creative workers (Grant and Kronstal 2010).

During the period from 2006 to 2008 we conducted ninety semi-structured interviews in Halifax as part of the national study to examine the social dynamics of economic performance (Gertler et al. this volume). The study focused on trying to understand the factors that attract talented and creative workers to the city-region: how do the social qualities of place encourage innovation and build commitment to local economic development? One theme that respondents raised consistently in our first year of interviewing – when we focused on government departments and independent agencies involved in promoting development in the city-region – was the significance of live music performances in making Halifax an exciting place to visit and live (Grant and Kronstal 2010). Consequently, in the second and third years of the study we targeted some interviews on people in the music industry in the city-region to understand the factors that make Halifax attractive to them: we completed nineteen interviews with music promoters, managers, administrators, and musicians from several genres. We recorded interviews for transcription and subjected the transcripts to thematic analysis. The quotes presented here derive from our transcripts.

Until the 1990s Halifax was largely associated with what Canadians know as Maritime music: heavy on fiddles, sea shanties, and Celtic tunes. At that time the university and art college scenes spawned some innovative musical forms. Local taverns provided venues for performance. Ambitious acts with a chance of making it nationally or internationally traditionally left the city: hence, singers such as Anne Murray and Sarah McLachlan, and bands like April Wine and Sloan, moved to advance their careers.

By the end of the first decade of the twenty-first century, Halifax had become known in Canada as a destination for musicians, as a place with an excellent independent music scene (Flinn 2009; Grant et al. 2009). What attracts musicians to a small city over twelve hours' drive from the nearest large city? Interviews with those in the scene have provided insight into the role of geography in the choices that musicians make about where to live and work. Like other respondents interviewed, those in the music sector talked about the character of the place, highlighting the natural beauty of the ocean and the heritage quality of the city. A music promoter explained:

> First of all the physical geography of the place is breathtaking – the province itself. The history and all of those intangibles – those things are all fantastic. There's a certain exotic-ness about it, plus the fact that it's established in the brains of all kinds of people. You talk to musicians from all over the world, everyone's heard of Halifax ... If you talk to most of them, they have always wanted to come here or play here.

Explicit contrasts with other music cities revealed the attractions musicians see in Halifax with its small scale and laid-back atmosphere. A musician compared Halifax with Toronto:

> I think it's an East Coast thing again. I think that there's something unique about the people in the East ... There's some kind of friendliness here that's almost naive – in a nice way – that I don't find in other places. You know, Toronto is so big. I think when you're in a larger city and the pace is faster ... maybe your blood pressure isn't as low. You know, you're not as able to take in the moment and say, "Hey!"

Many musicians acknowledged the national reputation that Halifax has gained as a place for music. Several cited the success of the grunge rock group Sloan – signed by Nirvana's label DGC at the peak of that boom – as creating awareness about Halifax. One musician/promoter described Halifax's attraction to university students: "I think we've got a good reputation where a lot of the … indie cool kids in Toronto have Sloan songs for their passwords on their email accounts."

For its size, Halifax has a significant number of live music venues that pay musicians to play: some musicians noted that in larger cities like Toronto and Montreal musicians sometimes have to pay to play (Morton 2009; Hracs et al. 2011). Supportive audiences in bars, in coffee shops, and on street corners provide musicians with positive reinforcement as they work to refine their material. Several respondents described Halifax as a town where people go to bars to listen to music and drink, where residents value music. With a slower rate of growth than Toronto or Vancouver, Halifax offers less expensive accommodations. The city also attracts talent from smaller regional cities like St John's, Newfoundland (Lepawsky et al. this volume). Musicians suggested that relatively inexpensive housing and rehearsal space made the city-region attractive to them. Those touring outside the region saw easy airline access to the American northeast and to Europe as another asset. In sum, musicians suggested that Halifax provided a good base for them to develop their talent.

The Periphery Rocks

The traditional structure of the music industry before the 1990s meant that producers and record labels in major cities like Toronto, Los Angeles, and London defined popular tastes (Bishop 2005). They determined what hit the record charts and who became famous, producing a "musical monoculture" (Burkart 2005, 491). Regional outposts such as Halifax played a limited role as places that lost their best talent to the big cities. By 1992, however, the success of singers and bands coming out of Halifax began re-defining the character of the local music scene. A music administrator explained the shift in perspective:

> There used to be more problems with people's attitudes about what Eastern Canada was like, but those are gone. Musically speaking, those have been gone for 15 to 20 years and Eastern Canada is really a kind of Mecca for interesting music. We're not seen as being hicks anymore:

down-homers. Bands like Sloan and people like that did huge things to change that picture that people had. Cool stuff comes out of Halifax as much as traditional stuff comes out. It's known for quality.

With the advent of the computer and the Internet revolution in the music industry, Halifax developed a network of producers who work with local musicians to package their work. The regional radio network of the Canadian Broadcasting Corporation (CBC) provided facilities to develop and promote local talent. To recognize excellence the East Coast Music Association set up an awards program that rapidly gained national prominence. Under the leadership of Ronald MacDonald, a traditional fiddler who became minister of tourism and later premier of Nova Scotia, the provincial government invested resources in programs designed to support a music sector strategy. The government set up an agency, Music Nova Scotia, to help musicians enhance their business skills in exporting cultural products. By the early years of the twenty-first century, many musicians seeking opportunities to develop their talent recognized Halifax as a music destination.

In the contemporary context, where independent musicians post their music on social media sites and sell songs through the Internet, being located in large cities no longer seems essential. One musician/booking agent explained:

> I think Halifax is being recognized as starting to create a Mecca, so to speak, for artists ... There are a lot of bands ... There is some good stuff coming out ... They're getting noticed in the indie scene. I don't know if it's because of Facebook that we're all becoming more apparent, but definitely the Internet has a lot to do with it. It's easy to make a band look good on the computer.

The Internet has created what musicians perceive as an increasingly democratic space where consumers decide what they do and do not like. A music promoter provided a compelling contrast with an earlier era:

> In old school music so-and-so would get a record, then the radio station would decide to play it or not. If they decided not to play it, you didn't hear it. If that record got a bad review, you may choose not to buy it. Now the filters are gone ... You don't need someone from Toronto telling you that it's really good in order to hear it any more. All you need is somebody with a MySpace page ... It takes away all the limits and boundaries and borders.

Halifax musicians rely increasingly on the Internet to reach fans and build audiences for their music. While Halifax has various venues, once bands become more established they typically seek larger venues and bigger audiences. Some tour in the European and American markets, as a music producer explained:

> You will find that in the last couple of years some musicians have chosen not necessarily to concentrate on Canadian markets but are turning to the European market much more. There's more back and forth now between here and Europe because you can – if you can situate yourself for a couple of weeks, say in Germany, in a two-hour drive you probably have access to 700 million people. Whereas Canada, although it's a large country geographically, is one of the smallest music markets in the world – 30 some million people. That's tiny.

In the age of the Internet, a good video or catchy song can garner a solid fan base for a musician. Local musician Dave Carroll, of the band Sons of Maxwell, wrote a song that "went viral" in 2009. After months of frustration in trying to get United Airlines to pay for damage to his guitar in 2008, Carroll wrote a song, "United Breaks Guitars." His band's cheesy $150 video of baggage handlers tossing his gear and unsympathetic agents dismissing his claim for his broken Taylor guitar became popular on YouTube.[1] *Rolling Stone*'s online report a week later reported the video already had 2.5 million hits (Bliss 2009). While the video gave United Airlines a black eye, it did wonders for Carroll's career, boosting CD sales and landing him new touring opportunities.

Circumstances in the contemporary industry leave few musicians with lucrative record deals. Most face years of struggle to make a go of a music career. Given that the large centres prove especially challenging, musicians may instead seek affordable and supportive places in which to be creative and to hone their skills. While the large music cities have dynamic and diverse scenes, peripheral places may generate opportunities for creativity, performance, and affordable living that attract musicians.

Isolation and Authenticity

In describing the characteristics of Halifax that contributed to creativity and innovation, those in the music scene often talked about isolation: "I think the isolation of this area means people work on their own sound without being directly influenced by a bigger outside scene. The music from here tends to be fairly unique."

Local musicians suggested that they could develop their own styles far from acknowledged centres of the industry. With Halifax being a long drive or expensive flight from major markets, relatively few bands came through on tour. A music producer explained:

> When I first moved here, it was the kind of thing where a band like the White Stripes, for instance, would never come to Halifax. So ... people had to make their own thing. It was insular. I don't know if that's the case any-more. *Q: Was that an asset?* ... Yeah, because people just kind of had to create their own entertainment on their own. There were no out-of-town bands coming to entertain people so people had to basically imagine what that band would be. People's only experience would be going to performances of people that they knew. You know if you don't have any precedent ... sometimes, you probably make it better than what you can imagine.

Some respondents worried that improving airline connections could undermine the isolation that they thought had benefited Halifax over the decades. One music promoter noted: "Part of why I think that peo-ple are so creative here – and I'm worried that will disappear as the airlines and travel links get better – is that we've had to entertain our-selves for so long because people don't come here."

Others acknowledged Halifax as the musical centre of a region of iso-lated small towns. Musicians wend their way to Halifax after developing their interest in music in the rural areas or in regional cities like St John's (Lepawsky et al. this volume). A musician described the process:

> When you are more isolated you're a little less distracted and you're more focused on your art. I think we benefit from that. I think it's a Maritime thing or an Atlantic Canadian thing that we bring to Halifax: ... we all bring that. There is that isolation that you have if you're growing up in [village X]: there's nothing to do. It's cold in the winter and playing music is a great outlet to express yourself and to put your energy into.

In this passage the musician explicitly links isolation and harsh cli-mate with creativity. As the regional centre, Halifax constitutes a step up the spatial ladder to a community with a vibrant music scene. Musicians' portrayal of remoteness and winter as generating creativity and authenticity provided a stark contrast to the need Canadian screenwriters identified to be in particular cities like Toronto, Vancouver, or Los Angeles to advance their careers (Davis et al. this volume).

The same musician continued on the theme of cosmopolitanism to explain why a vibrant city like Vancouver may not provide appropriate conditions for developing creativity:

> I've been to Vancouver and I don't think there are that many great bands from Vancouver. I almost know why. We would spend a couple months out there and everyone is biking around. People are like "Oh man, let's go down to the juice bar." Whatever. "Oh, the Dalai Lama is giving a talk to-day." Everyone is so active it's almost sickening [laughing]. Here we would grab a beer and grab a guitar, and think about what you're going to write. I picture writing lyrics in my house in January: there's nothing else to do. They don't get that much snow out there, but then they're skiing. I just think that there's something to that. We benefit from that isolation. We suffer a little more for our songs and I think we're better for it.

Some respondents suggested that living in large cities replete with music industry infrastructure can distract musicians from an essential focus on creativity. A music writer explained: "You go to Toronto and it's all about the industry. Everyone is trying to get noticed. Down here that is not as big a priority. It's more about working on your music … If you're living in Ohio or Iceland, places that are far away often come up with the most interesting stuff. I think Halifax is definitely in that category."

Such comments suggest that whereas isolation sparks creativity, larger centres may promote status seeking. Fringe cities, far from the acknowledged centre of the music industry, may offer musicians space to innovate. Of course, not all distant places have the ability to attract clusters of musicians. Cities with universities have an advantage in developing alternative music scenes (H. Kruse 1993; McLeay 1994). NSCAD University in Halifax, internationally renowned for its arts programs, lures artists from across Canada and well beyond. As Leyshon (2009) noted, some university towns and small regional centres are developing vibrant independent music scenes as the music industry restructures. Respondents, such as one music promoter, saw Halifax as a beneficiary of this process: "The university situation we have here and the art school has helped … create a much more global city compared to its size. So with the art school and 35,000 students – whatever it is – coming in September, there's a huge creative pool that comes and you combine that with a fringe market."

Although musicians often described Halifax's remoteness as an asset, several acknowledged the challenges of trying to advance careers from the edge. One musician answered a question about financial challenges and advantages in Halifax by pointing to the difficulty of finding business assistance:

> The challenges would be that we're not Toronto, we're not Vancouver, and as such we're not in the middle of the machine which is where you get the most attention and where you do business. Where your manager is meeting with people and they're giving opportunities – whereas if you're up here you have to make a lot of extra effort to stay in the limelight … business-wise. People don't remember you. People are like "Oh yeah, you guys were really good, but whatever. They're in Halifax and I haven't talked to them in awhile." Running into people in clubs and networking dies off a bit here. We're sort of like "those hermit artists." But if you're good enough and you can do that – the advantages of being in Halifax are that it's obviously cheaper. The rent is cheaper and the cost of living is cheaper than Toronto. The relaxed nature of a smaller city is just better.

Generating and maintaining a national or international profile is easier in a major centre with its music publishers and promoters constantly networking. For musical artists, however, peripherality offers rewards related to lifestyle and creative focus: technology such as the Internet provides the connections they need to participate in wider networks. Halifax-based musicians described themselves as developing an enhanced work ethic and attending to the quality of their product to avoid being seen as "hermit artists."

Character of the Scene

While affordability, isolation, and supportive audiences play important roles in creating positive conditions for musicians in Halifax, respondents emphasized the character of the music scene itself in attracting and retaining talented people. The community of musicians in Halifax has created a small but supportive subculture of mythic dimensions (Hracs et al. 2011; Grant et al. 2009; Morton 2009). Almost every respondent interviewed from the music scene commented on the collaborative and open nature of music activities in Halifax: musicians sharing instruments, mentoring newcomers, and volunteering on projects. Collaboration provides musicians with opportunities to cross genres in ways that may not be possible in larger scenes, as a music administrator noted:

It seems also that there is just a very creative group of people who are interested in making more than one type of music, and having different roles in those setups. Someone who might be the lead singer in their group might also just really want to play guitar in a group that plays different kinds of music ... All you have to do is take twelve CDs and read the credits and you won't believe you are looking at the same thirty names over and over and over again. But they are playing different instruments, they are singing different things. It's different kinds of music. It's bizarre, but it's wonderful. It's what makes this industry unique and saleable from my perspective. It becomes fascinating as a sales feature, part of our brand. We work it from all angles, that this is a community. We're selling a community.

As the administrator noted, collaboration has become Halifax's brand. While respondents described the Toronto music scene as competitive and cut-throat they said that Halifax offered musicians a sympathetic and cooperative musical home (Hracs et al. 2011).

Young musicians across Canada who are looking for places to develop their talent hear stories about the supportive musical culture and institutions in Halifax. A music promoter explained:

Strangely enough, in spite of everything, this part of the country is almost bordering on one of those places that you would want to go to – perversely because the cooperation between artists in this town is hugely supportive ... You can get a lot of attention out of this market. There are a lot of really good industry people here. The CBC [radio network] is probably more into the music side of things in this city than they are in any other city that I can think of. They help and foster those artists.

Some older respondents found Halifax reminiscent of the Greenwich Village scene that produced Bob Dylan and other great artists in the 1960s. A community of artists and musicians collaborating can spark dynamic creativity. Despite the challenges of making a living in Halifax, one musician described it as a good place to grow as an artist: "I would say it's a great place to be a musician if you maybe don't want a career. It's hard to make a career of it here at this time, but it is a great place to be a musician for sure: to play music, write music, to have people to play with and collaborate with."

The same musician acknowledged that living in Toronto might make touring easier, but it would mean sacrificing the inspiration and cachet the band found in Halifax. "[In Toronto] you would be one of thousands of bands that are trying to be awesome, or you could stay here and embrace your roots and that's a lot cooler. The perception is it's a lot cooler than being another Toronto band."

One musician was asked about how Halifax, compared to larger centres, valued the ability to be versatile in a career in a smaller city; the respondent was willing to sacrifice material reward for artistic opportunity:

> I really love being able to do the different things that I do. If I was in a bigger centre, I would be in competition for every one of those [gigs] with somebody else. I would have to focus on a specific thing. This would probably help me discover what my strengths are, but it could also make me just go to where the opportunities are. They might not reflect my strengths, just that there is more demand for it. Here you can go between all these different things. I would get more money but ... I once had this student who told me it's all about the money, and I refused to teach him anymore. I just couldn't do it. Why take music lessons if it is all about the money?

Some musicians saw commitment to their art as a cultural practice which required economic sacrifice but generated loyalty to Halifax.

Although many respondents talked about successful colleagues who had moved to larger cities like Toronto, New York, and Nashville to further their careers, comments revealed sentiments that suggested that moving on often entailed creative compromises. Several respondents noted that Sloan had broken with its major label over creative differences, and suggested that the band produced its best work when it had greater independence. Respondents from the Halifax music scene revealed attitudes that Hibbett (2005) associated with indie rock. Musicians saw Halifax as providing them with "authenticity and otherness" (ibid., 56) not possible in Toronto (cf. Hracs and Stolarick this volume). Halifax affords musicians time to develop sound and songs; by contrast, major music centres were described as forcing musicians into accepted formulas that undermined creative focus. Rather than embracing their roots and creating original material, musicians said, those in larger scenes get trapped by industry conventions; in a similar way, screenwriters avoid telling authentic Canadian stories in order to make it in American TV and film (Davis et al. this volume). By contrast, fringe scenes such as Halifax encourage experimentation, as one musician argued:

> I think you get an all-star team of the best writers of that geographical range ... That's pretty impressive. Now the industry side really lacks so

you don't hear of Tyler Messick. You don't hear of Dog Day across the country as much, but they're world class. But that doesn't mean that they're ever going to be successful …You ask your friends about their songs. "How did you get that sound? That's really cool." You have access to really great artists. And at the end of the day which side would I rather fall on, or what would anyone want to fall on? I'd rather fall on the side of the artists and be less successful than be Nickelback[2] – to be honest.

Those who stayed in Halifax clearly adopted the indie sentiment that they refused to sell out for commercial success.

The Advantage of Distance

Isolation can only help Halifax if it is more perceptual than real. At varying points in their careers musicians have to travel to tour, meet with managers or advisers, or advance their careers. Distance then becomes an issue. A mid-sized city cannot provide the array of opportunities that musicians may need to develop their acts as they become more successful.

As Florida et al. (2010) noted, live venues, exciting musicians to learn from, and availability of funding or supports may lure musicians to places: such elements contribute to Halifax's attraction (Grant and Kronstal 2010). Musicians need audiences: thus, Halifax's ability to attract university students and tourists fuels its music scene. The supportive musical subculture that attracts acolytes eager to learn from established artists depends on the leadership of key figures in the local scene and on the continuing availability of live music venues that pay artists for their work. Affordable housing and rehearsal space near the city centre helps musicians create strong local networks. If those elements began to dissipate, then the Halifax scene could decline. In the interim, however, Halifax attracts artists passionate about their work and committed to creative development. Many who land in the city come to view it as home. They have generated a scene known for its edginess, both in its songwriting qualities and in terms of its position on the rim of the continent.

The music industry needs an "artistic elsewhere" (Hibbett 2005, 65). Those "hermit artists" squirrelled away on cold January afternoons writing music in remote Halifax articulated a discourse of centre and periphery that gave the city a special cachet. The changing dynamics of centre and periphery in the music industry is affecting location choices for some musicians. While before the 1990s musicians relocated to larger music scenes like Toronto to refine their acts and launch careers, the digital revolution enabled by file sharing, home recording, and social networking has created conditions that can make smaller cities attractive to musicians. Smaller cities that attract musicians could take advantage of the opportunity to reconfigure economic development strategies to support the local music scene so that they can capitalize on the edginess their locations provide.

ACKNOWLEDGMENTS

The authors thank Aaron Pettman, Rebecca Butler, and Robyn Holme for help with interviewing and Brian Hracs for comments on an earlier draft. We appreciate the assistance of many people who made time in their busy schedules to talk with us.

NOTES

1 The video is on YouTube at http://www.youtube.com/watch?v=5YGc4zOqozo.
2 Nickelback is a Vancouver-based hard rock band that has been commercially successful under the EMI label. They have won Canadian and international music awards and several Grammy nominations.

REFERENCES

Bathelt, Harald, Anders Malmberg, and Peter Maskell. 2002. *Clusters and knowledge: Local buzz, global pipelines and the process of knowledge creation.* Danish Research Unit for Industrial Dynamics, Working paper no. 02-12. http://ideas.repec.org/p/aal/abbswp/02-12.html.
Bishop, Jack. 2005. "Building international empires of sound: Concentrations of power and property in the 'global' music market." *Popular Music and Society* 28 (4): 443–71. http://dx.doi.org/10.1080/03007760500158957.
Bliss, Karen. 2009. "Dave Carroll's airline mishap goes viral in 'United Breaks Guitar.'" http://www.rollingstone.com/rockdaily/index.php/2009/07/13/dave-carrolls-airline-mishap-goes-viral-in-united-breaks-guitars/.
Brown, Adam, Justin O'Connor, and Sara Cohen. 2000. "Local music policies within a global music industry: Cultural quarters in Manchester and Sheffield." *Geoforum* 31 (4): 437–51. http://dx.doi.org/10.1016/S0016-7185(00)00007-5.

Burkart, Patrick. 2005. "Loose integration in the popular music industry." *Popular Music and Society* 28 (4): 489–500. http://dx.doi.org/10.1080 /03007760500159013.

Carney, Court. 2006. "New Orleans and the creation of early jazz." *Popular Music and Society* 29 (3): 299–315. http://dx.doi.org/10.1080/03007760600670331.

CIRAA (Canadian Independent Recording Artists' Association). 2010. FAQ. http://www.ciraa.ca/faq.php.

Connell, John, and Chris Gibson. 2003. *Sound tracks: Popular music, identity and place*. New York: Routledge. http://dx.doi.org/10.4324/9780203448397.

Connell, John, and Chris Gibson. 2004. "World music: Deterritorializing place and identity." *Progress in Human Geography* 28 (3): 342–61. http://dx.doi.org /10.1191/0309132504ph493oa.

Currid, Elizabeth. 2007. *The Warhol economy: How fashion, art and music drive New York City*. Princeton: Princeton University Press.

Currid, Elizabeth. 2009. "Bohemia as subculture; 'Bohemia' as industry. Art, culture and economic development." *Journal of Planning Literature* 23 (4): 368–82. http://dx.doi.org/10.1177/0885412209335727.

Dowdy, Michael. 2007. "Live hip hop, collective agency, and 'acting in concert.'" *Popular Music and Society* 30 (1): 75–91. http://dx.doi.org/10.1080 /03007760500503459.

Drake, Graham. 2003. "'This place gives me space': Place and creativity in the creative industries." *Geoforum* 34 (4): 511–24. http://dx.doi.org/10.1016 /S0016-7185(03)00029-0.

Flinn, Sue Carter. 2009. Halifax. "Cities of song: Get into the groove in these hot cities for music lovers." *CAA Magazine*, Summer: 28–9.

Florida, Richard. 2002a. "Bohemia and economic geography." *Journal of Economic Geography* 2 (1): 55–71. http://dx.doi.org/10.1093/jeg/2.1.55.

Florida, Richard. 2002b. "The economic geography of talent." *Annals of the Association of American Geographers* 92 (4): 743–55. http://dx.doi.org/10.1111 /1467-8306.00314.

Florida, Richard. 2002c. *The rise of the creative class and how it's transforming work, leisure, community and everyday life*. New York: Basic Books.

Florida, Richard. 2005a. *Cities and the creative class*. New York: Routledge.

Florida, Richard. 2005b. *The flight of the creative class: The new global competition for talent*. New York: Harper Business, HarperCollins.

Florida, Richard, and Scott Jackson. 2010. "Sonic city: The evolving economic geography of the music industry." *Journal of Planning Education and Research* 29 (3): 310–21. http://dx.doi.org/10.1177/0739456X09354453.

Florida, Richard, Charlotta Mellander, and Kevin Stolarick. 2008. "Inside the black box of regional development: Human capital, the creative class and tolerance." *Journal of Economic Geography* 8 (5): 615–49. http://dx.doi.org /10.1093/jeg/lbn023.

Florida, Richard, Charlotta Mellander, and Kevin Stolarick. 2010. "Music scenes to music clusters: The economic geography of music in the US, 1970–2000." *Environment & Planning A* 42 (4): 785–804. http://dx.doi.org/10.1068/a4253.

Frith, Simon. 1987. "Towards an aesthetic of popular music." In *Music and society: The politics of composition, performance and reception*, ed. Richard Leppert and Susan McClary, 133–49. Cambridge, UK: Cambridge University Press.

Gibson, Chris, and John Connell. 2003. "'Bongo fury': Tourism, music and cultural economy at Byron Bay, Australia." *Tijdschrift voor Economische en Sociale Geografie* 94 (2): 164–87. http://dx.doi.org/10.1111/1467-9663.00247.

Glaeser, Edward L., and Joshua D. Gottlieb. 2006. "Urban resurgence and the consumer city." *Urban Studies* (Edinburgh, Scotland) 43 (8): 1275–99. http://dx.doi.org/10.1080/00420980600775683.

Grant, Jill L., Jeff Haggett, and Jesse Morton. 2009. "The Halifax sound: Live music and the economic development of Halifax." http://theoryandprac-tice.planning.dal.ca/pdf/creative_halifax/isrn/halifax_sound.pdf.

Grant, Jill L., and Karin Kronstal. 2010. "The social dynamics of attracting talent in Halifax." *Canadian Geographer* 54 (3): 347–65. http://dx.doi.org /10.1111/j.1541-0064.2010.00310.x.

Hibbett, Ryan. 2005. "What is indie rock?" *Popular Music and Society* 28 (1): 55–77. http://dx.doi.org/10.1080/0300776042000300972.

Hracs, Brian J. 2010. "Working in the creative economy: The spatial dynamics of employment risk for musicians in Toronto." Doctoral dissertation in geography, University of Toronto.

Hracs, Brian J., Jill L. Grant, Jeffry Haggett, and Jesse Morton. 2011. "A tale of two scenes: Civic capital and retaining musical talent in Toronto and Halifax." *Canadian Geographer* 55 (3): 365–82. http://dx.doi.org/10.1111/j.1541-0064 .2011.00364.x.

Jones, Steve. 2002. "Music that moves: Popular music, distribution and network technologies." *Cultural Studies* 16 (2): 213–32. http://dx.doi.org/10.1080 /09502380110107562.

Kruse, Holly. 1993. "Subcultural identity in alternative music culture." *Popular Music* 12 (1): 33–41. http://dx.doi.org/10.1017/S026114300000533X.

Kruse, Robert J., II. 2005. "The Beatles as place makers: Narrated landscapes in Liverpool, England." *Journal of Cultural Geography* 22 (2): 87–114. http://dx.doi.org/10.1080/08873630509478240.

Leyshon, Andrew. 2001. "Time-space (and digital) compression: Software formats, musical networks, and the reorganisation of the music industry." *Environment & Planning A* 33 (1): 49–77. http://dx.doi.org/10.1068/a3360.

Leyshon, Andrew. 2009. "The software slump? Digital music, the democratisation of technology, and the decline of the recording studio sector within the musical economy." *Environment & Planning A* 41 (6): 1309–31. http://dx.doi.org/10.1068/a40352.

Lorentzen, Anne. 2009. "Cities in the experience economy." *European Planning Studies* 17 (6): 829–45. http://dx.doi.org/10.1080/09654310902793986.

Markusen, Ann. 2006. "Urban development and the politics of a creative class: Evidence from a study of artists." *Environment & Planning A* 38 (10): 1921–40. http://dx.doi.org/10.1068/a38179.

McLeay, Colin. 1994. "The 'Dunedin sound': New Zealand rock and cultural geography." *Perfect Beat* 2 (1): 38–49.

Morton, Jesse. 2009. "'There's a reason why I love this town': Exploring the Halifax music scene." Master's research project, Dalhousie University. http://theoryandpractice.planning.dal.ca/pdf/creative_halifax/jmorton_thesis.pdf.

Peterson, Richard A. 2005. "In search of authenticity." *Journal of Management Studies* 42 (5): 1083–98. http://dx.doi.org/10.1111/j.1467-6486.2005.00533.x.

Scott, Allen J. 1999. "The cultural economy: Geography and the creative field." *Media Culture & Society* 21 (6): 807–17. http://dx.doi.org/10.1177/016344399021006006.

Scott, Allen J. 2000. *The cultural economy of cities*. London: Sage.

Scott, Allen J. 2007. "Capitalism and urbanization in a new key? The cognitive-cultural dimension." *Social Forces* 85 (4): 1465–82. http://dx.doi.org/10.1353/sof.2007.0078.

Shank, Barry. 1994. *Dissonant identities: The rock'n'roll scene in Austin, Texas*. Hanover: Wesleyan University Press.

Stein-Sacks, Shelley. 2006. *The Canadian independent music industry: An examination of distribution and access*. Ottawa: Canadian Heritage.

Storper, Michael, and Anthony J. Venables. 2004. "Buzz: Face-to-face contact and the urban economy." *Journal of Economic Geography* 4 (4): 351–70.

Straw, Will. 1991. "Systems of articulation, logics of change: Communities and scenes in popular music." *Cultural Studies* 5 (3): 368–88. http://dx.doi.org/10.1080/09502389100490311.

Wynn, Graeme. 1998. "Places at the margin: The Atlantic provinces." In *Heartland/hinterland: A regional geography of Canada* (3rd ed.), ed. Larry McCann and Angus Gunn, 169–226. Scarborough: Prentice Hall Canada.

PART III

Attracting High-Technology Workers

7 Attracting Knowledge Workers and the Creative City Paradigm: Can We Plan for Talent in Montreal?

SÉBASTIEN DARCHEN AND
DIANE-GABRIELLE TREMBLAY

Introduction: What Motivates Junior Knowledge Workers?

In this chapter, we anticipate some consequences of implementing the creative city paradigm in urban planning practice to attract talent. The paper reports on the results of research on factors influencing the attraction and retention of junior knowledge workers – students in science and technology professions – in Montreal. There are three main sections. First, we define the creative city paradigm based on the most recent literature on the subject. We draw on the creative class thesis to explain that the debate also concerns urban regeneration. Next, we summarize our findings on factors influencing the mobility of junior knowledge workers in Montreal; amenities may not be as important as some think, while job opportunities seem to dominate mobility decisions. We also differentiate the views of students according to their origin (from Canada, Quebec, Montreal, or outside Canada). Third, we discuss the transferability of creative city ideas into urban planning practice and the possible social and economic outcomes of such an approach to city planning. Implementing creative city ideas in regeneration initiatives might contradict the concept of a diverse city that integrates different classes, cultures, and tastes within urban environments – considered by many to be more conducive to innovation and creativity than a city that is relatively homogeneous or segregated in terms of ethnicity (Pilati and Tremblay 2008; Tremblay and Pilati 2008a, 2008b; Tremblay and Tremblay 2010). Moreover, since our data suggest that junior knowledge people (talent) migrate in search of meaningful work, it is unlikely that city-building initiatives based on the creative city paradigm will affect migration between cities; rather, it may increase gentrification processes in a neoliberal context where there are limited public funds for improving the built environment (Battaglia and Tremblay 2012, 2011).

The Creative City Paradigm and Attracting Talent

Edensor et al. (2010) state that the two most influential works that have shaped the concept of the creative city are the publications of Landry and Bianchini (1995), *The creative city*, and Landry (2000), *The creative city: A toolkit for urban innovators*. Their basic tenet is that cities are facing immense challenges with the transition from an industrial to a post-industrial era and need to be creative in thinking of solutions to urban problems.

Costa (2008) describes the creative city as a concept characterized by three basic components: the first is the idea of creativity as a toolkit for urban development; the second is the notion that the creative city is based on the use of creative activities and industries; and the third supports the concept of the creative city as having the capacity to attract creative competences as human resources. It is the third component that we analysed in our study. However, we also took into consideration the first component, which concerns the implementation of the creative city paradigm in city planning.

The Creative Class Thesis in Economic Development

Initially, as the creative class thesis concerns urban economics, it can be considered an extrapolation of the human-capital model, although it remains a thesis of economic development. The creative class thesis was introduced by the American economist Richard Florida (2002; 2005; 2008), and has been disseminated widely. Both Florida and Charles Landry have promoted their ideas through extensive marketing (Gibson and Klocker 2004). Florida's work has had an impact on the field of urban economics, especially in regard to the creative capital thesis, but also increasingly on the field of urban planning, urban development, and urban policy.

There is not yet a clear consensus on the nature of the relationship between the quality of place as defined in Florida's criteria and economic development at the regional level. Beckstead and Brown (2006) indicate that human capital (e.g., knowledge workers associated with professionals working in the cultural sector) remains a better indicator to predict urban growth than urban amenities. They demonstrate links between the size of a city, the percentage of people employed in science and technology fields, and its potential for growth. They conclude that city size is the best indicator of urban growth, as larger cities have a larger number of firms which require more specialized types of human capital, such as scientists and engineers. Such research indicates that economic growth can be predicted on the basis of the concentration of human capital; however, growth is not necessarily linked to the influence of urban amenities, since metropolitan areas have experienced rising wages with or without urban amenities (Glaeser et al. 2001; Glaeser and Saiz 2004).

The creative class thesis can thus be considered as a complementary approach to the human-capital model. Florida (2002, 2005) and Florida et al. (2008) suggest an alternative measure of human capital based on the professional occupations included in the acronym TAPE: Technology and Innovation, Arts and Culture, Professionals and Management, Education. Florida sees the creative capital perspective as a better approach than the human capital model (Thomas and Darnton 2006), but Shearmur (2010) says it has not been empirically tested. The model links the concentration of human capital and economic growth at the regional level, but only accounts for level of education as a measure of human capital (Glaeser and Saiz 2004; Shapiro 2003; Simon 1998), whereas Florida integrates specific categories of human capital. Indeed, there are very few studies on the impact of actions related to creative initiatives, one of the few being the work on TOHU in Montreal (Tavano et al. 2012).

Florida (2003, 8) indicates that his theory of creative capital differs from the human capital model in two ways. First, he affirms that it identifies a specific type of human capital, people who occupy "creative" professions, as critical to economic growth. Second, he identifies the underlying factors that shape the locational decisions of people in these professional categories. Creative capital is thus an important output from the theory. Various professional categories of these creative workers are said to be attracted to metropolitan areas that have such characteristics as high levels of tolerance of cultural diversity and a large variety of social activities. According to Florida (2002), creative capital is attracted to locations where creativity can flourish. We have analysed the main criticisms of this thesis in economic development elsewhere (Darchen and Tremblay 2010a, 2010b, 2010c).

The Creative City Paradigm in City Planning

The ideas and principles of the creative class have now translated into city planning, and especially into city regeneration, to form an influential and quasi-universal paradigm. This paradigm has had, for approximately ten years, a growing influence on economic development policies and urban regeneration strategies. What are the possible outcomes if we plan for attracting talent? This is an emerging field of research and the consequences of creative city concepts on city planning are still poorly understood, despite the growing popularity of the paradigm. Research has mainly focused on the consequences of creative city ideas on urban policies, but seldom on planning practice. Landry (2000, 2006) defines a creative city as a city that promotes urban environments designed and suitable for talent because they fulfil particular criteria: openness to creativity, high levels of tolerance, abundant cultural activities, a concentration of gay and bohemian populations, and so on. However, recent works have indicated that the creative class conceptual model (from which is derived the creative city paradigm) does not hold up under empirical analysis: for instance, standardized indicators do not work in the Quebec case (Reese et al. 2010). Keil and Boudreau (2010) note that regardless of its weaknesses the creative city is influential in urban politics and entrepreneurial governance, particularly in Toronto.

According to Edensor et al. (2010), creativity has become part of the language of regeneration experts, urban planners, and urban policymakers. However, Rantisi and Leslie (2008) warn that there is a major risk associated with the creative city script, and its governance paradigm can hinder the potential for long-term sustainable policies. According to Miles and Paddison (2005), the idea that culture can be used as a driver for economic development has become part of a new orthodoxy for cities to enhance their position in a context of economic competitiveness, with the creativity agenda becoming an organizing principle for urban economic development (e.g., job creation and skills development). The popularity of creative city ideas and the appeal of arts and culture to local planners and regional economic development policymakers has already been documented (Evans 2003, 2009; Gibson and Klocker 2004; Gibson 2008). Gibson and Klocker point to the lack of critical thinking in the creative city discourse in city planning; they suggest that policymakers might brush aside local cultures by applying creative approaches to city building that have previously been applied elsewhere, in different local contexts. Christopherson and Rightor (2010) argue that culture and the arts are becoming tools for a wide variety of economic goals, including the revitalization of downtowns. However, critiques have also flourished regarding the possible outcomes of culture-led development (Peck 2005; Miles 2005) and about the manner in which culture and creativity have been commodified and neoliberalized (Zukin 1995; Hetherington 2007; Christophers 2008).

The works of Boudreau et al. (2009) and Peck (2005, 2009) emphasize that creative city strategies constitute new objects of governance and reinforce neoliberal forms of politics. Peck (2005) discusses the possible consequences of urban policies that embrace the creativity package. According to Peck, creative city strategies actually commodify arts and cultural resources to serve urban competition. He warns that creative city strategies constitute new objects of governance that lead to gentrification and are organized around short-term projects rather than progressive goals, such as poverty alleviation and environmental sustainability. Peck (2009, 159) argues that these strategies – which he labels as "fast [fixes] in a neoliberal urban conjuncture" – are based on facilitating localized life-styles instead of promoting meaningful social action on a broader scale. His arguments are highly critical of Florida's discourse, but his point regarding the transferability of the creative city approach is relevant. In the context of Toronto, Boudreau et al. (2009) view the creative city strategy as a discourse crafted to foster economic competitiveness, which they label "creative competitiveness," in the period following the economic austerity of the 1990s. The creative city discourse is undoubtedly very attractive to elected officials, especially in a context of recession.

Rantisi and Leslie (2008, 2009) identified the material dimension of neighbourhoods (referring to the case of Mile End in Montreal) as a key component in attracting creative workers, such as artists and designers, but the authors emphasize that spaces of creation and socialization within these neighbourhoods tend to develop spontaneously. If that is true, can we plan for the emergence of creative neighbourhoods? Mommaas (2004) suggests that the most historically recognized creative neighbourhoods (Soho, New York; Montmartre, Paris) have never been planned. Thus, effectively translating creative city ideas into city planning is questionable. Based on our results on the attraction and retention of junior knowledge workers in Montreal, we turn now to discuss the transferability of the creative city paradigm into city regeneration initiatives. The findings suggest that the creative city paradigm may be highly questionable from an empirical perspective in the Montreal case.

A Study of Montreal Talent

In order to evaluate whether various characteristics of cities have an influence on the attraction of scientists and engineers – one specific part of the creative class related to creativity in technology – we conducted empirical research using qualitative and quantitative methods. Our data collection began with an online questionnaire filled out by students in science and technology programs. The sample includes 529 students from programs in science and technology in universities in Montreal: UQÀM, Université de Montréal, École de Technologie Supérieure, and École Polytechnique de Montréal. We developed the questionnaire to evaluate the criteria influencing the mobility of students once they graduate. Therefore, we asked them to anticipate some of the decisions they would make (e.g., the place of work and the factors influencing this choice) regarding their career once they had graduated. The questionnaire aimed at analysing the following: the criteria influencing the attractiveness of Montreal as a place to study, retention factors for graduate students, the factors influencing attraction of the workforce, the influence of lifestyle in Montreal as a retention factor, their preferred residential location in the metropolitan area (city centre versus suburbs), and factors influencing their choice of destination once graduated.

Regarding the criteria used in the questionnaire, we proposed the following definitions. *Quality of the university* referred both to the institution and to the quality of the programs available in science and technology disciplines. *Quality of work* refers to employment that is stimulating and corresponds to the academic background of the student and to career objectives. *Quality of life* refers to characteristics such as the level of security, social welfare, the quality of the urban environment, the quality of public transport, and so on. *Level of tolerance* refers to low barriers of entry to human capital (e.g, ethnic and cultural diversity). *Lifestyle* refers to the elements offered by a city, including the possibility of access to cultural and social activities, a diverse array of restaurants, and urban amenities in general. *Openness to creativity* is linked to the level of tolerance of a city and includes the ability to attract people from a wide range of backgrounds. *Authenticity of the urban milieu* refers to the capacity of the urban milieu to offer opportunities in terms of entertainment, nightlife, and cultural activities.

For the data analysis, we did statistical tests (Wilcoxon tests) to determine the order of ranking for the different criteria used in the questionnaire.[1] To complement the information obtained with the questionnaires, we also conducted nine interviews; we analysed these data with a thematic analysis using NVIVO8 software. We used the interviews to further explore the interpretation of concepts that are central in the construction of the conceptual model of the creative class thesis: the

Table 7.1 Mobility according to the origins of students (per cent)

	Montreal ($n = 115$)	Quebec ($n = 252$)	Abroad ($n = 116$)	Total ($n = 483$)
Mobile	59.1	46.8	59.5	53.2
Non-mobile	40.9	53.2	40.5	46.8

openness to creativity, the authenticity of the urban milieu, the level of tolerance, the lifestyle, and so on. We interviewed students who were not necessarily drawn from the survey sample but were studying in francophone programs in science and technology in Montreal.

The Attraction of Creative Capital: Results with Junior Knowledge Workers

The quantitative analysis confirmed that science and technology students ranked the criteria related to the quality of place as secondary compared with criteria regarding career opportunities (Darchen and Tremblay 2010a, 2010c). We complemented the results with an analysis of interviews, which demonstrated that the criteria related to the quality of place played a part in the decision of choosing a place to work, but that these criteria alone cannot explain the attraction or retention of graduate students in science and technology.

The theory of human capital or of the creative capital implies that the workforce in science and technology is mobile and, according to Florida (2002), looking for cities which offer urban environments with characteristics appealing to creative workers. In our sample, however, students did not necessarily consider themselves a mobile workforce. Table 7.1 gives details on this, while describing the sample.

About half of the students already had an idea of the place where they wanted to work after their studies, and were less influenced by the criteria related to different places in the process of looking for employment; we considered these students as rather non-mobile. Participants in the sample considered mobile did not have a clear idea where they wished to work once graduated and were still hesitating between different destinations. Our data show that students from abroad or born in Montreal tend to be more in the category of the mobile in comparison with students coming from the rest of the province of Quebec, who have a tendency to be less mobile (or already have a clear idea where they intend to realize their career objectives).

Table 7.2 Montreal as a place to work: Retention
factors (*n* = 525)

Quality of work	2.02
Social network	2.69
Lifestyle	3.09
Quality of life	3.30
Cost of living	3.88

Scale: 1 = very important; 2 = important; 3 = somewhat
important; 4 = not so important; 5 = not at all important

Table 7.2 shows the results regarding the factors influencing the retention of students in Montreal once they have graduated. Students
were asked to rank five factors. There are significant differences between these factors. The quality of work comes first, followed by the
social network, the lifestyle, the quality of life, and finally the cost of
living. In contrast to the creative class hypothesis, the criteria regarding
the quality of place (the lifestyle and the quality of life) were less important than the quality of work or of the social network.

The interviews confirmed that students see the quality of work as the
most important criterion related to a decision to stay in Montreal upon
graduation. The students attested that they often compromise and that
they considered different elements in their choice of staying in Montreal.
They prioritized the criteria related to the quality of work, but they also
took into consideration the quality of life in Montreal, in terms of ethnic
diversity, cultural activities, and social interactions (six respondents).
The interviews thus confirmed that the quality of work (related to program of studies and to career objectives) would be the main criterion.
To summarize, students interviewed balance the different criteria (those
related to social network, career opportunities, and quality of place) in
their choice of whether or not to stay in Montreal. While elements related to the quality of place are part of this decision, these criteria alone
are not significant enough to explain the decision.

We asked the students, if they were not living in Montreal, what would
attract them to this city as a place to live. They were asked to rank four
factors: quality of work, level of salary, openness to creativity, and level
of tolerance (table 7.3). The criteria related to the quality of work still
came first, then the level of salary, and only after, the openness to creativity and level of tolerance. The interviews confirmed that the quality of
work is more important than the level of salary to explain the attraction

Table 7.3 Montreal as a place to work: Attraction
factors (*n* = 528)

Quality of work	1.53
Level of salary	2.35
Openness to creativity	2.82
Level of tolerance	3.28

Scale: 1 = important; 2 = somewhat important;
3 = not so important; 4 = not at all important

of students to Montreal. Salary was mentioned in two interviews, yet quality of work remained a priority. The openness to creativity was mentioned twice in interviews; students referred to it as a characteristic linked to social interactions in the urban environment and contributing to better productivity at work. The level of tolerance was mentioned in three interviews and was understood as the capacity of a city to welcome newcomers. Respondents saw the ethnic diversity and the two cultures (francophone and anglophone) of Montreal as an asset.

The students were asked to rank the four factors that would attract them to a city in general. According to the Wilcoxon tests, there are significant differences between the four factors proposed (525 respondents). The criteria related to the quality of work came first (1.44), followed by the level of salary (2.22), the authenticity of the urban milieu (2.86), and the level of tolerance (3.46).

The authenticity of the urban milieu was never mentioned directly in the interviews, but students referred to the lifestyle characterizing Montreal, and mentioned that ethnic and cultural diversity contribute to creating a vibrant living environment that is not necessarily found outside of the city or elsewhere in the province. The lifestyle of Montreal is viewed as an asset because of the multitude of entertainment activities. However, one student mentioned that one does not have to be in an urban environment to find entertainment.

We asked the students to rank various activities that contribute to the quality of the city's lifestyle: they estimated that international festivals (2.03) are more important than the variety of restaurants (2.24), followed by nightlife (2.56) and finally art galleries (3.15). Our aim was also to measure if these activities could have an impact on retaining students compared with career opportunities available in another city. We then asked the students if they would hesitate to leave Montreal if another city had better career opportunities but lacked the above-mentioned activities. They had four choices: 13.5 per cent answered Yes (they would hesitate); 23.7 per cent said it is likely (that they would hesitate); 38.5 per cent said it is unlikely (that they would hesitate); and finally 24.3 per cent said No (they will not hesitate).

Career opportunities still dominated; indeed, a majority of students (62.8 per cent) consider that they would not hesitate to leave Montreal for better career opportunities. The results indicate that the lifestyle factors that characterize Montreal are assets in the retention of students, but that career opportunities have a stronger impact on attracting students.

We asked the students where they would rather live once they have graduated: in the suburbs or in the city-centre. We wanted to see if the workforce in science and technology is attracted towards an urban living environment. Almost two-thirds of the students indicated they would rather live in the suburbs of Montreal than in the city-centre. This confirms that students in science and technology are not necessarily looking for vibrant living environments, even if they appreciate the lifestyle of Montreal; this appears to contradict the creative class thesis. Regarding their reasons for choosing the suburbs as a place to live, students indicated that the space available in the suburbs is significantly more important than the lifestyle, and the cost of living is less important. As for those who chose the city-centre, the lifestyle is significantly more important than the proximity of commercial activities, and the level of tolerance comes last. The findings confirm Markusen's (2006) argument that the creative class includes professional categories with different tastes regarding ways of living.

Our interviews offer a little more qualitative information. For example, students mention the fact that living in the city-centre offers better opportunities regarding access to transportation and cultural activities, as well as more social interactions. It is mainly when students consider having a family that they might find the suburbs more attractive.

Our results show that criteria related to the quality of work are most relevant to understand the mobility of students in science and technology once they have graduated: graduate students will go where they can find work corresponding to their career objectives. It seems likely this can be considered an indicator of the factors influencing the mobility of knowledge workers. Although the level of salary has an effect, it has a lesser influence on the mobility of students than does the quality of work. The criteria related to the quality of place are thus less relevant than criteria related to work opportunities to explain the mobility of students once they graduate.

The criteria related to the quality of work and to the social network are more relevant in the retention of students in Montreal than criteria related to the quality of place (lifestyle and quality of life). Activities contributing to the quality of the lifestyle are not considered by a majority of students (62.8 per cent) as having a major impact on their decision to leave Montreal if they had better career opportunities elsewhere.

We also observed that a majority of students in science and technology would rather live in the suburbs than downtown. This is a clear indication that students in science and technology are not necessarily looking for vibrant urban environments to live in. Other criteria may influence the mobility of graduate students. We found that students coming from the province of Quebec tend to be less mobile than those coming from abroad or from Montreal (table 7.1). It is interesting to note that the origins of students has an influence on the results, something which has not been highlighted before to our knowledge, although there is a need for further investigation of this point.

Our results concur with the conclusions of chapters 8 and 9 (this volume, regarding Saskatoon and Calgary): junior knowledge workers move for the job opportunities. The quality of place and criteria associated with the creative class thesis play a minor role in explaining the mobility patterns of junior knowledge workers. As Ryan et al. (this volume) argue, mobility patterns result from complex decisions not easily reduced to a set of criteria. As Hracs and Stolarick (this volume) note, some criteria from the creative class thesis (e.g., authenticity of place) are difficult to nail down and thus to evaluate empirically. The comparison indicates that musicians attach greater importance to criteria linked to the quality of place than do knowledge workers in their decisions to move to a city to perform their art.

Discussion: Can We Plan to Attract Talent?

Based on the Montreal results, it seems likely that policies based on the creative class thesis and the city-building goals of improving the appeal of urban environments would have no major impacts on the migration of junior knowledge workers between cities. Thus, it is improbable that the translation of the creative class thesis into urban policies is achieving its goal: namely, to attract talented science and technology workers. It is not likely to influence the mobility patterns of this population.

In this discussion, we attempt to anticipate how the creative city paradigm might translate into planning practice and what might be the benefits or the negative effects of such an approach. First, there is no consensus yet on either the definition of a creative city or the ways in which to implement it. Smith and Warfield (2008) identify two orientations: the culture-centric and the econo-centric orientations. The lack of clarity regarding the definition of what exactly is a creative city is likely to lead to different interpretations in practice; in a neoliberal context where local governments are less involved with planning matters, it is likely that the private sector will take the lead in implementing the paradigm in practice.

Little has been written about the translation of the creative city thesis into planning practice in the case of Montreal, so we refer here more to the Canadian and international context, as well as to our results. In implementing creative city strategies[2] in city planning, especially in the context of urban regeneration, the literature in urban planning has emphasized the possible outcomes. Peck (2005) is probably the most critical of implementing the creative city paradigm; he anticipates that creating innovative and tolerant milieux could also lead to dislocating low-income households. Rantisi and Leslie (2008, 2009) state, in the case of Montreal, that even if creative workers might look for urban environments conducive to creativity, it is another story to say that we can plan for talent or plan to foster creativity. Research on creative neighbourhoods has already emphasized that spontaneity is a key component of success.

The translation of creative city ideas into planning practice is likely to lead to a piecemeal approach to urbanism, as in the case of Toronto and to a lesser extent in Vancouver. The appropriation of the idea by city boosters from the private sector, Business Improvement Area associations especially, results in the use of the paradigm as a means for producing distinctive upper-class areas and thus often forces local artists to relocate (Catungal et al. 2009; Darchen 2010; McLean 2010), as was the case in the Montreal Multimedia City (Tremblay and Rousseau 2006). Recent research in different areas of the world has warned of the possible outcomes of implementing creative city strategies (Atkinson and Easthope 2009).

The rush to implement creative city ideas is not based on solid empirical research. Our research in Montreal suggests it is likely that the city planning initiatives on urban environments without incentives to create job opportunities will not lead to an effective economic development strategy. As Smith and Warfield (2008) note, the creative city paradigm is too generic and does not make any distinction between arts and culture values and creative industries values. In the case of Toronto, where there is a shortage of public funding, the creative city rhetoric is taken over by private stakeholders in city planning, and the paradigm deviates from its initial objective to produce distinctive urbanscapes (e.g., Liberty Village, Toronto Entertainment District). While Florida's discourse initially helped push the arts and culture scene to the forefront of economic development in Montreal, the media and population became more critical by the time of his speech at the Montreal Chamber of Commerce in 2009. Many organizations are now distancing themselves from his theory; researchers are highlighting the importance for Montreal to maintain its preoccupation with social cohesion and inclusion in governance processes and to take this into account when thinking of the creative sectors and development of the city (Klein and Tremblay 2010). This results in many projects focusing on the local community, and not solely considering the attraction of outside talent.

Directions for Future Research

Let us start by mentioning a few limitations and future research directions. Our research has analysed the intentions of students who will soon be part of the creative class and population of knowledge workers as scientists and engineers. Certainly, a study of students' aspirations may be different from the actual behaviours of these students in the future. Nevertheless, the results present an exploratory analysis of the impact of criteria related to the quality of place in the decision process of these professionals when they choose a place to work. We are also aware that other classes of creative workers may respond differently to these questions.

The origins of students influenced their answers concerning their mobility and their destinations upon graduation. Further studies might compare the results for Montreal with those for other cities. We have collected the same kind of data for Ottawa and compared the results on these two cities (Darchen and Tremblay 2010c), but the potential for further illuminating research on other cities remains.

The creative cities paradigm has certainly opened a new field in urban economics and urban research, but its benefits and potential have been exaggerated. The research reported here identifies some of its weaknesses. City planners and economic development staff need to assess the hype and the promise against the risks and realities.

NOTES

1 Given limited space, we do not go into technical details: refer to the details
  and tables in Darchen and Tremblay (2010b). We evaluated the size of the
  difference between the criteria using the scale of Cohen's standard. Criteria
  are ranked in the tables according to their level of relevance. The tables
  present the means regarding the ranks; we discuss the results according to
  the two types of tests presented here.
2 We actually prefer the term creative city paradigm, which emphasizes a
  paradigm shift from the modernist paradigm in city planning.

REFERENCES

Atkinson, Rowland, and Hazel Easthope. 2009. "The consequences of the cre-
    ative class: The pursuit of creativity in Australian cities." *International Jour-
    nal of Urban and Regional Research* 33 (1): 64–79. http://dx.doi.org/10.1111
    /j.1468-2427.2009.00837.x.
Battaglia, Angelo, and Diane-Gabrielle Tremblay. 2011."22@ and the Innova-
    tion District in Barcelona and Montreal: A process of clustering development
    between urban regeneration and economic competitiveness." *Urban Studies
    Research*, vol. 2011, article ID 568159, 17 pp. http://dx.doi.org/10.1155/2011
    /568159. http://www.hindawi.com/journals/usr/2011/568159/.
Battaglia, Angelo, and Diane-Gabrielle Tremblay. 2012. "El Raval and Mile
    End: A comparative study of two cultural quarters in Barcelona and Mon-
    treal, between urban regeneration and creative clusters." *Journal of Geogra-
    phy and Geology* 4 (1).
Beckstead, Desmond, and W. Mark Brown. 2006. *Capacité d'innovation: L'emploi
    en sciences et en génie dans les villes canadiennes et américaines.* Ottawa: Statis-
    tique Canada.
Boudreau, Julie-Anne, Roger Keil, and Douglas Young. 2009. *Changing Toronto:
    Governing urban neoliberalism.* Toronto: University of Toronto Press.
Catungal, John, Deborah Leslie, and Yvonne Hii. 2009. "Geographies of dis-
    placement in the creative city: The case of Liberty Village in Toronto." *Urban
    Studies* (Edinburgh, Scotland) 46 (5–6): 1095–114. http://dx.doi.org/10.1177
    /0042098009103856.
Christophers, Brett. 2008. "The BBC, the creative class and neoliberal urban-
    ism in the north of England." *Environment & Planning A* 40 (10): 2313–29.
Christopherson, Susan, and Ned Rightor. 2010. "The creative economy as
    'big business': Evaluating state strategies to lure filmmakers." *Journal of*

Planning Education and Research 29 (3): 336–52. http://dx.doi.org/10.1177 /0739456X09354381.

Costa, Pedro. 2008. "Creativity, innovation and territorial agglomeration in cultural activities: The roots of the creative city." In *Creative cities, cultural clusters and local economic development*, ed. Philip Cooke and Luciana Lazzeretti, 183–201. Cheltenham, UK: Edward Elgar Publishing Ltd.

Darchen, Sébastien. 2010. "The creative city approach and the production of urban designscapes: A comparison of redevelopment processes in Toronto and Vancouver." Paper presented at the City Institute Seminar, York University, 3 December, Toronto, Canada.

Darchen, Sébastien, and Diane-Gabrielle Tremblay. 2010a. "Attracting and retaining the workforce in science and technology: The case of Montreal." In *Knowledge-based development of cities and societies: An integrated multi-level approach*, ed. Kostas Metaxiotis, Francisco Javier Carrillo, and Tan Yigitcanlar, 42–58. Hershey, PA: IGI Global.

Darchen, Sébastien, and Diane-Gabrielle Tremblay. 2010b. "La thèse de la classe créative: Revue des écrits et perspectives de recherche." In *La classe créative selon Richard Florida: Un paradigme urbain plausible?*, ed. Rémy Tremblay and Diane-Gabrielle Tremblay, 13–35. Rennes, France: Presses Universitaires de Rennes.

Darchen, Sébastien, and Diane-Gabrielle Tremblay. 2010c. "What attracts and retains knowledge workers/students: The quality of place or career opportunities? The cases of Montreal and Ottawa." *Cities* (London, England) 27 (4): 225–33. http://dx.doi.org/10.1016/j.cities.2009.12.009.

Edensor, Tim, Deborah Leslie, Steve Millington, and Norma Rantisi. 2010. *Spaces of vernacular creativity: Rethinking the cultural economy*. London: Routledge.

Evans, Graeme. 2003. "Hard branding the culture city – From Prado to Prada." *International Journal of Urban and Regional Research* 27 (2): 417–40. http://dx.doi.org/10.1111/1468-2427.00455.

Evans, Graeme. 2009. "Creative city, creative spaces and urban policies." *Urban Studies* (Edinburgh, Scotland) 46 (5–6): 1003–40. http://dx.doi.org/10.1177 /0042098009103853.

Florida, Richard. 2002. *The rise of the creative class and how it's transforming work, leisure, community and everyday life*. New York: Basic Books.

Florida, Richard. 2003. "Cities and the creative class." *City & Community* 2 (1): 3–19. http://dx.doi.org/10.1111/1540-6040.00034.

Florida, Richard. 2005. *Cities and the creative class*. New York: Routledge.

Florida, Richard. 2008. *Who's your city? How the creative economy is making where to live the most important decision of your life*. New York: Basic Books.

Florida, Richard, Charlotte Mellander, and Kevin Stolarick. 2008. "Inside the black box of regional development human capital, the creative class and tolerance." *Journal of Economic Geography* 8 (5): 615–49. http://dx.doi.org /10.1093/jeg/lbn023.

Gibson, Chris. 2008. "Creative arts, people, and places: Which policy directions?" In *How are we going? Directions for Arts in the Creative Edge*, ed. Lisa Anderson and Kate Oakley, 42–56. Cambridge, UK: Cambridge Scholars Press.

Gibson, Chris, and Natascha Klocker. 2004. "Academic publishing as 'creative' industry, and recent discourses of 'creative economies': Some critical reflections." *Area* 36 (4): 423–34. http://dx.doi.org/10.1111/j.0004-0894.2004 .00242.x.

Glaeser, Edward Ludwig, Jed Kolko, and Albert Saiz. 2001. "Consumer city." *Journal of Economic Geography* 1 (1): 27–50. http://dx.doi.org/10.1093/ jeg/1.1.27.

Glaeser, Edward Ludwig, and Albert Saiz. 2004. "The rise of the skilled city." *Brookings-Wharton Papers on Urban Affairs*: 47–105.

Hetherington, Kevin. 2007. "Manchester's urbis." *Cultural Studies* 21 (4–5): 630–49. http://dx.doi.org/10.1080/09502380701278996.

Keil Roger, and Julie-Anne Boudreau. 2010. "Le concept de la ville créative: La création réelle ou imaginaire d'une forme d'action politique dominante." *Pôle Sud* 32 (1): 165–78.

Klein, Juan-Luis, and Diane-Gabrielle Tremblay. 2010. "Can we have a 'creative city' without social cohesion? Some avenues of reflection." *Plan Canada* 52 (2): 27–9.

Landry, Charles. 2000. *The creative city: A toolkit for urban innovators*. Sterling, VA: Earthscan Publications Ltd.

Landry, Charles. 2006. *The art of city building*. Sterling, VA: Earthscan Publications Ltd.

Landry, Charles, and Franco Bianchini. 1995. *The creative city*. London: Demos.

Markusen, Ann. 2006. "Urban development and the politics of a creative class: Evidence from a study of artists." *Environment and Planning A* 38: 1921–40.

McLean, Heather. 2010. "The politics of creative performance in public space: Towards a critical geography of Toronto case studies." In *Spaces of vernacular creativity: Rethinking the cultural economy*, ed. Tim Edensor, Deborah Leslie, Steve Millington, and Norma Rantisi, 200–13. London: Routledge.

Miles, Steven. 2005. "Interruptions: Testing the rhetoric of culturally led urban development." *Urban Studies* (Edinburgh, Scotland) 42 (5–6): 889–911. http://dx.doi.org/10.1080/00420980500107375.

Miles, Steven, and Ronan Paddison. 2005. "Introduction: The rise and rise of culture-led urban regeneration." *Urban Studies* (Edinburgh, Scotland) 42 (5–6): 833–9. http://dx.doi.org/10.1080/00420980500107508.

Mommaas, Hans. 2004. "Cultural clusters and the post-industrial city: Towards the remapping of urban cultural policy." *Urban Studies* (Edinburgh, Scotland) 41 (3): 507–32. http://dx.doi.org/10.1080/0042098042000178663.

Peck, Jamie. 2005. "Struggling with the creative class." *International Journal of Urban and Regional Research* 29 (4): 740–70. http://dx.doi.org/10.1111/j.1468-2427.2005.00620.x.

Peck, Jamie. 2009. "The cult of urban creativity." In *Leviathan undone? Towards a political economy of scale*, ed. Roger Keil and Rianne Mahon, 159–76. Vancouver: UBC Press.

Pilati, Thomas, and Diane-Gabrielle Tremblay. 2008. "Le développement socio-économique de Montréal: La cité créative et la carrière artistique comme facteurs d'attraction?" *Canadian Journal of Regional Science* 30 (3): 475–95.

Rantisi, Norma, and Deborah Leslie. 2008. "The social and material foundations of creativity for Montreal Independent Designers." Presented at the annual meeting of the Innovative Systems Research Network, Montreal, Canada. http://www.utoronto.ca/isrn/publications/NatMeeting/NatSlides/Nat08/slides/RantisiN_LeslieD_Foundations_Creativity.pdf.

Rantisi, Norma, and Deborah Leslie. 2009. *Montreal: The small, big city. Theme II report on the social foundations of talent attraction and retention*. Research report for the Innovative Systems Research Network project. (Unpublished manuscript).

Reese, Laura A., Jessica M. Faist, and Gary Sands. 2010. "Measuring the creative class: Do we know it when we see it?" *Journal of Urban Affairs* 32 (3): 345–66. http://dx.doi.org/10.1111/j.1467-9906.2010.00496.x.

Shapiro, Jesse M. 2003. *Smart cities: Explaining the relationship between city growth and human capital*. (Unpublished manuscript).

Shearmur, Richard. 2010. "L'aristocratie du savoir: Quelques réflexions sur les thèses de Richard Florida." In *La classe créative selon Richard Florida: Un paradigme urbain plausible?* ed. Remy Tremblay and Diane-Gabrielle Tremblay, 107–26. Québec: Presses de l'Université du Québec.

Simon, Curtis J. 1998. "Human capital and metropolitan employment growth." *Journal of Urban Economics* 43 (2): 223–43. http://dx.doi.org/10.1006/juec.1997.2048.

Smith, Richard, and Katie Warfield. 2008. "The creative city: A matter of values." In *Creative cities, cultural clusters and local development*, ed. Philip Cooke and Luciana Lazzeretti, 287–312. London: Edward Elgar.

Tavano Blessi, Giorgio, Diane-Gabrielle Tremblay, Marco Sandri, and Thomas Pilati. 2012. "New trajectories in urban regeneration processes: Cultural capital as source of human and social capital accumulation. Evidence from the case of Tohu in Montreal." *Cities* 29 (6): 397–407.

Thomas, June Manning, and Julia Darnton. 2006. "Social diversity and economic development in the metropolis." *Journal of Planning Literature* 21 (2): 153–68. http://dx.doi.org/10.1177/0885412206292259.

Tremblay, Diane-Gabrielle, and Thomas Pilati. 2008a. "Les centres d'artistes autogérés et leur rôle dans l'attraction de la classe créative." *Géographie, économie et société* 10 (1): 427–47.

Tremblay, Diane-Gabrielle, and Thomas Pilati. 2008b. "The Tohu and artist-run centres: Contributions to the creative city?" *Canadian Journal of Regional Science* 30 (2): 337–56.

Tremblay, Diane-Gabrielle, and Serge Rousseau. 2006. "The Montreal multimedia sector: A cluster, an 'innovative milieu' or a simple colocation?" *Canadian Journal of Regional Science* 28 (2): 299–327.

Tremblay, Remy, and Diane-Gabrielle Tremblay, eds. 2010. *La classe créative selon Richard Florida: Un paradigme urbain plausible?* Québec, Rennes: Presses de l'Université du Québec and Presses de l'Université de Rennes.

Zukin, Sharon. 1995. *The culture of cities*. London: Wiley-Blackwell.

8 Talent, Tolerance, and Community in Saskatoon

PETER W.B. PHILLIPS AND GRAEME WEBB

Introduction: Why Do High Tech Workers Come to Saskatoon?

There is a hot debate in academic and policy circles about the emerging hypothesis that the social dynamics of city-regions constitute the foundations of economic success in the global economy. While the literature hypothesizes that three dimensions – that is, the social nature of the innovation process; the social foundations of talent attraction, integration, and retention; and the degree of social inclusion and civic engagement – work in tandem to drive development at the local level, the purpose of this chapter is to examine the characteristics and features of the Saskatoon city-region that prove to be salient to talented and creative workers. In short, why do high-technology workers move to Saskatoon? And what makes them stay?

In order to facilitate the examination of these questions we have divided the chapter into six sections. First we discuss the socio-economic background of Saskatoon. Then we review the theory related to our study. The next section outlines the nature of the surveys administered. After we report on the results of the surveys of individuals and institutions, the final section offers some concluding comments.

Saskatoon Emerges as a Fast-Growth Community

This is an interesting and volatile time to examine the structures and dynamics in the Saskatoon market. After the better part of two decades of extreme economic volatility in the core commodity markets relevant to the Saskatoon economy, the city entered a period of robust and volatile growth. A major commodity boom and bust characterized the 1972–86 period, triggered by the Great Grain Robbery of 1971 (when the USSR cornered the global grain market before releasing news that it had suffered a massive crop failure), increased with the founding of OPEC in the early 1970s, and ended with the collapse of almost all commodity prices in 1986. Consequently, Saskatoon faced the better part of two decades of relatively stagnant socio-economic development. Per capita incomes lagged behind national growth and employment and demographic growth was more related to intra-provincial restructuring than to net provincial economic growth.

Before the debt crisis and the global fiscal and economic meltdown of 2008–10, the demand for most commodities had been growing strongly, at least partly owing to economic strength in Asia. While other parts of Canada were seriously affected by the global downturn, the continued strength of key commodity markets (particularly in oil and gas, potash, and uranium) allowed Saskatchewan to maintain a robust level of growth. Furthermore, new and potentially more profitable resource deposits have been delineated and an array of technologies has emerged that make some local product markets more profitable. In recent years more than $1 billion of new investment has been directed to the University of Saskatchewan and related research facilities to take advantage of these new opportunity areas, while oil, heavy oil, potash, uranium, gold, and diamonds have all been targeted for further development and the agri-food sector has rebounded (both owing to higher world prices and the end of the US embargo on beef trade).

The result has been a continued boom in Saskatchewan and Saskatoon in what has proved to be a rather uncertain and tentative global economic recovery. The province and the city have slightly bettered the national rate of growth in population (especially in 2008 and 2009), employment growth (up 24 per cent in 2000–9, compared with only 14 per cent for Canada as a whole and just marginally behind Calgary and Edmonton), and property-market price rises (more than doubling in the 2006–8 period and holding steady between 2008 and 2010). In the twelve months ending in July 2010, Saskatoon had the fastest population growth rate of any urban centre. Given this context, we should not be surprised to see a bit of disconnect between the recorded data on socio-economic vibrancy and the local perception thereof. Most of the available data for Saskatoon was collected during the 2001 census; even the more contemporary data comes from annual statistical measures that lag the economy by up to a year (table 8.1).

Table 8.1 Socio-economic indicators, Saskatoon and Canada

Key indicators	Period	Saskatoon	Canada
Population change*	2000–10	14.0%	11.2%
Per cent foreign born	2001	7.5%	18.2%
Per cent BA or higher	2001	17.5%	15.4%
PhDs per 1000	2001	10.9	5.4
Employment rate*	2009	70.6	61.7
Unemployment rate*	2009	4.7%	8.3%
Per cent creative occupations	2001	33.4%	29.2%
Per cent science &technology (S&T) occupations	2001	5.8%	6.4%
Bohemians per 1000 in the labour force	2001	11.6	13.1
Number clusters	2001	4	263
Per cent employment in clusters	2001	15.5%	22.1%
Average household income	2001	$53,025	$58,360

Sources: Spencer and Vinodrai 2006; *Statistics Canada 2011a and 2011b.

Nevertheless, the data in table 8.1 shows a few notable features in Saskatoon in the context of talent and tolerance. Saskatoon presents a different situation from many other centres in Canada. It has a higher degree of talent, as measured by those with advanced degrees (BA or higher) and those with PhDs (10.9/1000 in Saskatoon versus 5.4/1000 for Canada). Similarly, Saskatoon has a higher percentage of its population engaged in creative occupations (33 per cent versus 29 per cent for Canada), even though it has a somewhat smaller share in the S&T occupations. Saskatoon has both self-labelled and been singled out by others as Canada's Science City, at least partly thanks to the city's research park, Innovation Place and the Canadian Light Source, one of only six third-generation synchrotrons in the world and the only one in Canada.

In contrast, on other measures the city presents a picture of a lower level of diversity. Only about 7.5 per cent of the Saskatoon population is foreign born, compared with more than 18 per cent for Canada. (One should note, however, that Saskatoon's Aboriginal population represents an estimated 15 per cent of the total population, which adds a different but significant type of diversity.) Similarly, Saskatoon has only 11.6 bohemians (defined as artists and artisans) per 1000 labour force, compared with 13.1/1000 for Canada. Nevertheless, Saskatoon was picked as Canada's cultural capital for 2006 in the category of cities over 125,000 and is judged by many to have a vibrant cultural community relative to its size.

This divergence from national patterns leads to a mixed picture of economic performance. Based on national measures, Saskatoon in 2001 supported only four identifiable industrial clusters, which employed about 15 per cent of the local workforce (compared with 22 per cent in identifiable clusters in Canada). Saskatoon's average household income also lagged behind the national average by 9.1 per cent in 2001: this gap has likely closed somewhat, as the provincial GDP per capita has risen from 93 per cent of the national average in 2001 to 21 per cent over the national average in 2009, and the Saskatoon economy has been more vibrant than that of the province as a whole. Nevertheless, Saskatoon has one of the highest labour force participation rates, with 70.6 per cent of the potential labour force working in 2009, 14.4 per cent higher than the national average. Its employment growth rate was 70 per cent higher than the national average over the 2000 to 2009 period.

In some ways, the choice of Montreal, Calgary, and Saskatoon as three comparator cities for investigating the role of talent, tolerance, and technology in attracting high-technology workers is inspired. While the candidate pool was limited (given Canada only has about 33 census metropolitan areas with more than 100,000 population), the cities offer interesting contrasts. All three aspire to attract and mobilize talented high-tech workers, yet each represents a different stage of industrial and economic development. Montreal, the oldest, largest, and most cosmopolitan of the three, has a large, traditional manufacturing base that, while part of a large market area that extends well into the American heartland, has been challenged to retool in recent years with new technology and new skills in response to lower tariff barriers and the stronger Canadian dollar. As a large metropolitan area with a global presence, Montreal represents an obvious location where tolerance and community vitality could be a strategic asset in transformation. Calgary, in contrast, is a relatively young, vibrant, Great Plains city that over the last generation emerged on the global stage, primarily as a major oil and gas player. With a relatively small manufacturing sector, Calgary has had the unique advantage of attempting to leapfrog the traditional stage of manufacturing and move directly to a service- and knowledge-based economy. This has been helped by the strong terms of trade that unambiguously favours resource-rich Alberta. Some assert that this may also be a weakness, as Calgary may suffer from the Dutch disease of having such strong returns in the petroleum sector that it absorbs the bulk of creative energy in the community. Ultimately, the majority of its knowledge and high-technology workers remain focused on optimizing economic returns in the primary sector. Saskatoon, as the smallest and least cosmopolitan of the cities, is only recently benefiting from the resource boom, and is testing the waters about how to sustain and build upon this good fortune.

This brief review of the socio-economic situation in Saskatoon sets the stage for addressing the question about the role of talent and tolerance in the economic development of a creative science city.

Theory

Scholars have examined innovation systems through an array of approaches. Some are interested in the role of innovation systems in minimizing transactional costs (e.g., Phillips 2005) or generating economies of scale and scope (e.g., Porter 1990). A wide range of approaches have been adopted, including industrial/managerial investigations of geographic concentrations of competing and cooperating companies, suppliers, service providers, and associated institutions that create industrial interdependencies (e.g., Porter 1990); analyses of networks and their relationships between markets and the visible hand of organizational authorities; study of industrial milieux that exhibit synergies of economic and technological interdependencies; modelling of value-chain industrial clusters involving an extended input-output or buyer-supplier chain; comparative institutional analysis; and investigations of innovation systems as learning regions acting as collectors and repositories of knowledge and ideas that facilitate the flow of knowledge, ideas, and learning (e.g., Florida 2002).

Ultimately, all these lines of research examine the role of untraded interdependencies (Dosi 1984; Lundvall 1988, 1992), a term now extensively used to refer to an array of externalities of scale and scope. These interdependencies are often characterized as involving region-specific conventions, informal rules and habits that coordinate economic actors in localized production systems (see Ryan and Phillips 2004 for a further discussion). The resulting analyses examine how central actors, networks, culture, alliances, and other relationships manage uncertainties, thereby lowering transaction costs or increasing the rate and scope of innovative activity. There has been extensive research on specific innovation systems around the world, many focusing on biotechnology, an array of ICTs (information and communication technologies), new media, wine, food, automotive parts, clothing, and advanced materials agglomerations in Europe (e.g., Asheim and Gertler 2006; Cooke 2002; Porter 1990), the United States (e.g., Saxenian 1994; Porter 1990; Audretsch and Feldman 1996), and Canada (e.g., Wolfe and Gertler 2004; Phillips 2002). Although these studies have shown various potentially key relationships between and among firms and other institutions, there is little in the evidence that is definitively causal or universally applicable.

Although most investigations of innovation systems have focused on examining the components of the system (through an institutional review) or outputs (using share analysis of value added or employment), we find increasing interest in examining what happens inside the black box of the system. This approach has tended to start with increasingly sophisticated surveys of the actors in and outside a system. The survey results have been used then to correlate business practices against outcomes, to determine if and how connections between actors enhance or impede invention and innovation. The approach has yielded several observations about the various roles actors may play.

The untraded interdependencies in these systems are largely governed by two mutually supporting types of actors: centrally located institutions and formal or informal leaders (sometimes called talent or creatives). Leaders are present in the system in different areas and guises. In many instances, centrally located institutional actors provide a platform for exchange. Central actors could be public research laboratories, formal or informal research collaborations, or industry associations. The price of admission and rules of engagement will vary widely, but ultimately these structures thrive and add value if they are able to generate an environment where participants can feel comfortable exchanging knowledge about what they know and what works (or sometimes, more importantly, what they don't know or what doesn't work). Many such systems are formalized via legal contracts or partnerships, which make the rules transparent and enforce the agreements. A number of models have been tried. Australia has Cooperative Research Consortia and the Commonwealth Science and Industrial Research Organization. Canada has created Networks of Centres of Excellence and National Research Council regional laboratories. The European Union has framework collaborations to complement the research facilities operated by its member states. Japan and South Korea have actively encouraged their *keiretsu* and *chaebol* (post–Second World War business models defined as horizontally integrated corporate alliances across many sectors) to create collaborative ventures. The United States has legally sanctioned and supported industry collaborative research and development agreements. Each is designed at least partly to create a platform for exchange.

Other systems operate less formally, with collaborative relationships revolving around industry associations or informal research groups. In these cases, the rules are often not formalized, but rather the systems operate on an implicit golden rule of "do unto others as you would have them do unto you." That type of governing system only works where there is a high likelihood that opportunistic action will not lead to large windfall gains and that the community or network will have a sustained life. Essentially, the system operates in the context of a repeated game, where there is a non-trivial probability that participants will need to interact on a sustained basis, so that one-off opportunistic action will seldom compensate for being ostracized and the attendant loss of opportunities and higher operational costs that would follow.

A second group of actors are the formal and informal leaders in a community. The position of a leader will vary depending on the nature and stage of development of an agglomeration. The leader could be a research star, a venture capitalist, an angel investor, an industrial actor, or a social entrepreneur. Different agglomerations need different leaders at different times. The difficulty is that there is no conclusive way to identify a leader. Each leader exhibits different idiosyncrasies and capacities, which tends to make most analyses highly subjective and value laden. At one level, we are forced to fall back on the psychological, sociological, and economic underpinnings to individual and group action. Some individuals will be driven by economic reward such as the biotechnology research stars in the 1990s who crystallized and capitalized their reputational equity through their roles in new venture startups (Zucker et al. 1998). Other actors seek different returns, in the form of reputation, social standing, and various other soft benefits.

The focus on the individual rather than the supply chain in some analyses leads to a wider discussion about the role of society in creating the conditions for technology and talent to come together to generate innovations that go on to generate economic and social value. Florida (2002) suggests the key factor is tolerance for all kinds of diversity (e.g., beliefs, values, epistemologies, morals, races, cultures, and lifestyles). Innovation requires change, which requires some antithetic actors or features. Hence, the system must be able to attract, engage, and retain a plurality of voices that contest the norms.

The challenge for analysis is that talent and tolerance seldom map cleanly onto any single community or, within a community, upon any clearly identified supply chain, industrial agglomeration, or cluster. Tolerance is more likely a reflection of the broader social milieu, while creative talent often lives and operates within, among, and between communities and clusters. Hence, the methodological challenge.

Although the focus in many supply chains, geopolitical regions, and technology fields is on building creative environments that will produce optimal inventive effort, we lack the tools to understand how to intervene appropriately. Ingenious, creative people and communities arise almost serendipitously, typically outside any formal governance system. Once they emerge, they often are captured by government, industry, or civil authorities, either during the inventive stage, or more often in the gestation period. When the ideas are reduced to practice, legal and regulatory compliance is achieved and the package is readied for commercialization (Phillips 2007).

As Darchen and Tremblay (this volume) suggest, the introduction of a Floridian style hypothesis has had a tremendous impact on how government and industry have viewed the cultural sector, yet the relationship between the cultural hypothesis and the attraction, retention, and integration of high-technology workers remains ambiguous at best. This part of the volume on talent attraction represents three attempts to further clarify the ambiguity. Darchen and Tremblay apply an urban planning lens. They examine the transferability of the creative city paradigm into city regeneration initiatives – "assess[ing] the hype and the promise against the risks and realities" and the implications for urban planners. Ryan, Li, and Langford (this volume) introduce the dynamic term of "embeddedness" and suggest that the failure to understand the relationship between a creative city–style hypothesis and the realities of urban social, cultural, and economic development stem from the lack of a sufficiently nuanced and complex investigative tool. Departing from these two lenses, our theoretical approach centres on a supply chain–oriented theory. This theoretical orientation, which we have coupled with the recognition of the importance of the individual, can provide a set of tools for policymakers to help drive sustainable economic, social, and cultural growth – providing realistic measures of the importance of environmental factors in the attraction of high-technology workers and allowing for more appropriate interventions.

One way to interpret Florida's concept of technology, talent, and tolerance is that talent is attracted and/or mobilized by the presence of a tolerant community and local pools of technology. In this chapter we identify a pool of talent and test how it is related to community tolerance and local pools of technology; then we look at the institutional mechanisms put in place to support tolerance and technology.

The Survey

We administered the Creatives Survey in Saskatoon in July–August 2007. Surveys were coded by organization, copied, and distributed to contacts in industrial, social, governmental, professional, service, and artistic organizations in Saskatoon. They were asked to distribute the survey to as many individuals as possible in their organization. While more than 115 surveys were returned, only 109 surveys were usable: rejected surveys were either incomplete or were answered from an institutional rather than individual perspective. The 109 respondents in the survey database had an average age of 35: 17 per cent were over 50; 24 per cent were in their forties; 19 per cent in their thirties; 39 per cent in their twenties.

The Creatives Survey included people with diverse backgrounds and experiences. Approximately one-fifth of the respondents were born and had lived most if not all of their lives in Saskatoon; another two-fifths or so were born in the province and migrated to the city at some point. The remaining 36 per cent came from outside the province: 16 per cent from Western Canada, 5 per cent from Central/Eastern Canada and 16 per cent from abroad. Based on the individual's stated date of arrival in Saskatoon, we were able to calculate that on average the survey respondents had spent 55 per cent of their cumulative living in Saskatoon; only 28 individuals reported having lived their lives in and around Saskatoon exclusively.

On the face of it, the survey would appear to have targeted and included at least one significant talent pool: namely, those with advanced degrees or high-technology workers. Only about 10 per cent had terminal education at the secondary level; 25 per cent had a technical diploma or degree; 36 per cent had an undergraduate degree; and 29 per cent had graduate training, including 21 individuals with PhDs or other higher doctoral training. Sixty respondents got all of their final education in Saskatoon. The average distance from Saskatoon for the 49 who did their final schooling elsewhere was 1325 miles (standard deviation = 2106).

The Creatives Survey also demonstrated how the talents of these high-technology workers were being applied in the local economy. Of the 109 respondents, 108 reported on their last 5 jobs and their tenure with those jobs. From these responses we found that all were employed – this is not surprising as the survey was administered through workplace institutions – and generally mobile. On average they reported 3.4 jobs, with an average tenure of 3.8 years per job: the tenure of the average worker in Saskatchewan is more than 10 years. Twenty-one individuals reported average tenure of more than five years (this group on average reported 3 jobs and an average tenure of 9.8 years per job); the other 87 individuals reported their average job tenure was 2.3 years (based on an average of 3.5 jobs). The data indicated that the high-technology workers captured in the survey were positively contributing to Saskatoon's economy both by directly putting their talent to use and by indirectly spreading knowledge and connecting people and institutions.

Given the direct and indirect impacts that these high-technology workers are purported to have on the city-region's economy (as seen in the literature and in the preliminary findings of the Creatives Survey), we developed a Talent Index to correlate talent against some of the measures of tolerance and other attractors in the community to determine how they may relate. In essence, the Talent Index is used to answer two questions: why high-technology workers moved to Saskatoon and what made them stay? There is no universally accepted definition of talent. In our study, we constructed a naive index that attempts to capture elements that may reflect talent. In particular, the talent index is a straight average of the percentage of a person's life spent outside of Saskatoon (which ranges from 0 to 98 per cent) and their highest level of education (senior matriculation = 0.2, technology diploma = 0.4, undergraduate degree = 0.6, masters = 0.8, and PhD = 1.0). The talent index ranges from 0 to 0.98, with an average of 0.53 (standard deviation = 0.25). While some investigators chose to focus on the professions or sectors the individuals work in (e.g., Florida 2002) or on individual responses to personal questions about attitudes and motivations (e.g., Webb 2009), we instead have focused on the role of creative people in industrial settings, where an individual's background education and willingness to match it to new opportunities are used as proxies for creative capacity. Mobility is used as a proxy for talent as it reflects an individual's opportunity cost and willingness to proactively move to match their skills with new opportunities. The farther they go, the more opportunity for hybrid vigour as they combine their background, knowledge, and skills with that of their new colleagues and neighbours. While education is not a perfect indicator, higher levels of accomplishment can reasonably be assumed to generate new opportunities for recombining knowledge that will generate inventions and innovation.

The three comparator cities – Montreal, Calgary, and Saskatoon – offer innovative comparative methods of analysis. The Saskatoon case investigates the creative background (mobility, training, and experience) of 109 individuals drawn from a few creative sectors and then undertakes correlation analysis to determine whether individual talent relates in any significant way to specific attributes of knowledge mobility. The Montreal study surveys a group of 529 wannabe technologists – students who have yet to have any significant applied experience – and undertakes a correlation analysis to determine the influence of a range of attributes posited to be important to knowledge workers (e.g., wages, taxes, community amenities, and other work and family-life variables). The Calgary analysis, in contrast, draws on the qualitative responses of a set of 48 interviews, investigating the relative importance of place-based factors and the linkage between different attributes. Each starts with a different subject group, uses a different research method, and investigates a different set of proxies for community attributes, yet offers comparable insights into the applicability of the creativity hypothesis.

Analysis of Saskatoon's Talent and Tolerance

One of Florida's fundamental assumptions is that talent is attracted by the presence of technology, other talent, and tolerance. Tolerance, by definition, can imply diverse views related to race, age, sexual orientation, and beliefs. Hence, no single, all encompassing measure of tolerance can be used. The survey probed this in several ways.

In the first instance, we asked all respondents: "Is Saskatoon a tolerant/welcoming place (i.e., in terms of race/ethnicity/secularity/general equality in your field)?" On a ten-point scale, where 1 is intolerant and 10 is tolerant, the average of all responses was 7.4 (standard deviation 1.7). The correlation coefficient between the talent measures for each individual and their response to this tolerance question was 0.07, which is not statistically significant from zero at 99 per cent confidence. Hence, the views related to tolerance are not significantly related to the respondent's level of talent.

As a second test of tolerance, we asked the respondents for their racial or ethnic background. The vast majority of the respondents reported their background as northern European or Caucasian. Ten respondents reported they were members of a visible minority. While fifteen individuals reported they had "encountered discrimination in Saskatoon in their field," we found no statistically significant evidence that this was related to race (the correlation coefficient between visible minority and discrimination was −0.0347, which was not statistically different than zero). Only one of those reporting personal discrimination was from a visible minority (an Aboriginal female). The others identified themselves as of European/Caucasian descent, but identified concerns related to race (8 respondents), gender (7, including one male referencing reverse discrimination), sexual orientation (2), and ageism (1).

Another measure of tolerance is whether the city is open to experimentation and creativity. Again on a scale of 1–10, with 10 being most tolerant, the average response was 6.3 (standard deviation of 1.6). We tested this with talent and found no statistically significant correlation between the talent index score and the view on this measure of tolerance.

We went on to test which characteristics of living and working in Saskatoon make it an attractive or unattractive place. We presented respondents with twenty specific community features and asked them to rank each on a five-point scale, from very negative to very positive. We also asked them to rank the top three positive features and the top three negative features. Table 8.2 shows the results. While all but the tax regime generated average positive responses, only four responses were statistically positive: commute time, community environment, suitability for raising children, and work environment in the firm. When respondents were asked to vote, four factors (commute time, suitability for raising children, work environment, and proximity to family) garnered the most net votes. Conversely, four factors generated the most net negative votes: natural environment/climate; tolerance; salary; and local and provincial tax regimes.

While table 8.2 is illuminating, it does not directly address the relationship between those characteristics and talent or creativity. Table 8.3 presents the results of a correlation analysis between the talent index and the individual responses to the attractiveness of the twenty identified characteristics. Only six of the twenty were statistically correlated. Salary, cutting-edge work, and affordable living were all positively correlated to the talent index (at the 95 per cent or 99 per cent confidence level), while restaurants/night life and proximity to family and friends were negatively correlated with talent. The positive measures are all about an individual's opportunities and would normally be viewed as part of one's

Table 8.2 Rating of community characteristics

	Avg	SD	Positive votes			Negative votes			Net + votes
			1	2	3	1	2	3	
Commute time	1.33	0.99	9	15	11	1	1	1	32
Community environment	0.94	0.85	4	4	4	1	1	3	7
Suitability for raising children	0.93	0.89	8	9	5	0	1	2	19
Work environment in firm .	0.91	0.88	4	6	6	0	1	1	14
Proximity to family	0.84	1.25	13	7	6	5	6	1	14
Proximity to friends	0.80	1.05	3	5	9	2	4	4	7
Recreational/cultural amenities	0.76	0.89	1	6	2	1	6	1	1
Ability of partner to find work	0.65	0.91	7	2	1	3	3	2	2
Quality of schools	0.63	0.78	2	3	3	1	0	2	5
Availability of job opportunities/ advancement	0.61	1.05	6	5	10	3	4	8	6
Community safety	0.58	1.07	5	5	5	4	3	7	1
Social and ethnic diversity	0.57	0.83	0	2	5	0	5	2	0
Cutting-edge work in the field	0.46	1.08	9	3	2	5	2	2	5
Affordable living	0.44	1.30	10	4	4	15	5	4	−6
Openness to experimentation and creativity	0.41	0.90	1	1	3	2	2	3	−2
Natural environment/climate	0.32	1.17	2	4	2	13	6	6	−17
Restaurants/nightlife	0.31	0.88	1	2	2	2	4	4	−5
Tolerance	0.30	0.91	0	1	2	6	4	7	−14
Salary	0.15	1.02	1	2	2	5	10	8	−18
Local and provincial tax regimes	−0.17	0.96	1	0	2	13	11	6	−27

Source: 2007 ISRN Creatives Survey

personal cost-benefit calculations of career and location. The positive correlations to talent would tend to suggest that the work environment in Saskatoon is a positive driver for talent attraction and that it is perceived to be appropriately compensated (perhaps both in absolute and purchasing-power terms). In contrast, Saskatoon is somewhat less attractive from the perspective of some talented individuals because of its limited nightlife and dislocation from friends and family (who often are in far-flung parts of the world). This result conforms to earlier work done by Phillips and Khachatourians (2001) and Phillips (2002).

Table 8.3 Correlation between talent index and community characteristics, 2007

	Correlation coefficient	Level of statistical significance
Salary	0.245	99
Cutting-edge work in the field	0.234	95
Affordable living	0.219	95
Restaurants/nightlife	−0.335	99
Proximity to family	−0.347	99
Proximity to friends	−0.383	99

Source: Authors' calculations

One way to test these results is to examine the responses about whether the local economy supports mobility of knowledge between jobs and sectors. The survey asked respondents whether Saskatoon's economy enables mobility between sectors. On a ten-point scale (1 = none; 10 = high), 58 individuals responded, with an average of 6.5 (standard deviation 1.6), that the economy facilitates mobility. When asked whether the respondent uses knowledge gained in other sectors in their current work (0 = never; 10 = frequently), 62 responded, giving an average of 6.6 (2.2 standard deviation). While earlier results seemed to demonstrate that high-technology workers enjoyed employment mobility, these responses tend to suggest that mobility (employment mobility and knowledge transfer) may not be overly effective within the Saskatoon city-region; there was no significant correlation between the responses and the talent index.

From these results we might infer that Saskatoon is not well positioned to tolerate creatives and innovators. Whether that is fundamentally true (and the evidence remains inconclusive), it is still possible to determine whether or not the perceived lack of tolerant, innovative zeal in the city has an effect on the economy. The survey asked respondents whether they ever started a new business or were employed by a start-up or early-stage business. Twelve respondents reported establishing a business (8 offered services; 1 produced goods; and 3 did not record the nature of the firm) and another 21 reported that they had worked for a start-up firm some time in their career. When the talent index was tested against an index of firm expansion (0 = never connected; 1 = employed or entrepreneur; 2 = employed and entrepreneur), a very small positive correlation was found (0.06); it was statistically insignificant.

Table 8.4 Industrial/institutional and community/cultural attributes that support creativity

	No. of cites	Specific attributes cited
Industry and institutions	26	• Inclusiveness; large scientific community; competition and cooperation
		• Biotech industry
		• Research infrastructure (e.g., university, federal labs); large research community relative to small city
Community, culture, and cultural amenities	31	• Size; amenities; lifestyle; pace; cost; sense of community
		• Cultural events; affordable and accessible activities
		• Rural/agrarian/small-town virtues (friendly, accepting, volunteerism)
Yes	5	Positive responses without any specific industry or community feature identified
None	20	Negative features included isolation, conservatism

Finally, the survey asked what "particular aspects of Saskatoon ... facilitate creativity in the city" (table 8.4). In all, 80 responses cited specific aspects about Saskatchewan that affected creativity. Of those who indicated specific institutions or features, 26 respondents reported that specific institutions (industry or infrastructure) facilitated creativity, while 31 reported that cultural aspects of the city supported creativity. Those citing institutions focused on the relatively large role the scientific community plays in the city, mentioning the infrastructure at the university (including the Canadian Light Source and federal research laboratories), the biotechnology firms, and the nature of a competitive yet cooperative community. Those citing the community and cultural aspects of the city mentioned amenities (cost, variety), rural/agrarian/ small-town virtues (e.g., friendliness, acceptance, and volunteerism), and access to affordable and engaging cultural events and facilities. Twenty-five respondents reported that they thought there might be some positive features, but they couldn't think of any or reported only negative features (e.g., small, isolated, and conservative community).

Statistical tests were done to look for relationships between the citations and the talent index. The correlation coefficient between the talent index and industry/institutions was 0.298 (statistically significant at the 99 per cent level), indicating that those who have higher talent measures see value generated by those institutional/industrial features that are unique to Saskatoon. No statistical correlation appeared between the talent index and community/culture or the negative responses. This does not necessarily mean that cultural and community attributes are not a contributory factor, simply that they are not differentially recognized by those who form the talent pool.

Talent and Tolerance: Important but not Definitive

We began this chapter by first identifying a pool of talent and then tested how it was related to community tolerance and local pools of technology. More specifically, we have begun to examine some of the underlying theories and hypotheses related to talent, tolerance, and community – using the Saskatoon city-region as a case study. While the theory suggests that social inclusion is a causal underpinning to attracting talent, the evidence from the Saskatoon Creatives Survey is mixed.

When examining the importance of tolerance, social/cultural vibrancy, and mobility to attracting, integrating, and retaining high-technology workers in Saskatoon, we found very little to support the literature surrounding place and creative workers:

- Tolerance: Views relating to tolerance levels in Saskatoon were not significantly related to level of talent.
- Social vibrancy: Restaurant/nightlife and proximity to family and friends were negatively correlated to the talent index.
- Mobility: We noted a perception among the high-technology workers that Saskatoon offered limited mobility opportunities (both employment mobility and knowledge transfer).

Rather than being attracted to the city-region by characteristics of place usually associated with members of the creative class, these individuals were essentially captured by the professional and commercial prospects of place – the positive correlation between salary, cutting-edge work, and affordable living. The talent index suggests workers were lured to the Saskatoon city-region because that is where the jobs are. However, the ability of the Saskatoon city-region to retain these high-technology workers suggests that once they are captured by aspects of place they find value in a broader spectrum of its attributes.

In summary, the Creatives Survey undertaken in Saskatoon shows that talent is differentially distributed across the community and is positively correlated to industrial and innovation infrastructure. Still, we found no statistically identifiable correlation between perceptions of tolerance or creative synergies in the community and talent. Nor is there any statistically significant correlation between talent (albeit measured by a naive index) and entrepreneurial engagement. While the Creatives Survey identified a non-trivial number of individuals who viewed the cultural and community attributes as positively contributing to creativity, this did not correlate in any way to talent.

While Saskatoon does have a highly recognizable biotechnology cluster, the boom in the province, and in the city of Saskatoon itself, has been largely resource-driven. Given the growth of Saskatoon and its continued attraction of high-technology workers, it is more than plausible that resource-boom cities such as Saskatoon and Calgary do not play by the same rules as other cities in Canada. Saskatoon is a city full of creative people, but does not exhibit the characteristics of a creative city. The most important aspect of place driving the attraction of high-technology workers is attractive jobs.

The Creatives Survey was undertaken in the summer of 2007 – immediately before the 2008 global economic meltdown – when Saskatoon shone as an economic star. While Canada has, in general, been relatively successful in weathering the proverbial economic storm, its recovery has been muted; however, the continued growth of Saskatchewan and the Saskatoon city-region in the post-2008 period provides an excellent counterpoint to other city-regions in Canada. It would be interesting to compare our pre-collapse findings with a post-collapse survey of high-technology workers in Saskatoon. Has the continued success of Saskatoon stoked the fires of attraction to the talented labour force? Is there an island-in-the-storm mentality for those who were already living in Saskatoon? If so, how have their views on the qualities and aspects of place changed? Lastly, and perhaps most important, are the levels of tolerance, social vibrancy, and employment mobility in a city-region only important when there are jobs to be had?

The findings of this section underscore the weakness of the creative city hypothesis in explaining the attraction of high-technology workers. It is largely pragmatism (of many differing kinds), not Floridian cosmopolitanism, that compels people to live in cities such as Saskatoon, Calgary, and Montreal. No single approach – either the cultural or the economic paradigm – can comprehensively explain or quantify what attracts high-technology workers to a city-region. Given these insights, along with our own understanding of the factors that attract high-technology workers to Saskatoon – a city full of creative people that does not obviously exhibit the characteristics of a creative city – we are compelled to ask questions about the limits of the creative city hypothesis. This is not to say that our findings refute the Floridian hypothesis, but rather that for some sectors and localities it may not be a necessary and sufficient story to explain the outcomes.

REFERENCES

Asheim, Bjorn, and Meric Gertler. 2006. "Regional innovation systems and the geographical foundations of innovation." In *The Oxford handbook of innovation*, ed. Jan Fagerberg, David Mowery, and Richard Nelson, 291–317. Oxford: Oxford University Press.

Audretsch, David, and Maryann Feldman. 1996. "R&D spillovers and the geography of innovation and production." *American Economic Review* 86 (3): 630–40.

Cooke, Philip. 2002. *Knowledge economies: Clusters, learning and co-operative advantage*. New York: Routledge.

Dosi, Giovanni. 1984. *Technical change and industrial transformation: The theory and an application to the semiconductor industry*. London: Macmillan.

Florida, Richard. 2002. *The rise of the creative class*. New York: Basic Books.

Lundvall, Bengt-Åke. 1988. "Innovation as an interactive process: From user-producer interaction to the national system of innovation." In *Technical Change and Economic Theory*, ed. Giovanni Dosi, Chris Freeman, Gerald Silverberg, and Luc Soete, 349–69. London: Pinter Publishers.

Lundvall, Bengt-Åke. 1992. *National systems of innovation: Towards a theory of innovation and interactive learning*. New York: Pinter.

Phillips, Peter. 2002. "Regional systems of innovation as a modern R&D entrepot: The case of the Saskatoon biotechnology cluster." In *Innovation, entrepreneurship, family business and economic development: A Western Canadian perspective*, ed. James Chrisman, J. Adam Holbrook and Jess H. Chua, 31–58. Calgary: University of Calgary Press.

Phillips, Peter. 2005. "The challenge of creating, protecting and exploiting networked knowledge." In *Crossing over: Genomics in the public arena*, ed. Edna Einsiedel and Frank Timmermans, 7–32. Calgary: University of Calgary Press.

Phillips, Peter. 2007. *Governing transformative technological innovation: Who's in charge?* Oxford: Edward Elgar.

Phillips, Peter, and George Khachatourians, eds. 2001. *The biotechnology revolution in global agriculture: Invention, innovation and investment in the canola sector*. Wallingford, UK: CABI Publishing. http://dx.doi.org/10.1079/9780851995137.0000.

Porter, Michael. 1990. *The comparative advantage of nations*. New York: Free Press.

Ryan, Camille, and Peter Phillips. 2004. "Knowledge management in advanced technology industries: An examination of international agricultural biotechnology clusters." *Environment and Planning. C, Government & Policy* 22 (2): 217–32. http://dx.doi.org/10.1068/c0343.

Saxenian, AnnaLee. 1994. *Regional advantage: Culture and competition in Silicon Valley and Route 128*. Cambridge, MA: Harvard University Press.

Spencer, Greg, and Tara Vinodrai. 2006. "Saskatoon city-region profile: Summary and highlights, 2001 census." http://www.utoronto.ca/isrn/city%20profiles/index.html.

Statistics Canada. 2011a. 91-214-X: "Annual demographic estimates: Subprovincial areas." http://www.statcan.gc.ca.

Statistics Canada. 2011b. 71-001: Monthly labour force survey. http://www.statcan.gc.ca.

Webb, Graeme. 2009. "Creative social entrepreneurs, social capital and collaborative governance: A Saskatoon based analysis." Unpublished MA thesis, University of Saskatchewan.

Wolfe, David, and Meric Gertler. 2004. "Clusters from the inside and out: Local dynamics and global linkages." *Urban Studies* (Edinburgh, Scotland) 41 (5–6): 1071–93. http://dx.doi.org/10.1080/00420980410001675832.

Zucker, Lynne, Michael Darby, and Marilynn Brewer. 1998. "Intellectual human capital and the birth of U.S. biotechnology enterprises." *American Journal of Economics* 88 (1): 290–306.

9 Exploring "Creative" Talent in a Natural Resource–Based Centre: The Case of Calgary

CAMILLE D. RYAN, BEN LI, AND COOPER H. LANGFORD

Introduction: The Dynamics of Creativity

Attracting and retaining talent is touted as a key factor for success in innovation systems from the level of the industrial cluster (Wolfe and Gertler 2003; Breschi and Malerba 2001; Maskell and Malmberg 1999), to the regional system (Florida 2002a, 2002b, 2002c, 2005; Cooke et al. 1997; Cooke and Leydesdorff 2006), to national systems (Freeman 1995; Lundvall 1992), and to global centres of excellence (Mahroum 2000a, 2000b, 2005). Innovation studies presume that talent, either generated individually or through teams, is the source of the creative activities that lead to innovation. In addition, past ISRN-related studies (e.g., Langford et al. 2003; Langford and Wood 2005; Holbrook et al. 2010; Phillips et al. 2008) found that the presence of the talent pool, or a thick labour market, is important for a firm's location decision. Therefore, assessing the factors that serve to attract and retain creative talent may effectively characterize a given innovation system.

We study creative actors thought to influence innovation within the Calgary census metropolitan area (CMA). The notion of creativity is multifaceted. According to Bassett-Jones (2005), creativity is a precondition to innovation. Creativity contributes to innovation through the development of ideas (West 2002). In its catalytic and interdependent relationship with diversity and competitive advantage, creativity facilitates the innovation process (West and Anderson 1996). Creativity extends beyond the arts and design arenas. Broadly speaking, creativity encompasses human potential for the original. Thus, identifying creative individuals requires finding those whose disposition or site of opportunity leads to the demonstration of original contribution.

The literature suggests two dominant approaches to study creativity in innovation systems. The first examines a region's quantitative characteristics that attract and retain creatives through simple market factors (Shearmur 2007). The second looks to the role of a rich, diverse culture (e.g., Florida 2000, 2002a, 2002b, 2002c, 2005; Gertler et al. 2002). While there are analytical strengths with each of these respective approaches, we explore a more holistic approach (à la Barnes 2001) to examine the human factors. We do, however, lean heavily on Richard Florida's (2005) interpretation of the term creative class:

> Some have criticized the idea of a creative class as elitist and exclusionary … It is neither … I came to use this term out of frustration with the snobbery of concepts such as "knowledge workers," "information society," "high-tech economy" … I find [creative class] to be more accurate in defining the real source of economic value creation – that is human creativity – and because it is an intellectual construct that extends to all forms of human potential: the vast storehouse that is human creative capacity. (Florida 2005, 4)

This chapter identifies factors of the Calgary CMA, as perceived by creative individuals who enable and build a creative talent base in an upstream oil and gas centre supporting knowledge exploitation beyond the CMA spatial unit. Calgary is an economic hub in oil and gas, yet there are no oil wells or refineries within 100 kilometres of the city. Rather, Calgary-based actors provide managerial, technical, and financial knowledge to resource extraction projects of regional, pan-Canadian, and global scope.

An analysis of knowledge-flow-related CMA factors through a spatial lens must consider both relational economic geography (Bathelt and Glückler 2003) and the systematic context. Calgary's talent attraction and retention occurs against social practices and processes grounded in its dominant natural resources sectors. Thus, the perceptions and expressed preferences of creative individuals about living and working in Calgary are a key data source for analysing the social circumstances that these individuals construct.

The chapter is structured as follows: in section one, we provide an overview of the Calgary CMA – its history and current state – and, most important, we conceptualize "creative" in this context. In the following section, we outline seven key driving categories for examining the Calgary CMA and provide a brief overview of our methodology. We next propose two unique indices for exploring the notion of attraction and retention in the Calgary CMA as well as outlining our twenty-eight "embeddedness" factors distilled through the interview process.

Conceptualizing Creative in the Calgary Context

In the literature, there are dominant ways of thinking about "creative" in a given innovation system. A common statistical approach employed by Florida (2002b) and others (Gertler et al. 2002) tallies employment numbers within certain sectors or people with advanced educational credentials[1] as a primary indicator of talent. According to Jaffe (1998), however, these are indicators by correlation and not direct measures. One claim is that talent relevant to innovation (and, by implication, growth)·is more concentrated in individuals with advanced education credentials than in the general population. Another claim is that particular kinds of employment indicate people are paid for doing creative work.[2]

The term creative often evokes ideas of the artistic. Since the type of innovation of interest here is over a broad spectrum of economically important activity, Florida classifies the artistic as bohemian; economic models take a similar line (Shearmur 2007). Although we draw on these theories in our study, we find statistical categories somewhat limiting. The statistical hypotheses do not necessarily deny that the process of innovation includes important individuals lacking key credentials. Neither do they imply that all employees in a given job category are consistently creative. Nevertheless, these statistical hypotheses have been essential for large studies and deemed useful in comparing performance across cities.

For the purposes of this study, our qualitative investigation does not include or exclude subjects strictly on educational credentials or job category, but instead focuses on direct evidence of creative contribution in working environments, recognizing that environments matter. From an operational perspective, and in our investigation, criteria for identifying those who work creatively include that they substantially control the direction, management, and quality of their work. Members of this population seek challenging opportunities, recognize new connections, and can defy current thinking and dominant paradigms. In short, creatives are presumed to think "outside the box."

Our intent was to explicitly identify workers whose contributions support innovation in many work contexts. We base our approach on the assumption that a creative individual's occupational role produces a vocational output that is not easily substitutable (Ryan et al. 2011).

Characterizing the Attractor City under Study

Discovery of oil and gas in the Turner Valley region south of Calgary early in the twentieth century, followed by the construction of pipelines in the 1950s, reinvented Calgary's economic, political, and social structures. From being one of the poorest agricultural provinces in Canada, Alberta became one of the richest over several decades. Exploration and development in oil and gas have largely spurred the rapid growth of the Calgary CMA (Foran and MacEwan Foran 1982). Calgary can be characterized as a resource-based centre, much like Saskatoon, which draws economic growth and development through agricultural and extended activities (Phillips and Webb this volume).

Through the 1970s, 1980s, and 1990s, Calgary's energy sector attained critical mass, attracting the sector's national head offices. Few well sites remain near Calgary. Local refineries, led by Imperial Oil, have since migrated to the Edmonton area. Instead, Calgary houses expertise in management, finance, and technology that provides a knowledge base for oil and gas exploration and extraction in its hinterland, the Western Canadian region, and globally. Calgary's economy has become a knowledge economy.

Phenomenal growth (noted by a marked change in prosperity in Alberta in the late 1940s) continued through the oil boom of 2006–7. The civic census of 1981 reported Calgary's population at 591,857. Twenty-five years later, the 2006 census (Statistics Canada 2007) reported that population had nearly doubled to 1,079,310. The in-migration from the rest of the country generally exceeded healthy natural increase.

In Canada, Calgary has the highest in-migration of science and engineering professionals, financial professionals, and business services professionals (Spencer et al. 2010) – all knowledge workers. Calgary's economy is concentrated in two senses. The headquarters of the major natural resource players and many minor firms are found in a compact city centre of high-rise office buildings bearing the logos of petroleum companies and major financial or engineering firms. An unusually high percentage of employment is concentrated in this core. Of over 700,000 jobs in the Calgary Economic Region, 138,500 are in Calgary's downtown core (City of Calgary 2008). Workplaces and public spaces in the core are linked by a network of enclosed pedestrian walkways above street level called the "Plus 15." This concentration facilitates informal networking and encourages open exchanges among firms and their creative workers.

The second sense of concentration concerns knowledge concentration versus knowledge diversity. The presence of six clustered industries identified by Spencer et al. (2010) from employment statistics of standard industrial categories suggests a diverse economy. However, interviews with firm leaders classified in the scientific and professional services industry (Langford et al. forthcoming) reveal that most scientific and engineering professionals focus on oil and gas activity. Similar remarks apply to firms in software and computer services. A large fraction of the business of financial and construction firms supports oil and gas activity. The technical, managerial, and financial knowledge to operate resource extraction locally and globally is not found only in oil and gas firms, but requires gathering creatives to mobilize a platform of *related knowledge diversity*. Such a platform (Cooke et al. 2007) places Calgary squarely between two conceptions of knowledge distribution conducive to innovation and growth. The first is that knowledge concentration in the leading industry drives innovation and growth, often called the MAR theory (Glaeser et al. 1992), after works by Marshall (1890), Arrow (1962), and Romer (1986). The second is that innovation and growth are promoted by a diverse distribution of knowledge over various industries, facilitating the injection of novelty and stabilization against the cycles of one industry (Jacobs 1970). This situation is a variant of the related knowledge platform discussed by Asheim (this volume). The concept of cognitive distance (Asheim et al. 2011) is particularly relevant. The diversity of the knowledge base for oil and gas might suggest that cognitive distances may grow large. However, this is mitigated by the common focus on the problems of oil and gas. Calgary has a diverse knowledge base related to a dominant industry that receives prices from global markets. Thus, its diversity does not offer protection from oil and gas fluctuation, and may not encourage the creative professionals recruited by oil and gas activity to direct attention to other areas (Asheim this volume).

Evaluating Embeddedness

To address the attraction and retention of creative talent in a complex environment, we propose and evaluate an indicator called *embeddedness*. In this study embeddedness relates to factors reported that might impact creative individuals' decisions to move to or to remain in the CMA. With embeddedness we capture direct evidence reported by creative individuals affecting their decisions to live, work, and remain in the CMA: commonly not any one overriding factor but rather a balance of professional, physical, and social amenities, and place and occupational circumstances. Embeddedness thus indicates a creative individual's desire to conduct most personal, social, and economic activities within the geographic locality based upon the advantages it provides (Ryan et al. 2011). This indicator echoes Mitchell et al.'s (2001) employment embeddedness in firms.

In contrast to approaches based on statistical categories, a qualitative investigation of individuals seeks direct evidence of the values and preferences informing creatives' affinity for place and occupational circumstances. Senior executives were asked to identify candidate individuals who would be difficult to replace. Candidates suggested for interview were filtered for those whose work is creative or innovative in either an individual or team capacity, not simply those hard to replace because of, for example, the long learning curves related to their position in communication networks. Several individuals were added to the interview list based on public recognition of their creative contributions to the Calgary CMA.[3] Thus, the operational definition of creative adopted for this study is two-pronged. It combines both the role of the individual informant (what they do) and the process for selecting creative informants to interview (the value they contribute to the firm or organization, or public documentation of their creative contributions).

We reorganized the ISRN research instruments (appendix A) to support open semi-structured interviews of approximately one hour in length designed with introductory open-ended questions to encourage individual narratives.

Based on notes and tags made from complete interview transcripts, via a grounded-theory approach, we developed a list of twenty-eight embeddedness factors and counted each factor's frequency of mention, grouped into seven overall categories (Ryan et al. 2011). We noted each mention of an embeddedness factor, and its positive or negative effects for the interviewee. Mentions of each embeddedness factor were tallied and, separately, the net frequency of positive or negative mentions was computed. For each category (C1 through C7), we gathered the relevant supporting embeddedness factors and computed the Weighted Aggregated Positivity Index (WAPI). Together, the product of the total number of mentions and the WAPI gives the Embeddedness Index (EI) as an indicator of the

Figure 9.1 Employment areas identified in interviews of creative individuals (*n* = 48)

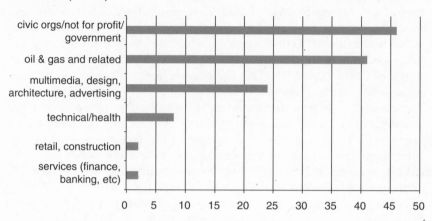

strength of the category of influence. Our methodology is outlined in more detail in Ryan et al. (2011).

The Words of Respondents

We interviewed forty-eight creative individuals in employment areas shown in figure 9.1. Some practised in more than one area. The largest single group of interviewees (not a majority) represented civil society and government organizations (i.e., government and charitable, cultural, or other not-for-profit organizations). A majority of interviewees were in the for-profit sector, strongly representing consulting/management, environmental/engineering, technical/manufacturing, and/or oil and gas.

We grouped nearly 600 preferences into seven high-level categories. These reflect the four theories of talent attraction summarized by Gertler et al. (this volume). One stream of research (C1) contends that local levels of tolerance and openness to diversity shape the flow of talent between regions. Another (C2) matches a key aspect of the body of research suggesting that the geographic distribution of talent is a response to thick labour markets with available diverse and high-quality jobs. For example, Shearmur (2007) advances economic hypotheses for attraction based on Canadian data. One closely relating to C2, but less prominent in the literature (Gertler et al. this volume), was suggested by the common reference to Calgary's spirit of entrepreneurship (C3). Two are related to social networks (C4 and C5) and the remaining two reflect factors of the local environment often discussed in the urban literature: amenities such as safe streets and good schools (C6) and the physical environment (e.g., proximity to the Rocky Mountains and ready access to outdoor activities) (C7). These latter categories follow the theme in the literature that a collection of amenities attracts talent (Gertler et al. this volume). In sum, the grounded-theory approach led to building a category set covering the factors most often addressed in the literature of urban talent attraction. These categories included:

C1: A sociocultural environment rich in diversity embeds creative individuals.

C2: Economic opportunity embeds creative individuals based upon opportunities and growth-driven growth.

C3: The local business environment or a spirit of entrepreneurship embeds creative individuals.

C4: The existence of professional networks (with strong links) provides a dynamic, adaptable, and flexible working environment.

C5: The existence of personal, leisure activity, and/or family networks (with strong links) embeds creative individuals.

C6: Structural amenities such as good schools, transportation, and safety are important factors for embedding creative individuals in a community.

C7: The physical environment provides opportunities for recreational activity for creative individuals.

Comments assigned to each of these categories are illustrated through individual interview quotes below.

Sociocultural diversity (C1) included openness to sociocultural novelty, perceived social issues such as homelessness and discrimination and responses to them, as well as opportunities for sociocultural participation. As a theatre professional said: "You've got festivals representing every kind of cultural ethnicity that I can think of which is fabulous ... We have representation in all these things, including the Gay Pride Parade ... the Disability Arts Festival and so on."

Economic opportunity (C2) included a collection of items from conditions afforded by a boom economy to opportunities for employment for creatives to practise their preferred vocational skill as in the case of this professional organization executive: "[Calgary is] a young, modern city. There's tremendous opportunity. It's a fast city … the financial centre, the oil centre, the business centre … It's a wonderful place, especially for young professionals. There's so much opportunity here."

Another person working in theatre offered: "It's the boom – it's the boom philosophy, the pioneering spirit … 'We try, we will'! We do have an abundance of heart in this town … corporate support … citizen support." A supportive local business environment (C3) with strong governance and business aspects is valued by creative talent. This includes government support for entrepreneurial and business activities. But in the case of Calgary, support – in the opinion of some interviewees – equates to a hands-off or indirect approach to supporting business. An example is provided here by an individual working in social services: "I think that this is what makes Alberta unique … In Alberta our political culture is such that we don't expect government to take care of things for us … We don't want government to take care of things for us."

Professional networks (C4) are valued informal relationships within a professional circle directly or indirectly connected to business activities. A corporate environment composed of networks of inter-firm and intra-firm relationships also supported professional networks enabling talent to connect to local customers and jobs. A geophysicist noted that "it's a great environment and again my number one reason for being here is the geoscience community." An engineering professional commented: "It's all about keeping your relationship open in Calgary. If you're a little bit of an extrovert and you're smart, you should have no problem networking yourself into never having to worry about work."

Personal networks (C5) embedded creatives in a community or in the CMA. They provide opportunities for personal (non-vocationally-driven) learning, volunteerism, civic activity, and other community participation. Personal networks include the presence of friends and, of course, that primary personal network: family connections. An interviewee in marketing reported on close personal relationships in the Calgary CMA as a tie to the community: "I have a really close network of friends. My family is here. We moved here when I was five [years old]; my parents are in their eighties."

Structural amenities (C6) embedding creatives in the Calgary CMA include features such as good schools, transportation, and safe streets. For example, a marketing professional stated: "The schools, the educational system, all of the things, call it the anthropology of an urban centre or a region as you might call it … are the fabric of what makes Calgary a great city."

Finally, the natural or geophysical setting (C7) includes the CMA's location adjacent to the Rocky Mountains, a feature valued by several interviewees, including this engineering professional: "Calgary … [has] so much available – the mountains, right next door … If you're into that kind of thing … the camping, skiing, climbing, etc."

Creatives also perceived less favourable features. The overall scoring of sociocultural diversity (C1) as a key embeddedness factor was associated with some negative comments. The positive impact of the economic boom has resulted in some countervailing social disparities according to this social services leader: "Calgary is a place where there is an opportunity for anyone. That said, I think that the scale of urban growth is causing a divergence … causing a gulf between the rich and the poor … Homelessness is the paradox of prosperity. The economically and socially disenfranchised can't keep up with the increasing costs."

The dominance of the oil and gas industry was also perceived to limit the establishment and growth of new firms and entrepreneurship. A serial entrepreneur engineering/environment professional told us: "I've learned over the years – never start into a business in Alberta that doesn't have direct implications and impact on the oil and gas business. This is an oil and gas town."

Despite the fact that many creatives viewed the hands-off role of government as effective in supporting the local business environment, others – such as this environmental engineering consultant – were more critical: "I think [the government] is really trying hard, but at some point they're going to have to give up their cheerleader role and actually step in and participate as partners."

Analysing Implications

In total, nearly 600 data points (observations) drawn from interview transcripts ($n = 48$) related to one or more of the identified factors. This sample allows appraisal of the indicators proposed. A key observation is that each of the forty-eight interviewees mentioned several aspects: an average of twelve. In other words, the strong conclusion well supported by the sample is that attitudes towards place attraction and retention are complex and nuanced. To illustrate the results of our calculations, table 9.1 summarizes the number of relevant mentions for each category and the calculated indices WAPI and the EI, while figure 9.2 represents these results visually.

Table 9.1 Categories, supporting mentions, and indices

Categories		Number of supporting mentions	Weighted Average Positivity Index (WAPI)	Embeddedness Index (EI)
C4	Professional networks	208	0.33	68.64
C2	Economic opportunities	306	0.18	55.08
C5	Personal networks	164	0.33	54.12
C3	Local business environment	119	0.15	17.85
C1	Sociocultural diversity	142	0.07	9.94
C7	Natural environment	47	0.11	5.17
C6	Structural amenities	60	0.05	3.00

Categories are ranked according to the calculated index. Interviewees have indicated that Calgary's networks (both personal and professional), together with its economic opportunities, were Calgary's most readily articulated and evident embeddedness factors.

The origins of the rankings begin to emerge if we now look at the characteristic remarks surrounding each category. To do this, we organize further discussion around summaries of our understanding of the respondents' attitudes towards each of the categories.

Creatives strongly value their networks – both professional (C4) and personal (C5). Personal networks ranked third in the index, while professional networks ranked first. Interviewees mentioned both types regularly. Personal networks were often linked to family and/or special-interest groups and grass-roots connections to the community, key factors in creative talent either staying in or returning to the Calgary CMA. As this information and communication technology (ICT) expert stated: "I am pretty established here … My family is here. No, I don't think that I would move." Professional networks included a valuable informal element. People working together value informal ties and connections in order to conduct and succeed in work-related activities according to another ICT creative: "What makes Calgary unique is that people are pretty open and honest here. Trust is important. It creates a foundation for 'deals [to] get done with a handshake.'"

Many creatives did not actively distinguish between professional and personal networks with respect to economic opportunity. This supports the impression that Calgary, as a city, tends to be always at work, even in the social context. In addition, professional networks appear particularly

Figure 9.2 Visualization of calculations by category

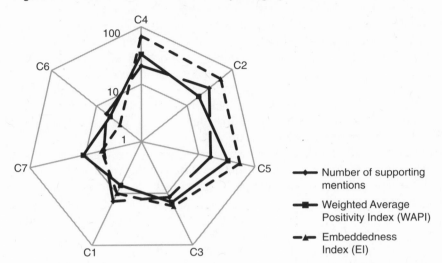

important in individual sectors. Geophysics, for example, is an oil and gas arena with a strong professional network that is fairly formalized, with regular meetings. As one interviewee explained: "Calgary has to be the most closely knit geo-scientific group in the world ... because the city [centre] is compact."

Interviewees also emphasized the importance of informal professional networking. A marketing professional noted: "It's during the three-hour cocktail session that we're actually going to learn something, exchange an idea, start a conversation that goes somewhere ... a lot of cocktail hours, shorter formal sessions, that's the ticket."

Beyond just pure networks, *creatives need economic opportunity (C2)*. The economic boom has created huge opportunities for enterprise and growth in Calgary. However, some respondents noted the expense of living and operating creative enterprises in Calgary. They illustrated the tension between fast-paced growth and the potential social and personal implications of a booming economy. One oil and gas professional said, "As you know, this city has struggled a lot with growth. Commercial space is expensive ... The health system that lacks availability of family doctors has a great impact."

The fact that creatives continue to live and conduct business in the Calgary CMA in spite of some adversity indicates that other factors in the environment are sufficiently valuable, economically or socially, to embed them. An architect stated: "Calgary is the most challenging place I've ever worked. I mean, I moved here to be near the mountains, to ski and to mountain bike and to do all those kinds of things."

Closely linked to individual economic opportunity, *creatives demand a structurally, politically, and professionally supported local business environment (C3).* Entrepreneurial spirit and available work niches appear important to several respondents, including this medical technologist: "There's an entrepreneurial spirit in Calgary which you just cannot beat … It's easy to raise money and run with an idea."

Relative to other large metropolitan centres such as Toronto or Vancouver, Calgary is easy to navigate according to an engineering professional: "I think there's a lot of advantages to its location and the transportation services. You can pretty much go wherever you want from here and you get there relatively quick." A marketing professional echoes the sentiment: "I like convenience, I like low stress. I think I can get that in Calgary more than any major city in Canada or the US." As Phillips and Webb (this volume) note, Saskatoon creatives also identify short commuting and convenience as key attraction factors.

However, Calgary creatives perceive social problems, the political environment, and dominance by the oil and gas industry (outside that sector) as detractors. In particular, higher-paying jobs in oil and gas may influence the talent needed by other industries and inhibit economic diversity within the CMA. An independent consultant stated: "The oil and gas sector has really made it difficult for businesses like myself [sic], because they're paying their assistants a hundred grand." Interviewees commented negatively on government awareness of or action in relation to backing new, existing, and necessary initiatives to enhance some aspects of Calgary's economic environment.

The factor often cited in contrast to economic ones is that *creatives would prefer a richer sociocultural environment (C1).* The calculated EI indicates sociocultural diversity as only weakly embedding creative talent in the Calgary CMA. This is reflected in comments by individuals in the arts community. One suggested: "Culturally speaking, Calgary really needs to have a thicker base of exciting things to do." Another added: "Arts is a bit of a rough sell here." Such impressions are not well supported by the statistics on the level of support for cultural organizations. We do have a concern about the reliability of the low ranking of C1. It may be that the issues, however important, are not the ones that come to mind first in responding to questions about the city as a site for the creative activities associated with innovation.

In addition, negative attitudes were reported with respect to government responsibility to address social issues such as poverty, ethnocultural discrimination, and economic disparity as outlined by one cultural organization professional: "Engaging [government] has not been easy. And getting minorities into positions of influence that could actually make changes is missing."

The next factor has been identified in qualitative cluster studies as a recruiting tool (Langford et al. 2003; Langford and Wood 2005). *A physically attractive environment provides opportunities for recreational activity for creative individuals (C7).* Despite the natural environment's low ranking in terms of the embeddedness index, Calgary's proximity to the mountains strongly embeds some creatives. An engineering professional characterized Calgary as a beautiful city, "a great place to live. And yet we all want to escape to the mountains or the lake on the weekends because you want to go back to nature ... And it's the simple things in life that are maybe the most important."

Finally, a factor often considered in the analysis of urban settings: *structural amenities appear to weakly embed creative individuals in a community (C6).* A local retail professional stated, "I'm happy in Calgary, it's vibrant, it's safe, it's clean," while an ICT professional asserted that Calgary is "a great place to raise kids. It still seems to me to be a friendly place."

Other amenities were lacking, as noted by a public relations professional: "I find that the entrepreneurial spirit that exists in Calgary is not conducive to social programming. Why aren't we developing low income housing?" A creative involved with a multicultural association raised concerns: "It's taking newcomers much longer to catch up than the average Canadian. More and more of them are homeless and their form of homelessness is different ... It manifests differently than [that of] the general population. A higher, vast, growing number of them are living in poverty." These quotes illustrated Calgary's imbalanced growth, aptly referred to by a creative as the "paradox of prosperity."

Finally, there is the issue of the significance of the diverse patterns of related knowledge in Calgary (similarly noted in Saskatoon by Phillips and Webb this volume). Networks (personal and professional) figured high in our analytical results. However, many of Calgary's creative professional networks did not appear to promote inter-sector interaction. For example, one quote above underscores the strength of the geophysical-based community network. Remarks about coffee meetings and similar informal networking tended to identify members of a sector's value chain (those in different firms working towards common goals), which may illustrate the attractiveness of the contexts created in the diverse but related knowledge platform. Interviewees from the independent sectors of multimedia/advertising and electronic manufacturing reported gaining reusable knowledge by working with the oil and gas industry. Previous studies of the origins of wireless telecommunications, global positioning systems, and several software activities demonstrate that sector-specific knowledge has spun into new independent sectors as the oil industry has reached out for new tools (Langford et al. 2003; Ryan et al. 2011).

Informal networks linked creatives from different sectors, including the cultural and charitable sectors, via such factors as outdoor recreation, volunteering, entrepreneurship, and other common interests. These associations appear to develop into what may be characterized in interviews as personally valuable and difficult to substitute weak links (Granovetter 1983). Such networks diffuse new and unique ideas and also gather diverse sources of support for new and innovative ventures. Interest in entrepreneurial activity may lead only to membership in one of many sector-oriented associations including the Petroleum Club or the WiTec wireless association, and may also be expressed through involvement in broader-based organizations like Calgary Technologies, Inc. and the Calgary Association for Advanced Technology, or in the not-for-profit sector or even in a motorcycle club. Each creative individual (and perhaps even their employer) who participates in these networks clearly receives a different combination of value attributable to their social, professional, and geographical context.

A final factor, in this vein of generating new ideas and innovation, emerged in interviews with people in cultural, charitable, and civic organizations. According to our research, firms in the Calgary CMA support the efforts of their employees as volunteers and board members of not-for-profits. This brings private-sector actors into engagement with the social and cultural organizations and, at the same time, brings employees of different firms together.

Complex Motivations

Earlier in the chapter, we outlined two dominant approaches to statistically analysing the attraction and retention of creative talent in Canadian cities. The first emphasizes cultural factors (Florida 2005; Gertler et al. 2002), while the other emphasizes economic factors (Shearmur 2007). We challenge these distinct and often diverging paradigms by suggesting that any approach to exploring creativity in the context of the city must, by definition, deal in aggregates that cannot distinguish the mixed motives of an individual from variations between individuals. Drawing on qualitative data, as we did here, serves to support the notion that neither the cultural nor the economic paradigm can alone explain or fully quantify the nature of the attraction and retention of creative talent within a given innovation region. Indeed, the subjects of our study might have positively supported either hypothesis as members of a population subjected to statistical analysis.

The results highlight the complexity of factors – both negative and positive – that serve to embed creatives in the city context. On average, twelve of any of the twenty-eight perceived factors characterized a typical single interview. There were favourable references to economic opportunity as well as to sociocultural diversity (some responses were positive while others were negative). One negative that appeared frequently in responses was the pervasiveness of the oil and gas industry; however, in some cases, respondents viewed a large and growing boom city as a positive factor. One particular interviewee, from the multimedia sector, remarked on what he perceived as a positive buzz associated with the Calgary CMA. Others commented on Calgary's positive attributes such as the CMA's overall openness to new ideas, its unique environmental factors (outdoors and recreation), relatively short commuting times, and, of course, the value associated with strong personal and professional networks. Our observations that both personal and professional networks are key perceived attraction and retention factors for creative individuals are comparable to findings about job embeddedness in which a social network provides professional benefits (Mitchell et al. 2001), and are consistent with literature about the high switching costs to changing social networks leading to locational attachment (Bolan 1997). These observations could imply a prediction that individual social considerations are important to creative talent in Calgary.

Despite these perceived positive attributes associated with the Calgary CMA, several respondents recognized that the boom economy came with negative externalities such as social problems, including increased homelessness and a lack of affordable housing. This naturally lends a cautionary note on the nature of a dominant entrepreneurial spirit in the context of a boom economy. The boom economy may, in many cases, strengthen perceptions of the entrepreneurial spirit. Indeed, the notion of an entrepreneurial spirit might seem far less convincing without the reinforcement of a sustainable economic reward. In Calgary, the entrepreneurial spirit has a complicated affiliation with the realities of an economic environment of received global prices. The fallout of the economic downturn that started in 2008 has not yet demonstrated whether the entrepreneurial spirit of the Calgary CMA can withstand major fluctuations in world commodity prices, environmental pressures on resource extraction, and global economic uncertainty. Unlike Calgary, Saskatoon has been able to enjoy some stability and economic growth since the economic downturn began (Phillips and Webb this volume). Saskatoon has not – as yet – suffered from a "boom" hangover.

Other points of comparison between Calgary and Saskatoon are the similarities in the industry base (noted earlier), common attractors, and the importance of institutions. Both CMAs are driven by the resource base. Common attractors are the professional or commercial aspects of place, which includes economic opportunities, the existence of dense and accessible professional networks, and a supportive business environment. Key organizations, clubs, and research institutions that support the respective industries in the CMAs serve an important role as resources and go-to's for creatives.

Sociocultural diversity attempts to capture factors associated with Florida's (2002a, 2005) influential work. Unfortunately, such factors may be under-reported in Calgary because they are not pervasive in everyday conversation. The interview data only weakly indicated the positive importance of these factors, either by direct reference or by supporting inference. While the interview results may be consistent with Shearmur's (2007) view that creative talent is attracted to economic growth, the qualitative comments about the natural environment and professional and personal networks, along with the overall complexity of perceptions and expressed motives, do not suggest a simple pull of economic opportunity and economic growth.

As for the indicators proposed here, statistics on the sizes of population classes or migration data alone using regression analysis provide limited information about causal factors. By the same token, simple explanatory propositions may mislead by suppressing diversity. The indicators employed in our case study provide an accessible tool to semi-quantitatively assess the qualitative data generated through interviews. They, too, have limits, most notably the rendering of positive and negative as binary. While they may not be generalizable in their application, they suggest an approach to the classification of factors and may be treated as hypotheses arising from a grounded-theory analysis, and perhaps deserve tests on other data.

The main lesson from the study deserves restating: motives are complex, revealing individual patterns of thought. It appears that a balance of personal circumstances and individual perceptions of the city determines each interviewee's overall expressed attitude about attraction and retention in the CMA. This is, perhaps, not a welcome message for policymakers seeking to enhance attraction. When situations are so complex, policy must be nuanced and multifaceted.

NOTES

1 For example, bachelor's degrees and beyond.
2 A major study of American cities (Florida 2005) found that creative class employment was a better correlate of income than human capital (education), whereas the reverse was true for total wealth.
3 For example, we sourced a list of probable Calgary creatives from the Tuesday, 1 January 2008 edition of the *Calgary Herald* that featured an editorial on the "20 Most Compelling Calgarians."

REFERENCES

Arrow, Kenneth J. 1962. "The economic implications of learning by doing." *Review of Economic Studies* 29 (3): 155–73. http://dx.doi.org/10.2307/2295952.

Asheim, Bjorn T., Ron Boschma, and Philip Cooke. 2011. "Constructing regional advantage: Platform policies based on related variety and differentiated knowledge bases." *Regional Studies* 45 (7): 893–904.

Barnes, Trevor J. 2001. "Retheorizing economic geography: From the quantitative revolution to the 'cultural turn.'" *Annals of the Association of American Geographers* 91 (3): 546–65. http://dx.doi.org/10.1111/0004-5608.00258.

Bassett-Jones, Nigel. 2005. "The paradox of diversity management, creativity and innovation." *Diversity Management, Creativity and Innovation* 14 (2): 169–75. http://dx.doi.org/10.1111/j.1467-8691.00337.x.

Bathelt, Harald, and Johannes Glückler. 2003. "Toward a relational economic geography." *Journal of Economic Geography* 3 (2): 117–44. http://dx.doi.org/10.1093/jeg/3.2.117.

Bolan, Marc. May 1997. "The mobility experience and neighborhood attachment." *Demography* 34 (2): 225–37. http://dx.doi.org/10.2307/2061701. Medline:9169279.

Breschi, Stefano, and Franco Malerba. 2001. "The geography of innovation and economic clustering: Some introductory notes." *Industrial and Corporate Change* 10 (4): 817–33. http://dx.doi.org/10.1093/icc/10.4.817.

City of Calgary. 2008. *Calgary and region economic outlook, 2008–2013.* Volume 2. Calgary: City of Calgary. http://www.calgary.ca/CA/fs/Documents /economics/socio_economic_outlook/socio_econ_outlook_2008_2013 _vol_2_econ_outlook.pdf?noredirect=1.

Cooke, Philip, Carla de Laurentis, and Franz Tödtling. 2007. *Regional knowledge economies: Markets, clusters and innovation. New horizons in regional science.* Aldershot, UK: Edward Elgar Publishing.

Cooke, Philip, Mikel Gomez-Uranga, and Goio Etxebarria. 1997. "Regional innovation systems: Institutional and organizational dimensions." *Research Policy* 26 (4–5): 475–91. http://dx.doi.org/10.1016/S0048-7333(97)00025-5.

Cooke, Philip, and Loet Leydesdorff. 2006. "Regional development in the knowledge-based economy: The construction of advantage." *Journal of Technology Transfer* 31 (Special issue): 1–15.

Florida, Richard. 2000. "The new economics of urban and regional growth." In *The Oxford handbook of economic geography,* ed. Gordon Clark, Meric Gertler, and Maryann Feldman, 83–98. Oxford: Oxford University Press.

Florida, Richard. 2002a. "Bohemia and economic geography." *Journal of Economic Geography* 2 (1): 55–71. http://dx.doi.org/10.1093/jeg/2.1.55.

Florida, Richard. 2002b. "The economic geography of talent." *Annals of the Association of American Geographers* 92 (4): 743–55. http://dx.doi.org/10.1111 /1467-8306.00314.

Florida, Richard. 2002c. *The rise of the creative class.* New York: Basic Books.

Florida, Richard. 2005. *Cities and the creative class.* New York, London: Routledge.

Foran, Max, and Heather MacEwan Foran. 1982. *Calgary: Canada's frontier metropolis.* Calgary: Windsor Publications.

Freeman, Chris. 1995. "The 'national system of innovation' in historical perspective." *Cambridge Journal of Economics* 19 (1): 5–24.

Gertler, Meric, Richard Florida, Gary Gates, and Tara Vinodrai. 2002. "Competing on creativity: Placing Ontario's cities in a North American context." Ontario Ministry on Enterprise, Opportunity and Innovation, Toronto. http://www.investinginchildren.on.ca/Communications/articles /Competing%20on%20Creativity.pdf.

Glaeser, Edward L., Hedi D. Kallal, José A. Scheinkman, and Andrei Shleifer. 1992. "Growth in cities." *Journal of Political Economy* 100 (6): 1126–52. http://dx.doi.org/10.1086/261856.

Granovetter, Mark. 1983. "The strength of weak ties: A network theory revisited." *Sociological Theory* 1: 201–33. http://dx.doi.org/10.2307/202051.

Holbrook, J. Adam, David Arthurs, and Erin Cassidy. 2010. "Understanding the Vancouver hydrogen and fuel cells cluster: A case study of public laboratories and private research." *European Planning Studies* 18 (2): 317–28. http://dx.doi.org/10.1080/09654310903491648.

Jacobs, Jane. 1970. *The economy of cities*. New York: Vintage Paperback (reprint of 1969 edition).

Jaffe, Adam B. 1998. "Measurement issues." In *Investing in innovation*, ed. Lewis Branscomb and James Keller, 64–84. Cambridge, MA: MIT Press.

Langford, Cooper H., Ben Li, and Camille D. Ryan. Forthcoming. "Firms and their problems: Systemic innovation and related diversity in Calgary." In *Innovating in urban economies*, ed. David Wolfe. Toronto: University of Toronto Press.

Langford, Cooper H., and Jamie Wood. 2005. "The evolution and structure of the Vancouver wireless cluster: Growth and loss of core firms." In *Global networks and local linkages: The paradox of cluster development in an open economy*, ed. David Wolfe and Matthew Lucas, 207–26. Kingston: McGill-Queen's University Press.

Langford, Cooper H., Jamie Wood, and Terry Ross. 2003. "Origins and structure of the Calgary wireless cluster." In *Clusters old and new*, ed. David A. Wolfe, 161–85. Montreal and Kingston: McGill-Queen's Press.

Lundvall, Bengt-Åke. 1992. *National systems of innovation: Towards a theory of innovation and interactive learning*. London: Pinter Publishers.

Mahroum, Sami. 2000a. "Highly skilled globetrotters: Mapping the international migration of human capital." *R & D Management* 30 (1): 23–32. http://dx.doi.org/10.1111/1467-9310.00154.

Mahroum, Sami. 2000b. "Scientific mobility: An agent of scientific expansion and institutional empowerment." *Science Communication* 21 (4): 367–78. http://dx.doi.org/10.1177/1075547000021004003.

Mahroum, Sami. 2005. "The international policies of brain gain: A review." *Technology Analysis and Strategic Management* 17 (2): 219–30. http://dx.doi.org/10.1080/09537320500088906.

Marshall, Alfred. 1890. *Principles of economics*. London: Macmillan.

Maskell, Peter, and Anders Malmberg. 1999. "Localised learning and industrial competitiveness." *Cambridge Journal of Economics* 23 (2): 167–85. http://dx.doi.org/10.1093/cje/23.2.167.

Mitchell, Terence R., Brooks C. Holtom, Thomas W. Lee, Chris J. Sablynski, and Miriam Erez. 2001. "Why people stay: Using job embeddedness to predict voluntary turnover." *Academy of Management Journal* 44 (6): 1102–21. http://dx.doi.org/10.2307/3069391.

Phillips, P.W.B., and D. Camille Ryan, Jeremy Karwandy, Tara Lynn Procyshyn, and Julie Lynn Parchewski. 2008. "The Saskatoon agricultural-biotechnology cluster." In *Handbook of research on clusters: Theories, policies and case studies*, ed. Charlie Karlsson, 239–52. Aldershot, UK, and Brookfield, US: Edward Elgar.

Romer, Paul M. 1986. "Increasing returns and long-run growth." *Journal of Political Economy* 94 (5): 1002–37. http://dx.doi.org/10.1086/261420.

Ryan, Camille D., Ben Li, and Cooper H. Langford. 2011. "Innovative workers in relation to the city: The case of a natural resource-based centre (Calgary)." *City, Culture and Society* 2 (1): 45–54. http://dx.doi.org/10.1016/j.ccs.2011 .03.002.

Shearmur, Richard. 2007. "The new knowledge aristocracy: The creative class, mobility and urban growth." *Work Organisation Labour and Globalization* 1 (1): 31–47.

Spencer, Gregory M., Tara Vinodrai, Meric S. Gertler, and David A. Wolfe. 2010. "Do clusters make a difference? Defining and assessing their economic performance." *Regional Studies* 44 (6): 697–715. http://dx.doi.org/10.1080 /00343400903107736.

Statistics Canada. 2007. *Survey of household spending*. Ottawa: Statistics Canada. http://www.statcan.gc.ca/daily-quotidien/081222/dq081222a-eng.htm.

West, Michael A. 2002. "Sparkling fountains or stagnant ponds: An integrative model of creativity and innovation implementation in work groups." *Applied Psychology* 51 (3): 355–87. http://dx.doi.org/10.1111/1464-0597.00951.

West, Michael A., and Neil R. Anderson. 1996. "Innovation in top management teams." *Journal of Applied Psychology* 81 (6): 680–93. http://dx.doi.org /10.1037/0021-9010.81.6.680.

Wolfe, David A., and Meric S. Gertler. 2003. "Clusters old and new: Lessons from the ISRN study of cluster development." In *Clusters old and new*, ed. David A. Wolfe, 1–36. Montreal, Kingston: McGill-Queen's University Press.

PART IV

Seeking Talent for Small Cities

10 Kingston and St John's: The Role of Relative Location in Talent Attraction and Retention

JOSH LEPAWSKY, HEATHER HALL, AND BETSY DONALD

Introduction: Placing the Creative Class

This chapter explores two related questions: What factors most strongly influence Canada's talented and creative workers – the mobile potential residents who contribute to city-region economies – to settle in particular cities? What particular characteristics or features of city-regions prove salient to the talented and creative workers who have decided to move there? In answering these questions, we make a theoretical argument based on empirical evidence from studies of Kingston, Ontario, and St John's, Newfoundland, two Canadian city-regions with similar population sizes and levels of ethno-racial diversity.

Advocates of creative class theory claim that the location decisions of the creative class are determined by quality of place (Florida 2002c). Quality of place includes thick labour markets (meaning high quantity, quality, and diversity of employment options), lifestyle amenities (e.g., parks, running trails, nightlife), possibilities for social interaction in "third places" such as cafés and book stores that are neither home nor work, diversity (e.g., in ethnicity, age, and sexuality), and authenticity (e.g., a distinctive music scene, historic built landscapes, and demographic mixture) (ibid., 228–9). Although creative class theory does not argue that quality of place perfectly substitutes for wages and employment, it does claim that a key shift has occurred: people are "not slavishly following jobs to places" (ibid., 223). Rather, firms and jobs are locating, relocating, or being created where the talent is. Proponents of creative class theory recommend to planning and economic development practitioners that regions should enhance quality-of-place characteristics to attract and retain the creative class so as to stimulate economic growth. We claim that place remains under-theorized in the creative class literature. In particular, we highlight the role of relative location as a key factor that conditions the choices made by members of the creative class about the places where they prefer to live and work. In so doing, we emphasize a relational theory of place in which qualities of place are contingent outcomes of relations with places elsewhere (Massey 1994). Creative class theory tends to understand places as bounded units into which the right mix of quality amenities can be poured in order to catalyse economic growth. In contrast, we argue that places – far from being bounded units – are more usefully understood as made up of relations that connect and/or disconnect them from places elsewhere.

Talking to the Creative Class

We draw on eighteen interviews with members of the creative class from each city-region. Creative class theory argues that members of the creative class share a common economic identity that operates as a fundamental determinant of their location decisions. Members of the creative class "engage in complex problem solving that involves a great deal of independent judgement and requires high levels of education or human capital" (Florida 2002c, 8) and share a common economic identity defined by occupational categories (e.g., Florida 2002a; Florida 2002b; Florida 2008; Florida et al. 2008; Martin and Florida 2009; Stolarick and Florida 2006). Florida (2002c) divides the creative class into two broad groups: the super creative core (e.g., computer and mathematical occupations, sciences, education, and arts) and creative professionals (e.g., management occupations, business and financial operations, legal, healthcare, and high-end sales).

We chose interviewees based on their representativeness of the economic clusters identified by Spencer and Vinodrai (2009a, 2009b) in each city-region. The city-regions differ in the number and type of economic clusters found. Indeed, in Kingston the only cluster that exists is higher education. While St John's also has a higher-education cluster, it exhibits additional clusters in arts, media, and culture industries; health industries and services; and maritime industries. The commonalities and differences between Kingston and St John's, rather than weakening the comparability of the cities, create the opportunity to examine whether members of the creative class share a common economic identity that determines their location decisions. If the proposition holds, then interviews with members of the creative class – albeit from different creative sectors – should elicit similar responses to questions about the qualities of place they perceive to be manifest in either Kingston or St John's.

Situating Kingston and St John's Provincially and Nationally

Canadian urban centres are conventionally represented as having undergone significant restructuring to accommodate the knowledge economy beginning in the 1970s, shifting from manufacturing and industry to a service-based economy (Bunting and Filion 2006; Wernerheim and Sharpe 2006). Yet the geographies of this shift have been highly uneven within Canada's urban system, where inter- and intra-urban variation is the norm. Though a broad shift to a service economy can be identified, economic and political change is also conditioned by contingent historical and contemporary processes.

Political and economic change in Kingston and St John's is tempered by public sector institutions in each city. Kingston's urban fabric reflects the city's historic dependence on public institutions such as Queen's University, the Canadian military, and the federal prison system. As the provincial capital and largest city-region in Newfoundland, St John's urban fabric is shaped by the political economy of extractive resource industries and tempered by the city's function as administrative metropole for the province. In contrast, Kingston's administrative prominence significantly diminished after 1848 when it lost its status as the national capital. Since then, the private sector in Kingston has struggled to adjust to broader changes in the Canadian economy, including the decline of waterway shipping and manufacturing (Osborne and Swaison 1988). Today, the city-region is often bypassed for Toronto (the provincial capital located 2.5 hours to the west) and Ottawa (the national capital two hours to the north). To further complicate Kingston's economic development, it depends on public institutional silos that were never designed to serve the local economy: the military trains soldiers to serve throughout the world; Queen's University educates the brightest young Canadians and prepares them for the Canadian workforce; and the federal prison system incarcerates people from across the country. This has led to a contemporary political economy that affords public sector stability, but struggles to attract innovative forms of private sector–led economic growth.

St John's, by contrast, plays a dominant role in the province's labour market and broader economy. In the wake of fisheries restructuring, the closure of two paper mills, and the ongoing shift from rural to urban and urban-adjacent areas, St John's dominates the province's economy more than ever and is a staging ground for migration out of the province. Today, 40 per cent of the province's population resides in communities within the St John's commuting area (Simms 2009). Significant wealth is still generated from the fishery and mining industries; however, oil production now underpins the province's economy. As of 2007, that sector alone accounted for 30 per cent of the province's real GDP (Stantec 2009). This shift will only solidify St John's dominance in the province's economy given that oil and gas fields have been found primarily on the Grand Banks, near St John's. The province's political, educational, and service centre is now also the home of the largest resource sector.

Between 2001 and 2006, the Kingston (2006 population of 152,350) and St John's (2006 population of 181,115) census metropolitan areas (CMAs) experienced population growth rates of 3.8 per cent and 4.7 per cent, respectively (Spencer and Vinodrai 2009a, 2009b). Like other small cities considered in this volume (see Bourgeois), both Kingston and St John's are less diverse than Canada as a whole in terms of ethnicity and place of birth. Kingston has a locational quotient (LQ) of 1.1 for its population born in Canada and approximately 0.7 for population born outside Canada. This means that Kingston has a higher proportion of Canadian-born residents than Canada as a whole, but a much lower proportion of foreign-born residents. For St John's the figures are similar or even weaker: an LQ of 1.2 for the population born in Canada and < 0.2 for population born outside Canada (Spencer and Vinodrai 2009a, 2009b). However, both city-regions' populations exceed the national average of 33.2 per cent of the population in creative occupations. In Kingston, the figure is 38.6 per cent and for St John's 37.4 per cent. Furthermore, a recent Statistics Canada study found that Kingston has the largest number of PhDs, scientists, and engineers per capita when ranked against other CMAs in Canada (McKenzie 2007). Meanwhile, the A1C postal code of downtown St John's has an artistic concentration four times higher than the national average and the second densest concentration of artists in Atlantic Canada after Halifax (Hill Strategies Research 2005). Members of the creative class live in Kingston and St John's, even if the two city-regions are not especially ethnically diverse.

The Creative Class in Relational Places

In what follows, we discuss key topics that arose under a broader theme of relative location in interviews with highly educated/creative workers and with employers of highly educated/creative workers and intermediary organizations: relative city size, (dis)connectedness, and mobility (a theme similarly relevant in Moncton; see Bourgeois this volume). This theme emerged in participants' discourse, where references were made to city-size and location characteristics of Kingston and St John's. Although we focus on the responses of particular individuals, the themes were common across interviews and discussed in myriad ways that highlight the place characteristics of Kingston and St John's as highly relational.

Our analysis finds some support for propositions about quality of place made by proponents of creative class theory. However, respondents' responses reveal greater complexity than the tenets of creative class theory help us understand. To some extent, the world is spiky (Florida 2008, 19; Martin and Florida 2009) for creatives in Kingston and St John's. They see a world populated by urban locales with desirable mixes of qualities of place. Yet interviewees' perceptions about the qualities of place manifest in each city are framed by how Kingston and St John's are situated in relation to places elsewhere. While we do not make any claims as to the direction of cause and effect between the relative locations of each city and the qualities of place that manifest there, our interviewees do. It is their perceptions that we report.

Kingston

Kingston is sandwiched between three major Canadian cities (Toronto, Montreal, and Ottawa), and its relative size is seen as too small for some and just right for others. For many, the size, affordability, location, natural surroundings, and compact urban form provide a welcome alternative to big-city living. For example, a professor describes the lifestyle associated with Kingston's small size as a huge asset:

> For someone who is married and has children, the compensation is unbelievable: the fact that we can afford a house. We can afford a house and be in walking distance of campus. We are two blocks to a day-care, two blocks to an elementary, two blocks to a high school and three blocks to campus. We could never have afforded that, and even if we move and go further

out, it's never more than a 10- to 15-minute drive anywhere in town. You can get to the airport in 15 minutes. I'm sure I gained wrinkles trying to get to the airport in Toronto trying to get to a job interview.

This professor continued:

> I think in terms of lifestyle that allows us to be the most productive at work because we don't have the commuting time, the smog, the traffic, the cost of living, and those are *big* … You know I sort of tracked all the hours I spent in Vancouver on a bus, and I was working another full day another day a week just taking the bus, and I lived in the *city*.

One professor elaborated on the advantages of size: "It's a small city, and it's beautiful, it's clean, it's quiet." Another mentioned, "I like the small-town feel where you can wander around the cafés and walk in to work or walk into centre town: the walking distance, that is nice." As a small city, Kingston offers affordability, which was also cited as an advantage for musicians in Halifax, where affordable housing and rehearsal space made the city more attractive (see Grant et al. this volume).

For others, however, the relative size of Kingston provides less diversity, fewer employment opportunities, and limited cultural amenities when compared to Toronto or Montreal (see also Leslie et al. this volume). In terms of diversity, one professor explained that

> if you were to compare Montréal to Kingston, well, they are two different worlds. And the truth is I've always lived in a very big city, so I'm very used to living in a very big city. Truth is that I'm used to very big cities partly because of the diversity of those cities. Kingston is not diverse, and that's a problem 'cause it makes it really tough to be in, and I find it a lot easier to lose myself in the context of a much bigger city like Montréal.

Many interviewees attributed the difficulties of finding opportunities for two-career households to the size of Kingston and its limited subset of private-sector employment. Large cities can offer cultural amenities to workers like one professor, who commented: "I like Toronto, I like the diversity, I like that I can go see a live band seven days a week. I like being able to see any movie I want … the film festivals and things like that. So … I like the life of Toronto more than I like the life of Kingston."

In-place creative amenities are perceived as lacking in Kingston. Yet the interviewees' perceptions assessed the desirability of Kingston *in relation to* and *in conjunction with* nearby cities. Their observations reinforce Massey's (1994) theory that places are constructed in relation to other places at various scales. Employing the theme of (dis)connection, some respondents explained that Kingston simultaneously pales in comparison to nearby, amenity-rich centres like Toronto, but provides opportunities to live a "hybrid" lifestyle that bridges Kingston and other cities.

In the Kingston city-region, (dis)connection is manifested both spatially and institutionally. This (dis)connectivity has both advantages and disadvantages for talent attraction and retention. Several interviewees discussed the importance of having connectivity to three large cities, as many of them have research or business connections. For example, one professor said, "So Kingston's location by virtue of being close to Ottawa is very beneficial to me for data and research"; while another emphasized that "one of the reasons we chose it is because we're within easy striking of … the three most important cities in the country in many respects." A manager of a bio-economy company noted that Kingston is "located between Toronto and Ottawa, which allows me a two-hour drive to any market that I choose. I'm close to the US border." Another interviewee said the train ride from Kingston to Toronto is equivalent to driving to downtown Toronto from the suburbs: "If you live on the outskirts of Toronto, getting downtown to go to a show is going to take a long time, and you can hop on a train in Kingston and in two hours you are in the middle, you go to Union Station … You're five minutes from most of the theatres … It's almost as easy to go to Toronto … from Kingston as it is to drive in from the suburbs and find a place to park."

There is, however, a downside to Kingston's connectivity to Toronto, Ottawa, and Montreal. New firms and talented graduates seeking business and employment opportunities often bypass the smaller city. As one professor discussed, "I think the proximity argument is a double edged sword … and that proximity I think … can work in favour of Kingston but also works against Kingston … Why incur this transportation cost when you can be there?" The irony of the city's location and difficulties in attracting young graduates was further emphasized by an independent visual artist: "It always surprises me how well situated Kingston is geographically, between Montréal and Toronto these major urban centres and you know … Lake Ontario. And it barely develops any kind of economy that can support individuals between the ages of 22 to 30." This contradiction of connectivity was elaborated by a professor: "I don't know why a city like Kingston, wonderful place, wonderful great size and great strategic location, why doesn't it become bigger in terms of attracting business and industry ... I think maybe being in the vicinity of Toronto, Ottawa, and Montréal, you would think Kingston would be a big hub economically."

For St John's, geographic isolation can significantly undermine talent attraction. The Kingston case shows, however, that proximity to larger urban centres can also present unforeseen challenges to economic development. Kingston suffers from institutional dis-connectivity that affects talent attraction and retention. The major local institutions do not serve the local economy. One interviewee described these institutions as "little Vaticans" within Kingston: separate and distinct spaces within the city. The military is largely confined to the eastern part of Kingston, with its own housing, parks, recreational facilities, and retail spaces. Queen's University students are largely located north of campus, while many of the families of prisoners live in an area known as North-of-Princess. Such spatial segregation seriously limits inclusive forms of community economic development.

Dis-connectivity is further exacerbated by the sometimes strained town–gown relations between Queen's University and the Kingston city-region. As one professor explained, "Well, as it stands now, Queen's students largely use Kingston as a sort of campground, right? I mean, they trash the houses, they go to the A&P [grocery chain], they go to the bars, they usé it for very specific purposes, but they're not linked into the community at all." Another interviewee, a company manager, discussed the lack of interaction between the military and the city: "We have 6000 people roughly in the military up on the base, many of whom have been to many parts of the world, who bring an awareness of what's going on in the world that we don't tap into very much." Many talented individuals commute to Toronto, Ottawa, or Montreal instead of fully committing to Kingston. As one professor explained, "I just don't relate to Kingston like that. It's not a place I think of: Wow, I don't want to live there, or I want to live there. I just don't have that relationship with it, I commute to it." Another professor discussed the problems associated with having a commuter culture: "One of the problems we have at Queen's is we have so many people who live in Toronto and commute. Frankly I don't think that those people, no matter how dedicated they are to their work, can ever make a commitment to the university community and the city, fully. They just can't do it."

The lack of commitment to Kingston has serious ramifications for economic development and retaining talented individuals, who fail to embed in the local community. But as one professor suggested, some assets in the city should be used so their talents can assist economically and socially in the city-region:

> Queen's University students are supposed to be the best and brightest in Canada, we keep getting told. Well, why not harness some of that, and start tutoring programs, where our students start helping the kids in this community who desperately need that kind of time and help and their parents can't do it, because their parents are just struggling to get food on the table. That would be, that could be an amazing thing.

While Queen's does have a history of engaging with the local community in many respects – from school tutoring programs to public health research – more can be done to engage locally for the benefit of both Queen's and community development. Recently, Queen's has initiated civic and social-responsibility programs inside and outside the classroom. These programs are promising for bridging the town-gown divide.

In Kingston's case, the role of connectivity has an impact on economic development that is alternately positive and negative for members of Kingston's creative class. One professor interviewed wondered whether the city could use this connectivity to large urban centres to attract and retain talented individuals and promote economic and social development. "My own feeling is that the city of Kingston should use that proximity rather than see it as a competition with those places." Yet, as another professor explained, Kingston is a quiet space to work and express oneself creatively, while Toronto is the locale for big-city amenities: "I live in two towns. I live in Toronto and Kingston. And so if I want to get a lot of work done, Kingston's great, because there are a lot of demands that happen in a lot of other cities that don't happen in Kingston ... And it does actually attract a lot of people who are artists and writers and creative people who like to come here for that purpose." Kingston is too small to compete with Toronto, but it provides an alternative quality of life to big-city living.

Collectively, these complicated, often contrary, perceptions of Kingston's position relative to other cities in central and eastern Canada underscore the complexity of national and international labour flows – mediated not just by discrete nodes of talent and amenities, but by relationships between cities and between the characteristics of the creative worker subject (age, race, economic sector) and the places they inhabit (see Massey 1994). Relative city-size, (dis)connectedness, and mobility have largely been overlooked as key determinants of quality of place in the talent attraction and retention literature. Yet, as the interviews from Kingston suggest, these factors are important in conditioning perceptions about the city's prospects for attracting and retaining creative people. Turning to St John's, we see the same factors of relative city size, (dis)connectedness, and mobility at play in perceptions of the city-region's economy and the location preferences of creative workers.

St John's

Unlike Kingston, the relative location of St John's is distinguished by a lack of proximity to other major cities within the province and the rest of the country. It is an eight-hour drive from St John's to Corner Brook, the province's next largest city. While the St John's International Airport was the eleventh busiest in the country in 2008 in terms of passenger traffic (Statistics Canada 2009), few direct connections with Canada's largest cities exist, except for Toronto, Montreal, and Ottawa. Flying time is about 1.5 hours to Halifax, 2.5 to Montreal, and 3 to Toronto. Air connections modify the relative location of St John's seasonally. A direct flight to London (Heathrow) brings the city closer to Europe in the summer than to Western Canada. At the same time, air fares between St John's and Canada's major cities often equal or exceed fares between those cities and major European or Asian destinations.

Compared with Kingston's interviewees, who consistently referenced the city's position vis-à-vis national and international urban metropolises, the creative workers of St John's perceive the city to be large in relation to the province's rural-urban system, yet small in relation to national and international urban systems; they find St John's advantaged in high-quality (rather than high-quantity) social networks, yet disconnected from places outside the province; and they observe that, taken together, these characteristics of relative city size and (dis)connectedness condition the mobility decisions of highly educated/creative workers in both positive and negative ways – a finding that resonates strongly with Bourgeois's investigation of Moncton (this volume).

When asked about mitigating the risks of unemployment, interviewees emphasized that characteristics of place condition the strength and density of family and social networks. For example, a successful musician, told us:

> I just have a lot of family here. I mean, my mom and dad are here and they helped me out big time; and, obviously, I just know a lot of people. There's just, like, a big social network, so getting a job really wouldn't be that hard. Just, you know, call my uncles and aunts … They have businesses or have brothers who own businesses, it's just such an incredible network of people. I mean, I could probably get a job in an hour.

He suspects, though he is not certain, that city size and what he refers to as the culture and isolation of St John's are key factors influencing the important social networks (i.e., forms of social capital) that reduce the risk of losing one's job:

> It's just a small sort of city where you know everybody, and there's just these social ties to so many different sectors and so many different businesses. I don't know if it's specific to this place because of the culture or because of the isolation, but everyone seems to be just incredibly interconnected, and you know dozens of people who own things or hire people and put in a word for you.

Within this response we get a sense that some of the factors suggested in the creative class literature are at play in St John's. For example, the musician draws attention to qualities of place and their influence on the strength and density of social relationships. But nuances colour his response. For example, he identifies city size as one probable factor explaining the strength and density of social networks that mitigate the risks of job loss. Yet his perception of St John's as a small city is critical to the character of these networks. The literature tends to associate increases in the density of social networks with larger city populations: in simplistic terms, more people means more networks. This musician's response hints at a potentially important point: that the quality of social networks – not just the number of them – is important. As Bourgeois also notes (this volume), the relative smallness of the city can play a positive role in facilitating strong, dense social networks that not only mitigate the risks of job loss but also enhance the flow of knowledge across sectors and increase the possibilities for experimentation. The city's relative size and isolation were also important factors in creating a collaborative and supportive music scene in Halifax to promote the growth of young musicians (see Grant et al. this volume).

A filmmaker made a similar case:

> What's so great about this place is, you know, you become part of this really small community and it's really wonderful and everybody knows each other and, you know, everybody supports each other ... The community that I work in is relatively small and close-knit, so there's a core group of people who always work on set ... But in terms of social networks, I mean everybody is extremely supportive of one another because everybody knows each other, and so everybody is always willing to help out on smaller projects.

The relatively small size of St John's plays a positive role in creating close-knit, supportive social networks that help overcome the precarious, boom-bust character of the film industry. These positive accounts of small-city social and cultural life in St John's stand in contrast to those from Kingston, where small city size was valued for logistical or environmental reasons (e.g., quiet, ease of transport).

At the same time, other interviewees saw the relative size and location of St John's as significant challenges for getting and keeping creative and highly educated workers. For example, a human resources manager in the higher education sector observed: "I think one of our strengths is also one of our weaknesses, which is our location, being located fairly remotely from everything else within Canada." This sentiment about location was echoed in other interviews. For example, the director of a health research organization told us: "This is a small place on the edge of the continent. There aren't a lot of jobs kicking around, but, when there are, it's often hard to find good talent. So you run an ad and get one or two applicants. It really is a problem, and the more specialized you get, the harder it is."

The human-resources manager reiterated the point about distance and dis-connectedness: "There's a big psychological barrier whenever you cross a body of water, so it's not as if you're moving from Ontario to Quebec. You know, you're moving from Ontario to a place that's very far away. So the distance is certainly a factor." Echoing the perceptions of creative workers like the musician and the filmmaker, both the human-resources manager and the research director speak to the issue of the relative size and location of St John's from the perspective of an employer and intermediary organization, respectively. On the one hand, the human-resources manager describes the remoteness of St John's in relation to other urban places. The research director, on the other hand, places the city-region on the edge of a continental geographic imaginary, suggesting a potential (yet perhaps unexplored) set of international relations between St John's and places elsewhere.

As in the case of Kingston, relative city size, (dis)connection, and mobility are perceived by members of the St John's creative class to shape the attractiveness of the city and influence the likelihood of people remaining there. Interviewees in St John's framed the city's relative size and location in comparison to provincial, national, and international urban systems. For them, the city exhibits both large- and small-city characteristics because of its size and functional role relative to the provincial urban system; however, the city-region's small size and isolation relative to larger, more connected national and international urban systems limits its ability to attract and retain talent.

The Practical Implications of Relative Location for Planning for the Creative Class

Empirically, this chapter engaged in a comparative exploration of factors described by members of the creative class as conditioning their decisions about where to live and work in two Canadian city-regions of similar population size and diversity. Through that analysis we find some support for one of the key propositions of creative class theory: that quality of place plays an important role in influencing where members of the creative class choose to live. Yet something that is striking about the responses our interviews elicited is the degree to which the quality of each city was described in relation to places elsewhere.

In Kingston, cultural amenities seemed to pale in comparison to those of its larger neighbours (perhaps even more so due to their close proximity), yet residents engaged with governmental (Ottawa) or cultural and economic (Montreal, Toronto) centres of power on an as-needed basis. Many used Kingston as a quiet living or working environment, travelling to other cities to fill the gaps in their geographically hybrid lives. In St John's, creative workers felt secure in the unique, relatively self-sufficient regional economy of the city – and enjoyed the cultural amenities it provided as a regional centre – but remained bounded by the isolation of the city. Both case studies also highlighted the ways in which characteristics of the individual creative subject (e.g., participation in a dual-income partnership, place of birth, proximity to family and social networks) mediated the negotiation of urban networks in central and eastern Canada. Thus, Kingston seems to represent a case of an improperly conceived creative city (i.e., it really forms part of a creative agglomeration or creative network), while St John's perhaps represents a case of untapped potential connectivity (e.g., with Europe or with other metropoles in the region).

The findings signal a need to engage more deeply with relational theories of place that have been elaborated by other geographers, but remained largely untapped as a theoretical resource for those interested in studying geographies of the creative class. In one way or another, interviewees in our study perceive relative city size, (dis)connection, and mobility to be key qualities of place that affect their location decisions. It is crucial to understand that qualities of place cannot be generated entirely in situ. They depend, by definition, on relations to places elsewhere. Consequently, conceiving of quality of place as a recipe of factors that can be poured into a place to catalyse economic growth is, we would argue, a risky proposition.

Our qualitative findings about place in this study resonate with a broad swathe of quantitative analyses of the Canadian space-economy that seek to understand why economic development (e.g., employment growth) happens in some places and not others (Delisle and Shearmur 2010; Shearmur 2010b, 2011). In brief, this work shows that both "local (endogenous) and structural (exogenous) factors" play significant roles in explaining differential economic growth across Canada, but that "there is no straightforward and unique approach to employment creation and retention at the local level" (Shearmur and Polèse 2007, 455; see also Gertler et al., Vinodrai, and Hracs and Stolarick this volume). In other words, economic development and the attraction and retention of talent to a place are conditioned by factors in that place and other places. In short, places are defined by relations between what is there and what is elsewhere: no single recipe will guarantee economic development in a particular place. This does not mean planning and policy devoted to such outcomes is futile, but it does suggest that practitioners should be cautious about adopting the propositions of creative class theory as if they provide a roadmap to guaranteeing enhanced growth in all city-regions.

With the above caution in mind, we offer some tentative recommendations for practitioners. First, be careful of misapplications of endogenous (i.e., internally driven) economic growth theory. That is, practitioners should treat sceptically two related ideas: that city-regions can or should be able to generate an appreciable portion of their economic growth from within their own boundaries; and that plans to enhance qualities of place in order to boost local economic development will necessarily capture the desired effects of those plans locally, even if they manage to attract and retain talent (Shearmur 2010a).

Second, if enhancing quality of place is going to be used as a vehicle to improve local economic performance, practitioners should find ways to measure and affect factors beyond those qualities proposed in creative class theory. Doing so would entail, inter alia, developing measures of relative city size, (dis)connection, and mobility relevant to the particular place in question. For example, while Kingston and St John's are quite similar in terms of absolute population size and diversity, they differ considerably in terms of relative city size, (dis)connection, and mobility. Kingston's relative location with respect to three of Canada's largest cities (Toronto, Montreal, and Ottawa) makes it a different, more contingent environment for attracting and retaining talent than St John's. Even qualities of place proposed as important in creative class theory (thick labour markets, lifestyle amenities, third places, diversity, and authenticity) are themselves relative. Kingston is a quiet, small city compared to nearby Toronto (or Montreal or Ottawa). St John's is the metropole relative to the province's outports, but the periphery relative to Ontario's Golden Horseshoe. By understanding each city's unique relative attributes, policymakers can find ways of capitalizing on the advantages of these relative differences. For instance, Kingston may consider lobbying CN Rail and other transportation organizations for better connection services between Kingston and the large urban centres of Toronto, Montreal, and Ottawa. St John's might consider subsidizing its seasonal direct air connection with London so that it is available year round to help foster and sustain better business connections with Europe.

Third, practitioners might consider the lessons to be learned from peer group comparisons, or – even more necessary – from benchmarking how peer places are defined through shared relational characteristics rather than absolute ones (i.e., relative rather than absolute size and diversity). Again, places need to be understood not as containers into which economic development recipes can be poured, but as relational sites in which practitioners lack straightforward ways to capture economic performance locally. This may mean that practitioners consider strategies other than trying to shape their place into a destination that attracts and retains talent. It might, for example, be more relevant – and realistic – to consider what might be gained from being a conduit (a place through which talent circulates) rather than a destination (a place to which talent is attracted and stays put).

In sum, we argue that creative class theory could be improved by examining the hitherto underrepresented relational theories of place. Relational theories may indeed become even more significant as researchers begin to document how certain cities and labour segments are faring in the current post–2008 financial crisis period. While our empirical research was conducted before the 2008 crash – and thus may convey a particularly prosperous and optimistic time for creative workers in these cities – insights from the largely untapped relational theories of place will provide future researchers with a new direction for thinking about creatives and their places in the uncertain times ahead.

REFERENCES

Bunting, Trudi E., and Pierre Filion. 2006. *Canadian cities in transition: Local through global perspectives.* Don Mills, ON: Oxford University Press.
Delisle, Françoise, and Richard Shearmur. 2010. "Where does all the talent flow? Migration of young graduates and nongraduates, Canada 1996–2001." *Canadian Geographer* 54 (3): 305–23. http://dx.doi.org/10.1111/j.1541-0064 .2009.00276.x.
Florida, Richard. 2002a. "Bohemia and economic geography." *Journal of Economic Geography* 2 (1): 55–71. http://dx.doi.org/10.1093/jeg/2.1.55.
Florida, Richard. 2002b. "The economic geography of talent." *Annals of the Association of American Geographers* 92 (4): 743–55. http://dx.doi.org/10.1111 /1467-8306.00314.
Florida, Richard. 2002c. *The rise of the creative class and how it's transforming work, leisure, community, and everyday life.* New York: Basic Books.
Florida, Richard. 2008. "Megaregions: The importance of place." *Harvard Business Review* 86 (3): 18–9.
Florida, Richard, Charlotta Mellander, and Kevin Stolarick. 2008. "Inside the black box of regional development: Human capital, the creative class and tolerance." *Journal of Economic Geography* 8 (5): 615–49. http://dx.doi.org /10.1093/jeg/lbn023.
Hill Strategies Research. 2005. "Artists by Neighbourhood in Canada." In *Statistical Insight on the Arts.* http://hillstrategies.com/content/artists-neighbourhood-canada.

Martin, Roger L., and Richard Florida. 2009. *Ontario in the creative age.* Toronto: Martin Prosperity Institute and Rotman School of Management at the University of Toronto. http://martinprosperity.org/media/pdfs/MPI%20 Ontario%20Report%202009%202nd%20Ed.pdf.

Massey, Doreen. 1994. *Space, place, and gender.* Minneapolis: University of Minnesota Press.

McKenzie, Michael. 2007. *Where are the scientists and engineers?* Ottawa: Statistics Canada, Science, Innovation and Electronic Information Division. Catalogue no. 88F0006XIE – no. 002. http://www.statcan.gc.ca/pub/88f0006x /88f0006x2007002-eng.pdf.

Osborne, Brian, and Donald Swaison. 1988. *Kingston: Building on the past.* Westport: Butternut Press.

Shearmur, Richard. 2010a. "On designing the perfect boat: Growth in the Canadian urban system, 2001–2006." Presented at Innovation Systems Research Network (ISRN) annual meeting, Toronto. http://www.utoronto.ca /isrn/publications/NatMeeting/NatSlides/Nat10/Slides/Session%20V _Richard%20Shearmur.pdf.

Shearmur, Richard. 2010b. "Space, place and innovation: A distance-based approach." *Canadian Geographer/Géographe Canadien* 54 (1): 46–67. http://dx.doi.org/10.1111/j.1541-0064.2009.00302.x.

Shearmur, Richard. 2011. "Innovation, regions and proximity: From neoregionalism to spatial analysis." *Regional Studies* 45 (9): 1225–43. http://dx.doi.org/10.1080/00343404.2010.484416.

Shearmur, Richard, and Mario Polèse. 2007. "Do local factors explain local employment growth? Evidence from Canada, 1971–2001." *Regional Studies* 41 (4): 453–71. http://dx.doi.org/10.1080/00343400600928269.

Simms, Alvin. 2009. "Functional regions and the regional capacity index. St John's." Presentation to the Federal Regional Council, 29 January 2009. (Copy available from the authors.)

Spencer, Greg, and Tara Vinodrai. 2009a. Innovation Systems Research Network City-Region Profile: Kingston (update). Program on Globalization and Regional Innovation Systems (PROGRIS): 1–13. http://www.utoronto.ca /isrn/city%20profiles/index.html.

Spencer, Greg, and Tara Vinodrai. 2009b. Innovation Systems Research Network City-Region Profile: St John's (update). Program on Globalization and Regional Innovation Systems (PROGRIS): 1–13. http://www.utoronto.ca /isrn/city%20profiles/index.html.

Stantec. 2009. "Socio-economic benefits from petroleum industry activity in Newfoundland and Labrador, 2005–2007." Petroleum Research Atlantic

Canada: 1–38. http://www.pr-ac.ca/files/files/MP08-01_NL_Benefits Update.pdf.

Statistics Canada. 2009. Table 1-1. "Passengers enplaned and deplaned on selected services – Top 50 airports." http://www.statcan.gc.ca/pub/51-203-x/2008000/t008-eng.htm.

Stolarick, Kevin, and Richard Florida. 2006. "Creativity, connections and innovation: A study of linkages in the Montreal Region." *Environment & Planning A* 38 (10): 1799–817. http://dx.doi.org/10.1068/a3874.

Wernerheim, C. Michael, and Christopher A. Sharpe. 2006. "The rural/urban location pattern of advance services in an international perspective." In *Services industries and the knowledge-based economy*, ed. R.G. Lipsey and A. Nakamura, 445–90. Calgary: University of Calgary Press.

11 Small Cities as Talent Accelerators: Talent Mobility and Knowledge Flows in Moncton

YVES BOURGEOIS

Introduction: Why Do Larger, More Expensive Cities Grow Faster in the Age of the Internet?

In less than a decade, Richard Florida's *Rise of the creative class* (2002) has ignited debates that have swept across the social sciences. At the core, Florida's arguments (2002, 2005, 2008) are that creative and technology-producing industries are the main drivers of the contemporary economy, and they grow and thrive most where creative and highly skilled workers cluster. Find what attracts this creative class of workers, and a city can become a magnet for creative and technological industries. What attracts these creative, knowledge workers, Florida further argues, are vibrant, diverse cities that provide a variety of cultural amenities and experiences.

Florida's insights invigorated location analysis that had been slowly orbiting around cost structures and hard infrastructure. His systematic analysis of employment, occupational, and other socio-economic data challenged a pervasive, anecdotal view that technological change was undermining the imperative of place. Rapid changes in Internet and other telecommunication technologies enchanted a generation of popular writers like Frances Cairncross (1997) and Thomas Friedman (2005) who saw technologies as making geography increasingly irrelevant, precipitating "the death of distance" or the "flattening of the world." Yet even the most compelling anecdotes could not explain why, in the age of the Internet, populations and economies were growing fastest in larger urban centres. The world's population grew four times faster in cities than in rural areas between 2005 and 2010 (UNFPA 2010). In the combined most industrialized nations, cities grew by 0.7 per cent while rural populations declined 0.6 per cent. If workers could telecommute, why would they move to large cities where the cost of living was higher, and why would employers locate where salaries and real estate would cost more?

Rather than conjuring anecdotes, Florida buttresses his hypotheses on statistical correlations between urban performance, the clustering of skilled-worker occupations, and indices of openness, diversity, and tolerance. By arguing that the cultural amenities of cities are magnets that attract workers with a particular set of creative skills, Florida presents a persuasive argument as to why higher-cost urban centres are growing faster at a time when telecommunications are supposedly making the world flatter.

The creative class hypothesis whetted the appetite of a generation of economic development scholars and practitioners endeavouring to unpack Florida's indices so as to understand or replicate the specific factors that seem to attract creative workers. At the same time, Florida's hypothesis has garnered criticism. Some deplore the resources that governments have diverted towards cultural amenities in attempts to attract creative workers: resources most often consumed by the wealthy. Hansen et al. (2009) question how Florida uses the concept of class and whether it is meaningful in class-diverse contexts such as in Europe. Boschma and Fritsch (2009) find support for a relationship between diversity, the presence of creative workers, and employment growth in European regions, but they suggest concentrations of workers based on formal education levels rather than creative occupations may better explain differentiated economic performance. Storper and Scott (2009) also buy Florida's premise that creative workers and economic performance are correlated, but they argue the causality is reversed: in other words, the presence of creative workers may not be causing urban economic growth, but rather cities where businesses do better at creating jobs are attracting mobile, creative workers who spend more on cultural products. Houston et al. (2008) argue that economic opportunities are a prerequisite to mobility. Musterd and Murie (2010) add that personal networks and relationships, as well as more classic conditions of jobs and accessibility, play a more significant role in explaining the mobility of creative workers than do "soft" conditions of diversity and tolerance.

The challenge remains to explain the concentration of demographic and economic growth in Canada's census metropolitan areas. Whether workers in creative occupations drive economic growth or follow it, the relationship between talented workers and urban performance needs to be expounded.

In this chapter I ask how knowledge and skills flow into city-regions and what role creative and talented workers play in facilitating these flows? Second, creative workers are often assumed to move from one city to the next at critical junctures in their careers, but do we need to distinguish creative workers in cultural occupations from those in technology occupations (Wolfe 2009, 90), and do their mobility patterns differ? Third, what role does urban hierarchy play in these flows of knowledge and talent, particularly in smaller cities such as Moncton, New Brunswick, that are much more dependent on connectedness to larger centres as sources of partnerships and new ideas?

To explore these questions, I first highlight knowledge flows as a source of innovation and creativity. Second, I describe the socio-economic background of the Moncton case study. Third, I group Moncton creative workers into broad categories according to their mobility patterns, discussing the implications for the flow of knowledge into the city-region.

I interviewed more than seventy-five Greater Monctonians as part of this research, including twenty-five creative and professional workers in five occupational groups. I focused on the culinary arts because of nascent haute cuisine establishments and their weathervane role in indicating the health of the local economy. A growing film and TV production industry warranted that sector's inclusion. I included dance and choreography as well as the literary arts because of an unusually high number of dance companies and publishing houses for a small metropolitan area. Greater Moncton's growth in knowledge-intensive business services firms made management and legal professionals the fifth set of occupations targeted.

Agglomeration Economies: Cities as Knowledge Accelerators

> But the economical advantages of commerce are surpassed in importance by those of its effects which are intellectual and moral. It is hardly possible to overrate the value, in the present low state of human improvement, of placing human beings in contact with persons dissimilar to themselves, and with modes of thought and action unlike those with which they are familiar ... Such communication has always been, and is peculiarly in the present age, one of the primary sources of progress.
>
> J.S. Mill (1848, 2.17)

These streets will make you feel brand new; big lights will inspire you.

Jay-Z et al. (2009)

J.S. Mill and Jay-Z are describing creativity advantages that cities afford accruing from the greater diversity in influences and experiences they enable. While Mill's treatise was extolling the virtues of commerce generally, in the passage quoted he was in effect linking space, diversity, and innovation (or progress). This link is at the basis of urbanization economies, one of two broad sets of agglomeration economies. That is, firms reap economic advantages not from their own internal decisions but by being close to others and benefiting from non-market exchanges (externalities).

Urbanization economies speak to those agglomeration economies based on the diversity of people, skills, and industries that large cities intertwine, and the speed of interactions dense urban areas can afford. They are attributed to Jane Jacobs (1970), although Mill had already etched out the relationship. Connections between urban diversity and growth are now indelibly linked to the works of Richard Florida. As one Moncton author said, "It's important for us [artists] to be concentrated geographically. There's an exchange of ideas, an exchange of cultures that happen. I inspire myself from the work of others. This is especially important for popular art." The city becomes a source of inspiration and renewal.

Specialization economies are the other broad set of agglomeration economies. Whereas urbanization economies privilege diversity, specialization economies accrue from clustering, which enables individuals and firms to specialize in relative strengths and exchange with related economic agents. Alfred Marshall (1890, 4.10.7) described them as the "advantages which people following the same skilled trade get from near neighbourhood to one another."

Both types of agglomeration economies compete and complement each other in explaining why cities are driving economic growth in the Internet age. The ability for city-regions to adopt and produce new forms of knowledge depends in part on the degree to which local actors interact meaningfully – collaborating and inspiring each other – and on the degree to which they are exposed to cutting-edge knowledge and ideas from outside. The mobility of workers – specifically creative and highly skilled workers who can learn, adopt, and adapt new ideas – helps cities stay attuned to changing market and technological trends as well as seize new opportunities.

The ability to attract creative, talented, highly skilled workers is a means not only to increase the size of a labour market and economy, but also to attract a more productive workforce that can sustain economic and per capita real wage growth. Perhaps more important, through their interactions within the local economy as well as along the urban hierarchy, creative workers accelerate knowledge spillovers: that is, the cascading of new, valuable knowledge into the region and circulation across local economic sectors, multiplying benefits to the local economy. They increase the ability of local firms to harness new ideas, create, and innovate.

How exactly do these talented workers move about, and how does mobility help circulate knowledge into and throughout the local economy? I return to how knowledge flows in a small metropolitan area like Greater Moncton after first providing some socio-economic background to the Greater Moncton case.

Moncton: A History of Flows

Throughout its history, Moncton served as a nexus though which goods, people, cultures, and ideas have flowed. For centuries Mi'kmaq Aboriginals used the bend in the Petitcodiac River to portage Fundy and Shediac Bays. The Petitcodiac River provided the pier for Moncton's first demographic and economic boom when the wooden shipbuilding industry anchored there in the mid-nineteenth century. Although iron and steam torpedoed Moncton shipbuilding soon thereafter, the city's strategic location on the Chignecto Isthmus connecting Nova Scotia and Prince Edward Island to the rest of Canada attracted the emerging Intercolonial railway and gave Moncton its second wind: the city became a hub for the region's railway system (Larracey 1991).

Expansion of Moncton's locomotive repair shops at the turn of the twentieth century secured the vitality of the railway industry and provided relative prosperity for generations. During this period, however, despite the funnelling of land transportation routes through the region, with the railway and the expanding network of highways exploding after the Second World War, there was little expansion of the city's manufacturing base to leverage new access to central markets. Moncton was born a ship manufacturing town, but it grew up as a service city: locomotive repair, warehousing, retail, an army base, and regional government offices were its major employers. Nor was it a capital city or a university town; for much of the twentieth century it remained a meat-and-potatoes, blue-collar service town and transportation hub.

Moncton weathered the perfect storm of the mid-1980s. Within a few short years it lost a tenth of its jobs, including its largest private-sector employer – the Canadian National locomotive repair shops – as well as other mainstays such as the Eaton's mail order catalogue, and the armed forces base. The CN shops alone represented 5000 jobs lost in a city with a workforce of 53,000 and in an economic region of 77,000 workers in 1987 (Statistics Canada 2011). The mood was dour. Even the local economic development agency's slogans dared not aspire beyond "Moncton – We're OK" (EGM 2005). The funeral was organized, but before the eulogy was spoken Moncton got up and carried on with steady population and economic growth.

Moncton's second revival in the 1990s led some to speak of the "Moncton miracle" (Farnsworth 1994). However, the credit for the economic resurgence owes less to Providence and more to an effort deployed by community and provincial leaders to put the economy back on its feet, as several local economic-development officials remarked in our interviews. Then New Brunswick premier Frank McKenna and local politicians banged on every door in Canada's financial centres and, capitalizing on Greater Moncton's large number of bilingual workers, returned with call centres and back offices. These were not the highest-paying jobs or easiest to sustain in the long term in a globalizing world, but they had an immediate palliative effect: they kept workers in Greater Moncton and attracted others at a time when employment rates were shrinking across the province. By the time CN closed shop for good, the greater Moncton economy was slowly transitioning into a higher-paying, professional business service centre, drawing Blue Cross insurance alongside Assomption Vie as large private-sector, financial services employers.

The French Connection

The city's large number of bilingual workers played a key role in attracting customer-oriented, professional, and government-services industries during the crisis of the mid-1980s. A bilingual, educated workforce had become a palatable economic tool, a marketable competitive advantage to the region. With growing demand for bilingual workers, more and more anglophones were graduating from French-immersion schools. International events such as the first World Acadian Congress, held in and around Greater Moncton in 1994, and the World Francophonie Summit, held in Moncton in 1999, further highlighted

the cultural significance of Moncton's Acadian population and the economic potential from bilingualism. "The 1999 summit was where many
young professionals were baptized and introduced to the world stage,"
remarked a former provincial civil servant now bridging arts and communications fields in Moncton. International exposure helped congeal
a growing cultural and economic *rapprochement* between francophones
and anglophones.

During this time the francophone artistic community had become
quite conspicuous in its contribution to the local arts and culture scene,
through its performing arts theatres, Aberdeen Cultural Centre in
Moncton, an international film festival, publishing houses, Université
de Moncton campus-based events, and a new cultural centre in Dieppe.
International events such as the Northrup Frye Book Festival provided
another venue for both francophone and anglophone artists to shine. A
bilingual workforce, new breed of Acadian entrepreneurs, French and
bilingual institutions, as well as a vibrant francophone arts and culture
scene have been instrumental in transitioning the Greater Moncton
economy from that of a railway town to a more highly educated city
with growing business and finance, health, and other service sectors.

Delayed Urbanization

According to the 2011 census, the Greater Moncton census metropolitan area (CMA) has 138,644 residents, scattered among the cities of
Moncton (69,074) and Dieppe (23,310), the town of Riverview (19,128),
and smaller adjacent communities (Statistics Canada 2012). It is one of
Canada's smallest (twenty-ninth of thirty-three) yet fastest growing
CMAs (9.7 per cent growth between 2006 and 2011), emerging in 2006
as New Brunswick's largest metropolitan area.

A sober second look at demographic trends suggests this population
growth rate will weaken considerably unless inter-provincial and international migration increases. In what could be called *delayed urbanization*, much of Greater Moncton's recent population growth has occurred
through migration within New Brunswick. By 2006, 12.4 per cent of
Greater Moncton's population had moved to the CMA from other parts
of the province in the previous five years, while 6 per cent had moved
from outside the province, and 1.1 per cent from outside the country.
Urbanization has been a dirty word in New Brunswick. Successive
waves of industrialization over the past 150 years saw job-seeking
New Brunswickers flee their own urban centres for New England, then

Central and Western Canada. Many New Brunswickers are now moving to the province's four southern cities – and Greater Moncton in particular – producing a noticeable effect on the city-region's built environment and transportation system.

Biculturalism materialized over many generations, and multiculturalism is a work-in-progress. Only 3.4 per cent of Monctonians were born outside Canada, compared to 7.4 per cent in Halifax, 19.8 per cent in Canada on average, 20.6 per cent in Montreal, and 45.7 per cent in Toronto. Only 2 per cent of Moncton's residents are from a visible minority, compared to 7.5 per cent in Halifax, 16.5 per cent in Montreal, and 42.9 per cent in Toronto. Only 2.2 per cent speak neither English nor French as their mother tongue, compared to 5.6 per cent in Halifax, 22.5 per cent in Montreal, and 44.5 per cent in Toronto (Statistics Canada 2007).

The story of Moncton is largely that of a small city whose past prosperity long depended on one main industry – first shipbuilding then the railway. When the closure of the railway repair shops in the mid-1980s threatened the city-region's existence, local and provincial leaders mobilized to transition the economy into a diversified financial-services sector, with burgeoning IT and light manufacturing, and buttressed by government, education, and healthcare institutions (table 11.1). "Monctonians wear their history," one writer quipped in an interview. "We're still blue collar workers. We just work in the services sectors now."

Given the slowing population growth and the widening real wages gap between Greater Moncton and the Canadian average, sustained economic growth in Greater Moncton will rely on capital investments – both physical and human – as well as innovation. The ability to produce and attract talented workers becomes paramount. Their higher levels of human capital increases productivity directly by increasing output per worker, as well as indirectly as higher levels of skills enable and enhance innovation. Productivity gains are the only means through which regional average wages and standards of living rise.

How Mobile Talent Facilitates Knowledge Flows in Greater Moncton

Most creative workers interviewed – those working as chefs, in TV and film production, or in literary, dance, and theatre arts – were highly mobile workers. In fact, many Moncton creatives could be considered migrant workers. Every few seasons or every few years they move between Moncton and New York, Toronto, Paris, or Montreal. The larger

Table 11.1 Percentage of workforce by occupation groups, Moncton CMA and Canada, 2006

Occupation groups	Creative	Service	Trades and manual	Agricultural and resources
Moncton	32.9	49.4	16.9	0.8
Canada	33.2	41.9	21.9	2.9

Source: Spencer and Vinodrai (2009)

world cities provide paying gigs in their field (such as writing TV dramas, performing in theatre, or making crafts), opportunities which are at best seasonal in Moncton. Unlike in St John's, where many artists viewed the city as free-standing (Lepawsky et al. this volume), many Moncton artists saw the city as a transient space of production. When in Moncton, they tend to work their craft either seasonally or part-time. They may engage in creative-leaning jobs such as stage lighting, art framing, museum work, graphic design, and so forth.

While it is more difficult to sustain full-time and year-long employment as a creative in Moncton compared to larger cities, many people interviewed suggested the smaller city afforded greater opportunities to collaborate than they found in large urban centres. As Grant et al. (this volume) found in Halifax, the arts and culture scene was less cutthroat and more nurturing in a smaller city like Moncton. In larger cities, artists have a greater chance to make a full-time living practising their art and are not always impelled to collaborate with artists outside their immediate realm. With few artists in any one field, smaller cities almost require artists to collaborate with others outside their discipline, accelerating the cross-fertilization of ideas. Several Monctonian writers considered indispensable the cross-sector collaborations between authors, musicians, and visual artists. Creatives in other fields, such as in dance and culinary arts, recognized the advantages of collaboration, but egos remained difficult to overcome, by their own admission. Moreover, a spatial dimension emerged in this cross-fertilization, as suggested by a relocated Moncton writer: "As a professional artist living in Montreal, I could confine myself to my neighbourhood. Here I *have* to move about, all around … and engage myself."

This provides two insights about the flow of knowledge into and across smaller cities like Moncton. First, it highlights how creative migrant workers are a major source of knowledge gleaned from larger metropolitan areas. From new lighting and cinematography techniques to genre development and business opportunities, creative migrant workers are constantly upgrading the local knowledge base by working elsewhere, importing new ideas and techniques, on the one hand, and exporting local cultural products, on the other. Second, even the most established artists in Moncton's cultural sectors have part- or full-time gigs in other local industries, and this maximizes the flow of knowledge from one cultural sector to the next, and throughout the broader economy.

Many of those interviewed pointed to the key but insufficient role institutions such as the Aberdeen Cultural Centre played in corralling together visual "artists, graphic artists, festival organizers, theatre troupes ... that all seem to feed off each other," as one art gallery curator observed. The success of the cultural centre masks a relative dearth of cultural infrastructure in Moncton (arts and convention centre, galleries, museums, exhibits), as several cultural festival organizers, artists, and venue directors lamented. This absence limits the meeting points of creative minds. However, makeshift venues, such as schools, and the deeper penetration of arts and culture workers into the labour market, may compensate for this paucity of physical cultural institutions.

Of course, this is not to say there are no struggling *creatives* juggling jobs and passions in larger cities, just that there are fewer *superstars* in smaller cities who can make their living solely from their art (Rosen 1981). In smaller cities, vertical hierarchies in creative sub-disciplines are short; there are fewer stripes to be earned and fewer opportunities to practise one's art full-time, which drives artists to interact horizontally across creative fields. "Montreal can be stifling – there are 1350 members of the writers union," confided a nomadic writer, who splits time between Moncton and other cities. For some artists interviewed, "working for the man" is a fact of life; for others it provides a grounding inspiration.

The following sections describe trends in the mobility patterns of the Greater Moncton creative and skilled workers interviewed. I discuss the main motives behind mobility patterns and what they represent for knowledge flows in the city-region, both vertically (into the city-region) and horizontally (across the city-region). These are further summarized in table 11.2.

Frequent Flyers

Legal, business, and IT professionals tend to be mobile workers in any city. Business professionals in particular travel as they cater to client

Table 11.2 Typology of talent mobility

Mobility type	Occupation	Move/ travel	Motivation	Knowledge flows
Frequent flyers	Legal and business Professionals	Weekly or monthly	Training, HQ needs, developing client base, implementing supplier technologies	Vertically from interactions with HQ, suppliers, clients, and other actors Horizontally through local business networking
Nomads	Writers	Events calendar	Promoting books and other literary works during fairs and trade events Inspiration through varied urban settings Interacting with like-minded souls.	Vertically from temporary clusters during international book fairs and literary events. Horizontally in local literary circles, artistic events as well as cultural centres.
Creative migrant workers	Theatre TV/ film production	Seasonal	Production schedules busy in Moncton area only during summer months because of agreeable weather and tourist venues	Vertically for those living in larger centres where they work during winter months Horizontally for those working locally in related occupations or industries during winter months
Rovers	Chefs Dancer/ choreographers	Every few years	New challenges once they plateau at current position Desire to introduce their specialty in underserved market	Vertically in bringing new ideas from cities where they worked last Horizontally (chefs) by sharing knowledge on techniques and varieties with local food producers and manufacturers

and supplier relationships, attend trade shows, and so forth. In smaller cities with many regional offices and divisions, they are also frequently asked to travel to company headquarters or other divisions for training, in preparation for new technology deployments or product commercialization. Because activities such as training and meeting with clients or suppliers are more likely to occur in the same city in larger metropolitan areas, travelling outside the region becomes relatively more important for professional services workers in smaller cities. Serving clients and "staying at the forefront of industry developments" were also reasons cited by legal professionals in motivating their travels.

A strong contingent of business professionals in Greater Moncton helps the local economy adopt, adapt, and grow. Their relatively short stints away limit the depth of the knowledge they can acquire while learning, learning-by-doing, and learning-by-interacting. This depth is further limited by the wider range of competencies business professionals develop in smaller cities.

However, there is an upside to lack of specialization. For legal professionals, small-town law firms "make you practise every kind of law there is," while big-city law firms can require undesirable hyper-specialization in a particular field. A smaller metropolitan area can make for a good career incubator for young professionals. Further, business professionals' intimate knowledge of the local economy helps sift the practicality and feasibility of ideas that can be generated into value. Thus, *frequent flyers* play a crucial role in gleaning new ideas and bringing them into the region. Their interactions with other local players through business networking activities and informal channels facilitate the spread of this knowledge horizontally. However, meaningful knowledge-sharing relationships were shown to be rather weak in Greater Moncton throughout the interviews. One successful IT firm owner admitted he stopped sending workers to networking events because "I realized my competitors were trying to poach my employees."

Nomads

Professional writers were very mobile as well. Their migratory patterns followed literary-events schedules, such as in New York, Montreal, and Paris, the destination often reflecting the language of the writer. Moncton hosts its own Northrup Frye international literary festival. Book fairs and other literary events are major venues to promote literary works, as well as to meet prospective publishers; for professional writers, attendance is paramount. The events themselves create temporary clusters (Schuldt and Bathelt 2011) where writers, publishers, publicists, and other players in the industry meet and exchange ideas, allow creative juices to flow, and provide inspiration for future literary works. Hence, such events serve as important venues for mercantile and knowledge exchanges alike.

Writers interviewed revealed that literary events served as the launch pads for much longer stays in vibrant cities such as Paris and New

York, where they may take up formal or informal artist-in-residence positions for several weeks or months. Many feel more valued and find inspiration in an eclectic "cultural Mecca." On this last point, however, writers seemed polarized. Some found such inspiration amidst the buzz of larger world cities, others in the serenity of Moncton's open spaces. Many Halifax musicians had found geographical remoteness an asset (Grant et al. this volume), as it minimized distractions to creativity and sheltered local bands from global competition for live music fans' attention. For all, the act of writing was an individualistic effort, but for some more than others, the ideas flowed from interactions with other people in dense urban settings. For those finding inspiration in "cultural environments with a human face," Moncton was described as a place of "symbiosis with other arts. Here we work closely with musicians and visual artists" in creating and producing work.

Overall, nomadic professional writers enabled the flow of knowledge and ideas into the region, and on to the world. From their participation in literary events and stays abroad, they uncover, appropriate, and incorporate ideas into their writings, disembodied in the printed word but embodied in the experiences they share upon their return. They forge relationships with other authors, publishers, and visual artists with whom they may collaborate. Writers also internalize much of this horizontally flowing knowledge: "It's different than when I lived in Montreal. Here artists have to be working on 10 different things at once. You learn a lot." The extent to which writers disseminate knowledge horizontally in the region varies significantly by author, as local involvement can vary depending on one's linguistic group as well as personal views of how they define community, and with whom and where they interact.

Creative Migrant Workers

Production schedules for theatre as well as TV and film are seasonal throughout most of Atlantic Canada. Cultural festivals, theatre runs, and venues such as Le Pays de la Sagouine are particularly active during the busy tourist season in the summer. Lower production costs and idyllic adjacent rural communities have attracted TV and film production opportunities, generally concentrated in late spring to autumn before the harshness of winter makes indoor production facilities and larger centres like Montreal the stage for camera shooting.

For actors, writers, stage hands, lighting technicians, and several other specialized technical workers, it is possible to practise one's craft and make a living in Moncton during the summer and the shoulder sea-sons. To pay the bills the remainder of the year, creative and skilled workers eke out a living by other means. Some find work locally in re-lated fields such as publishing, others in non-related fields such as ac-counting. Others follow production companies to Montreal and other locales where they can continue to practise their art.

By spending part of the year in other shooting locations, the creative migrant worker perfects her art, learns of new production techniques, and remains at the forefront of new technologies. Their return during summer months brings into the region new forms of knowledge that casual industry workers will learn in turn. This enhances the vertical flow of knowledge into the region. Those who stay in the region but work in other industries circulate new knowledge horizontally, putting new techniques and technologies to work in related and unrelated sec-tors. While their inability to sustain year-long employment in TV and film production may be a disadvantage for many workers, their role in bringing in new knowledge from larger centres and then disseminating it throughout the local economy becomes a major asset to the region.

Itinerants

Elite chefs master their trade over decades, in small part during formal training, but mostly by working years under experienced masters and experimenting on their own. Often they will change restaurants, cities, and countries altogether when scaling kitchen ranks (e.g., sous-chef, executive chef) or acquiring specialties (e.g., saucier, patissier, *grillar-din*). "Four years of *hôtellerie*, three years of exams, but by far the most important was learning-by-doing," one émigré made clear. "It was working with a chef that I really learned what was cuisine."[1]

Every two- or ten-year stint in other cities provides chefs with deep knowledge of local cultures and allows them to forge relationships with specialized food producers, from farmers at local markets to fish bro-kers. These relationships go beyond simply buyer-seller dealings, but can evolve into repeated knowledge interactions, a "symbiosis with sup-pliers" whereby chefs constantly learn from producers about local spe-cialties and then create new dishes accordingly. Food producers also learn from chefs about techniques or coveted and valuable varieties of foodstuff they can produce. "I give seeds to farmers," said one chef. Others coaxed agricultural producers in adopting different techniques, raising different varieties, or harvesting differently, such as tomatoes when they are green. Hence, when chefs move into a new city, they bring years of experience and knowledge they often seek to share with local producers in order to increase and improve the supply of ingredients and fresh local food products. The potential benefits of their knowledge are thus shared not only with restaurant patrons but with agriculturalists and food manufacturers throughout the broader economy.

Knowledge is thus easily shared vertically in the production chain, between chefs and food producers. Two chefs were eager to share their knowledge with students and the general public through food fairs and similar events. However, knowledge is shared with greater difficulty horizontally. Two chefs interviewed lamented that egos "get in the way of the greater good," as in the movie *Big Night*. Moncton's international seafood festival was seen as a closed event. "I win seafood competitions in other provinces, but I can't get myself invited to the one in my city." As a result of using the festival "to promote one chef and one restaurant" above the others, "the festival is moving backwards," with fewer participants.

Chefs are here described as *itinerants* because, unlike many business professionals who travel frequently from a home base, chefs travel less often but tend to do so continually searching for new experiences and challenges. The nature of the restaurant industry, open nearly 365 days a year, means that chefs do not wander far or often, especially not chef-restaurateurs. Some chefs interviewed mentioned that when they do travel, they often choose cities where there are other chefs they have met or heard of, and make it a point to meet them at their restaurants. Other prominent chefs, however, use the Internet as inspiration to compensate for distance, gleaning "perhaps not recipes themselves, but ideas for new variations." As another chef added, "never to copy, but to get sparks." Of all creative workers interviewed, chefs were the most likely to consider leaving Moncton, as opposed to changing jobs within the city, if a change of scenery became desirable.

The mobility of the dancers and choreographers interviewed mirrored those of chefs to a large extent. Their art is learned through some schooling, but mostly through years of informal training and practice. For most of those interviewed, many learning and employment experiences were acquired abroad. "You have to. You can only get to certain levels here in Moncton. You have to leave the province and country to learn and to master your field," suggested one choreographer and dance school owner. "There are lots of schools and opportunities here for amateurs to learn, but not for professionals," added another. "A creator has to rejuvenate oneself." Choreographers moving or returning periodically to Moncton allowed the region a window onto the world, opportunities to tap into knowledge and experiences impossible to forge endogenously. By the same token, next to chefs, choreographers were the most likely to leave Moncton in pursuit of other opportunities.

Despite the rather large number of dance schools for a smaller city, or perhaps because of it, opportunities for sharing knowledge horizontally were quite limited. Cut-throat competition for limited public funds, patrons, and students has chilled relations between several dance schools and troupes. One dance school director confided: "We live in conflict: strong personalities, funding, wavering between art and sport [to access funding and be eligible for tax credits], whether to have quality standards."

The Underappreciated Role of Talented Workers as Knowledge Brokers

Cities with higher concentrations of talent perform better with respect to innovation, the growth of creative and technological industries, as well as job and income growth. Current debates ponder whether it is the creative nature of the occupations (Florida 2002, 2008) or human capital as formal education (Boschma and Fritsch 2009) that best explains this relationship. We also wonder whether the chicken or the egg came first – is the presence of creative workers the cornerstone of successful economies (Florida 2005) or do creative workers simply move where jobs are created faster (Storper and Scott 2009)? Whether the drivers are place-based amenities or employment opportunities, this carries immense implications for governments who wonder how many scarce resources to devote to cultural amenities and how many to industrial growth and attraction.

In the case of Greater Moncton, employment opportunities were the main attractor for talented workers interviewed. Larger cities like Toronto have thicker labour markets for cultural and specialized workers (Hracs and Stolarick this volume), which makes it easier to find related work should an artist or cultural worker lose his or her job, thus making the gamble more reasonable if one is choosing where to live based on lifestyle. One Greater Moncton IT worker summarized a view shared by almost all those interviewed who moved to the region from another province and by all who had moved from another country: "I moved to Moncton for the job. It would have been ridiculous for me to move without it. If you have a job, it's a great place to live and work."

Cultural and leisure opportunities did have an impact on the decision to stay, however: perhaps more than employment opportunities given the shallowness of the labour market for specialized or cultural workers. This supports findings that urban amenities "do indeed play an important role in retaining [workers] once they have relocated" (Martin-Brelot et al. 2010, 854). The Moncton case study supports Storper and Scott's (2009) position, although this may be a testimony to small cities that lack the branding power to attract migrants of cities like Toronto, Montreal, and Vancouver.

Moncton's relative tolerance and openness to outside influences were not cited by migrants from other countries or provinces, but they were oft named by creative workers who moved to Moncton from other parts of the province. "Acadie cannot thrive without a metropolitan area such as Moncton ... where differences are more tolerated than in smaller Acadian towns and villages," noted a TV/film executive.

In these debates on the attraction of creative and talented workers, cities are often viewed as disconnected islands competing for talent. The flow of talent is couched in linear terms as one of workers moving from one city to another at critical junctures in their careers (Richardson 2009), such as upon completing university (Hansen and Niedomysl 2009; Comunian et al. 2010). The Moncton case study shows that we need to refine our understanding of talent mobility in a hierarchical system of world cities. In smaller metropolitan areas, talent flows are not linear – that is, occurring at key moments of workers' "personal trajectories" (Martin-Brelot et al. 2010). Rather, flows are in constant circular movement, and talented workers are continually travelling to learn and find inspiration. This greatly enhances creativity and the flow of knowledge into the city-region. Interconnected urban hierarchies (Lorenzen and Andersen 2009) thus become crucial to understanding these circular flows. Lepawsky et al. (this volume) further argue that creative class theory needs a relational perspective of place.

In the Moncton case, talented workers most frequently cited Montreal, Paris, Toronto, and New York as destinations. As one choreographer stated, "you *need* to go out and see Montreal, Canada's cultural Mecca. And you *need* to go to New York, which is really a country within a city." However, which cities were atop the food chain varied somewhat according to workers' creative fields and language. It also depended on cultural workers' success and income. Like St John's but unlike Kingston, Moncton is not an easy commute to cities further up the hierarchy, such as Montreal or Toronto. Air connections are costly. From Montreal, it can be cheaper to fly to Paris than to Moncton. Places of *resourcing* and *connections* are more accessible for the wealthier than for many cultural industry workers.

Where travel is costly, cost of living was cited as an advantage by artists and cultural groups, as the time needed working to pay the bills is shorter, leaving artists with more time to work on their creations. According to Vinodrai's (this volume) rankings of the percentage of household budgets devoted to housing, Moncton is Canada's fourth least expensive place to live, after Winnipeg, Regina, and Ottawa. However, sprawl has made public transit impractical. Only 2.8 per cent of Monctonians with jobs travel to work using public transit, compared to Halifax (11.9%), Toronto (22.2%), and Montreal (32.6%). Conversely, 87.1 per cent of employed Monctonians travel to work in personal vehicles. Hence, many lower-income Monctonians spend more on car ownership than people in other cities, making the cost-of-living differential less significant.

Social networks are double-edged swords. On the one hand, they can be easier to penetrate and to leverage in smaller cities like Moncton and St John's (Lepawsky et al. this volume) than in large ones like Toronto (Hracs and Stolarick; Davis et al. this volume). Many *creatives* also celebrated the fact that in smaller urban centres, sheltered from the rigid artistic hierarchies of larger metropolitan areas, there was more freedom to create. "It's easier to take chances, easier to experiment," said one performance artist. In major cities, where many artists had toiled and continued to do so periodically, it is often customary to work in the shadows of giants, pay tribute and earn one's stripes along the way, and perhaps one day get the chance to see one's play, music, or choreography performed. In smaller centres it was easier to sidestep these hierarchies and for upstarts to get their break.

On the other hand, the consequences are more severe should social-network connections be ruptured. "It's very difficult here to offer critiques without being ostracized," admitted one playwright. Cliques among established artists were viewed as exclusionary by several young artists. Moreover, while some artists cherish larger cities where the bar is set higher (Davis et al. this volume) and the disciplinary effect of competition pushes one to work harder, several Moncton authors, choreographers, and chefs lamented that the bar was too low and that the general population was "content with too little." "It's easy to feel alone ... There's little competition in our field – it keeps the bar low. We have to catch up by reading and travelling frequently, collaborate with outside firms to round out our experiences and skills."

Smaller cities make it difficult to sustain full-time, year-long employment in creative fields. Part-time creatives moonlight in their craft while working at administrative or technical jobs by day, often in related industries. This facilitates the horizontal flow of ideas and knowledge across sectors within the local economy. For seasonal creatives – such as writers and performance artists – summer festivals, stage, and TV production schedules mean they also live and work half the year in larger cities along Moncton's urban hierarchy. Their migratory patterns ensure a vertical flow of ideas and knowledge in and out of the local economy. For all creatives, residence or regular sojourns in larger metropolitan areas are seen as key to learning, renewal, and inspiration. It is an unfortunate irony that creative workers, especially those in arts and culture, can rarely make ends meet practising their trade, yet they play a key role as knowledge brokers: ambassadors while living in other cities, and returning with new ideas that sustain creativity and innovation in the local economy.

ACKNOWLEDGMENTS

I am indebted to the Social Sciences and Humanities Research Council of Canada for its generous funding, as well as Robert MacKinnon and Tracy Chiasson of UNBSJ, and Rodrigue Landry and Hélène Gallant of CIRLM, for administering the grant. Daniel Bourque provided much appreciated research support. I am indebted to David Wolfe and Meric Gertler for their admirable stewardship of this comparative project, to Jill Grant for her invaluable comments on the chapter, and to interviewees for volunteering precious time.

NOTES

1 Human capital as the accumulation of experience, while of course common to several fields, was most strongly cited by film and TV producers. One literary artist had suggested formal education diminished the worth of his human capital. "I actually had to unlearn what I was taught in school and university [in order] to make it as a writer. If I had to do it over, I wouldn't borrow money to go to university."

REFERENCES

Boschma, Ron, and Michael Fritsch. 2009. "Creative class and regional growth: Empirical evidence from seven European countries." *Economic Geography* 85 (4): 391–423. http://dx.doi.org/10.1111/j.1944-8287.2009.01048.x.

Cairncross, Frances. 1997. *The death of distance: How the communications revolution will change our lives*. Boston: Harvard Business School Press.

Comunian, Roberta, Alessandra Faggian, and Qian Cher Li. 2010. "Unrewarded careers in the creative class: The strange case of Bohemian graduates." *Regional Science* 89 (2): 389–410.

EGM (Enterprise Greater Moncton). 2005. *Annual report, 2004–2005*. Moncton.

Farnsworth, Clyde. 1994. "The 'Moncton miracle': Bilingual phone chat." *New York Times*, 17 July.

Florida, Richard. 2002. *The rise of the creative class and how it's transforming work, leisure and everyday life*. New York: Basic Books.

Florida, Richard. 2005. *Cities and the creative class*. New York: Routledge.

Florida, Richard. 2008. *Who's your city? How the creative economy is making where to live the most important decision of your life*. New York: Basic.

Friedman, Thomas. 2005. *The world is flat: A brief history of the 21st century*. New York: Farrar, Straus and Giroux.

Hansen, Hogni Kalso, Bjorn Asheim, and Jan Vang. 2009. "The European creative class and regional development: How relevant is Florida's theory for Europe?" *Creative Economies, Creative Cities* 98 (3): 99–120. http://dx.doi.org/10.1007/978-1-4020-9949-6_7.

Hansen, Hogni Kalso, and Thomas Niedomysl. 2009. "Migration of the creative class: Evidence from Sweden." *Journal of Economic Geography* 9 (2): 191–206. http://dx.doi.org/10.1093/jeg/lbn046.

Houston, Donald, Allan Findlay, Richard Harrison, and Colin Mason. 2008. "Will attracting the 'creative class' boost economic growth in old industrial regions? A case study of Scotland." *Geografiska Annaler: Series B, Human Geography* 90 (2): 133–49.

Jacobs, Jane. 1970. *The economy of cities*. New York: Vintage.

Jay-Z Shawn Carter, Janet Sewell, Angela Hunte, Sylvia Robinson, Burt Keyes, Alicia Keys, and Alexander Shuckburgh. 2009. "Empire state of mind. The blueprint 3." New York: Roc Nation/Sony Music Entertainment.

Larracey, Edward W. 1991. *Resurgo: The history of Moncton*. Moncton: City of Moncton.

Lorenzen, Mark, and Kristina V. Andersen. 2009. "Centrality and creativity: Does Richard Florida's creative class offer new insights into urban hierarchy?" *Economic Geography* 85 (4): 363–90. http://dx.doi.org/10.1111/j.1944-8287.2009.01044.x.

Marshall, Alfred. 1890. *Principles of economics: An introductory text.* London: Macmillan.

Martin-Brelot, Helene, Michel Grossetti, Denis Eckert, Olga Gritsai, and Zoltán Kovács. 2010. "The spatial mobility of the 'creative class': A European perspective." *International Journal of Urban and Regional Research* 34 (4): 854–70. http://dx.doi.org/10.1111/j.1468-2427.2010.00960.x.

Mill, John Stuart. 1848. *Principles of political economy.* London: Parker.

Musterd, Sako, and Alan Murie. 2010. *Making competitive cities.* Oxford: Wiley-Blackwell.

Richardson, Kathrine. 2009. "What lures and retains the international creative-class family? A case study of the family unit found in Vancouver's biotechnology sector." *Comparative Technology Transfer and Society* 7 (3): 323–45. http://dx.doi.org/10.1353/ctt.0.0041.

Rosen, Sherwin. 1981. "The economics of superstars." *American Economic Review* 71 (5): 845–58.

Schuldt, Nina, and Harald Bathelt. 2011. "International trade fairs and global buzz. Part II: Practices of global buzz." *European Planning Studies* 19 (1): 1–22. http://dx.doi.org/10.1080/09654313.2011.530390.

Spencer, Greg, and Tina Vinodrai. 2009. Innovation Systems Research Network City-Region Profiles: Moncton, 2006 census. Toronto: ISRN, University of Toronto. http://www.utoronto.ca/isrn/city%20profiles/2006%20City%20 Profiles/MonctonProfile2006.pdf.

Statistics Canada. 2007. *Moncton, New Brunswick (Code305)* (table). *2006 community profiles.* 2006 Census. Statistics Canada Catalogue no. 92-591-XWE. Ottawa. Released 13 March 2007. http://www12.statcan.ca/census-recensement/2006/dp-pd/prof/92-591/index.cfm?Lang=E.

Statistics Canada. 2011. *Table 282-0054 – Labour force survey estimates (LFS), by provinces and economic regions.* CANSIM (database). Ottawa: Statistics Canada.

Statistics Canada. 2012. *Moncton, New Brunswick (Code 305)* (table). *Census profile.* 2011 census. Statistics Canada catalogue no. 98-316-XWE. Ottawa. http://www12.statcan.ca/census-recensement/2011/dp-pd/prof/index. cfm?Lang=E.

Storper, Michael, and Allen Scott. 2009. "Rethinking human capital, creativity and urban growth." *Journal of Economic Geography* 9 (2): 147–67. http://dx.doi.org/10.1093/jeg/lbn052.

UNFPA (United Nations Population Fund). 2010. "State of world population 2010." http://www.unfpa.org/webdav/site/global/shared/swp/2010 /swop_2010_eng.pdf.

Wolfe, David. 2009. *21st century cities in Canada: The geography of innovation.* Ottawa: Conference Board of Canada.

PART V

Innovating in Talent Attraction

12 What Does the Creative Class Approach Add to the Study of Talent, Creativity, and Innovation in Canadian City-Regions?

BJØRN T. ASHEIM

Evaluating the Contribution of Richard Florida

A decade after the publication of his seminal book *The rise of the creative class*, Richard Florida's (2002) major contributions can be summarized in three key points.

1 He brought urbanization economies – especially Jane Jacobs's (1969) emphasis that diversity in the urban environment stimulates creativity – back on the scene after a decade in which localization economies promoted by Porter's (1990, 1998) cluster approach and Krugman's (1998) new economic geography had dominated.
2 He transcended the understanding of human capital by adding the concept of creative capital, thereby arguing that the economy depends on inputs from a creative class that includes more than just the highly educated (i.e., what is typically defined as human capital) (Glaeser 2005).
3 He enlarged what was traditionally understood as the factors that made cities attractive to people to include social diversity, openness, and tolerance.

Taken together these contributions not only underlined the significance of city-regions and urbanization economies for creativity, innovation, and competitiveness, but also placed people – talented and creative workers – under the spotlight of academics and policymakers. Florida expressed this most clearly in his argument that in the global knowledge economy "jobs follow people," rather than the other way around. After ten years of discussion, research, and policy application, what influence has Florida's work had? To what degree can his arguments be useful in a study of creativity and innovativeness in Canadian city-regions of various sizes, industrial composition, and location? In this chapter, I briefly touch upon this problematic both in general and with non-Canadian eyes examining the Canadian regional mosaic.

The Relevance of Florida's Work for Canada

How relevant are urbanization economies (i.e., the exploitation of external economies from the co-location of different activities in an urban environment) for the creativity, innovativeness, and competitiveness of city-regions? Is the concept only germane for larger cities and city-regions, or has it something to offer mid-sized and smaller city-regions and towns? There is nothing new in the observation that size, superior educational achievements, and high income levels create a critical mass in many industries and occupations in large cities and city-regions, leading to innovation and growth that is normally above the national average. In a European research project I coordinated,[1] Florida's US results (Florida 2006; Florida et al. 2006; Florida, Mellander, and Stolarick 2008) were confirmed in the larger city-regions in the participating European countries (Finland, Norway, Denmark, Sweden, the United Kingdom, Germany, the Netherlands, and Switzerland) (Boschma and Fritsch 2009). In Nordic countries, his approach proved most valid for the capital cities (Andersen et al. 2010). We did not find support for the attractiveness of smaller city-regions and towns for the creative class broadly defined, and, consequently, for its impact on investment and growth, nor for the hypothesis that jobs follow people. Thus, we concluded that in mid-sized city-regions and smaller towns the authorities should be careful in applying the creative class approach in city policy-making and regional planning.

This picture is more or less confirmed by the chapters in this volume, based on extensive research in Canada. With respect to geography, settlement structure, and industrial composition Canada is more similar to the Nordic and European context than to the United States (Asheim 2009). Canada has only a few major cities: some of the largest display a strong geographical concentration (Toronto, Ottawa, and Montreal), while the remaining are geographical outliers (such as Vancouver and Calgary). The urban hierarchy does not offer the same opportunities for career mobility between large and diverse labour markets as seen in the United States: this has consequences for the number of creative class members who can afford to move around trusting that "jobs follow people." As seen in the Nordic study (Andersen et al. 2010), the Canadian research presented here demonstrates that most members of the creative class indicate that they follow job opportunities when they move.

What parts of the creative class move without thinking of job opportunities because they believe that jobs will follow them (or will be self-organized)? A Swedish study found that it was primarily members of the creative class belonging to occupations and industries based on the symbolic knowledge base, such as fashion, music, media, and advertising (Asheim and Hansen 2009). These people seek large dynamic cities where new ideas often originate and develop before being diffused through the urban hierarchy; consequently, their work tends to be in large cities such as Toronto (see Leslie et al., chapter 3, and Davis et al., chapter 4). This group of creative workers offers the best support for Florida's argument that the creative class is larger than traditional measures of human capital (e.g., higher degrees) suggest, as some of the actors and artists working in these occupations may not be highly educated. Since much of the work in these occupations is temporary and project based, income levels and job security for members of this group of the creative class are not among the best. The chapters here offer insight into some of the factors that influence super-creatives in the geographic context of Canada. Hracs and Stolarick (chapter 5) offer a model of mobility, based on their analysis of musicians in the largest centres. The mobility of highly creative workers and the great distances between Canadian urban centres may explain the small clusters that form in some more affordable city-regions like Halifax (chapter 6), St John's, and Kingston (chapter 10).

Large city-regions attract global talent to academia (e.g., researchers at university and research institutes) and large businesses: however, this group of the creative class – often belonging to analytical knowledge-based occupations – follows a different logic. These workers are primarily attracted to high-quality and well-paid jobs in the city-region. Because they often have many jobs to choose among, the quality of the urban environments (including national laws and regulations), and the nature of the social environment (including questions of diversity, openness, and tolerance) can influence where workers decide to go.

What then is the more general relevance of the first two original contributions of the creative class approach for Canadian city-regions? With the exception of the largest city-regions, localization economies – that is, the exploitation of external economies from the co-location of firms from the same and closely related industries (see Porter's 1990, 1998 cluster definition) – generally will be more important than urbanization economies. This is especially true in a resource-based economy such as Canada's. The challenge is to make sure that exploiting localization economies avoid negative lock-ins (that would limit capacity for innovation) and promote positive lock-ins. Positive lock-in or path extension represents a continuous strengthening of the competitiveness of industries in a region (Narula 2002). This could be achieved drawing on non-local connections, both nationally and internationally, to provide the necessary diversity and breadth in knowledge bases, absorptive capacity, and cognitive distance, securing not only path extension (positive lock-ins) but also path renewal (changing technological trajectories). This is, however, not at odds with the creative class approach, since Swedish studies (Asheim and Hansen 2009) have shown that creative class members with a synthetic knowledge base (e.g., engineers) do move for interesting and challenging job possibilities independent of the size and atmosphere of city-regions. Thus, smaller city-regions and towns can attract members of the creative class when good job opportunities are available. The cases included in this book add to our understanding of these dynamics. Evidence from Calgary (chapter 9) and Saskatoon (chapter 8) illustrates the logic at work for synthetic knowledge–based creative workers.

Innovations occur through combining new and existing knowledge, skills, and resources. Broader and more diverse knowledge bases enhance the scope for innovation (Asheim and Gertler 2005). Lorenz and Lundvall (2006) have shown that firms combining a science- and experience-based mode of innovation perform best, and other studies have demonstrated that firms sourcing broadly from both R&D and experience-based knowledge are the most innovative (Laursen and Salter 2006). An important goal for policy may therefore be to contribute to the necessary variety in the knowledge available for innovation, which could increase the transformative capacity of innovation systems, making them more dynamic and open, and thus better able to support new initiatives in the economy. In all economies, except possibly a few very large ones, the most important source of variety in knowledge bases is found abroad. The ability of a country's entrepreneurs and firms to tap into global networks of knowledge, and to use knowledge productively (open innovation), which depends on the absorptive capacity of the firms and regions, will often prove more important than creating new knowledge at home. Thus, the international dimension of globally distributed knowledge networks has increased dramatically in importance over the last decade.

This means that it is more than ever vital to understand how the international context interacts with nation- and sector-specific conditions in affecting competitiveness and economic growth. Arguably, an efficient knowledge economy depends on innovation systems with a high degree of openness and diversity, not only concerning knowledge strictly defined, but also with respect to tolerance towards the cultural, religious, and ethnic characteristics of the carriers (e.g., entrepreneurs and researchers) of that knowledge (Fagerberg and Srholec 2008; Florida 2002).

What about the third of Florida's original contributions on the importance of diversity, openness, and tolerance for attracting the creative class to city-regions? Countries that practise an open and liberal immigration policy – such as Canada and Sweden – have and will in the future likely benefit in the battle for attracting global talent, while those – first and foremost, Denmark, but followed by other European countries such as France, Italy, the Netherlands, Belgium, the United Kingdom, and Hungary with influential right populist parties – that succumb to anti-immigration or anti-immigrant policies will not. An OECD study on the attraction of global talent to European cities compared Amsterdam (the most open and tolerant Dutch city), Stockholm, and Copenhagen, and found that it was much easier for Amsterdam and Stockholm to attract global talent than for Copenhagen (Zick et al. 2011). With many elements related to tolerance and openness, however, policy is set at the national or state level: city-regions cannot, for instance, usually set immigration policy or permit same-sex marriage. What is left to the local and regional levels is the implementation of national laws and regulations. This aspect should not be ignored, as proactive and open-minded local governments can make a difference in how members of the creative class perceive the level of openness and tolerance they encounter in a city-region. Windows of opportunity are obviously greater in larger city-regions than in smaller ones, as the large ones benefit from a greater diversity of people, industries, and occupations, which gives them a solid position for further developing policy measures to attract and retain members of the creative class. Policy initiatives on the local and regional levels – even in elements such as school board or recreational policies – can influence whether national or international audiences perceive city-regions as welcoming.

Talent, Creative Cities, and Economic Innovation

What is the potential for seeking talent for creative cities, as the title of this book asks, and what effect does talent have on economic innovation? So far I have suggested that all city-regions, independent of size, industrial structure, and location, can attract members of the creative class. The knowledge base approach (Asheim and Hansen 2009; Asheim, Coenen, and Vang 2007; Asheim and Gertler 2005) implies that the creative class is heterogeneous, with occupations and industries drawing on three knowledge bases: analytical (e.g., science); synthetic (e.g., engineering), and symbolic (e.g., art). While large city-regions with diverse industrial structures would attract talent belonging to all knowledge bases, smaller city-regions and towns may be more interesting to people seeking employment in industries based on synthetic knowledge, as this category of the creative class gives good job opportunities the highest priority.

What should be understood by a creative city? This is a fuzzy concept never properly defined: when attempts are made, the definitions prove either too narrow or too broad to make theoretical, empirical, and practical sense. On the one hand, Florida (2002) applies a broad definition of the creative class, which implies that all human beings potentially are creative. This seems rather banal for a theoretical definition. On the other hand, in his work on the geography of creativity, Törnqvist (2004) defines places of creativity so narrowly as to only accommodate universities producing Nobel Prize winners. Neither definition is especially useful in making sense of what should be understood by a creative city as well as what it means with respect to promoting economic innovation.

One way to proceed would be to differentiate between creativity, innovativeness, and competitiveness using an evolutionary economic approach that discusses variety creation, adaptation, selection, and retention. Variety creation enjoys the best potential conditions in the largest city-regions where diversity in every aspect is greatest: this is strengthened by institutional factors ranging from proactive policy to promote creativity to formal and informal institutions supporting diversity, openness, and tolerance. In this connection we could raise the interesting discussion of cognitive distance. Asheim, Boschma, and Cooke (2011) argue that the advantage of a related-variety perspective over Jacobs's (1969) urbanization economies is that related variety builds on the idea of optimal cognitive distance promoting maximum knowledge spillover: that is, the distance is neither too narrow (as in specialized localization economies where everyone does the same task and therefore cannot learn from each other) nor too broad (as in urbanization economies where activities can be so disparate that the cognitive distance is too remote to absorb new knowledge, limiting the potential for knowledge spillovers). However, in the case of path-breaking or radical innovations, knowledge spillover may take place precisely in environments characterized by very disparate activities, where the cognitive distance is great enough to provide the impetus to think in radically new ways: this likely occurs within large city-regions exploiting urbanization economies. In the Canadian context this is most commonly achieved in the three largest city-regions (Toronto, Montreal, and Vancouver): by such definition these would be the only creative cities in Canada.

Then we have the question of adaptation. Only a limited number of inventions end up as innovations: the same could be said about many creations. Transforming inventions into innovations may be seen as a selection process, which occurs at multiple levels. Failure does not necessarily imply that the attempted innovation carries little promise, but may have to do with resistance from other actors involved in the selection process. The strategic dimension of adaptation involves the absorptive capacity of people at firm and regional levels. Here the question of optimal cognitive distance becomes highly relevant, as does related variety (i.e., sectors with shared or complementary knowledge bases and competences). In short, some degree of cognitive proximity is required to ensure that effective communication and interactive learning takes place, but not too much cognitive proximity, to avoid cognitive lock-in (Nooteboom 2000). Thus, it is not regional diversity in urbanization economies (which involves great cognitive distance) or regional specialization in localization economies per se (resulting in too much cognitive proximity) that stimulates real innovations, but regional specialization in related variety, which is more likely to induce interactive learning and innovation. As such, the concept of related variety goes beyond the traditional dichotomy of localization economies and Jacobs's urbanization economies (Asheim, Boschma, and Cooke 2011). City-regions that have these characteristics could be described as innovative and competitive. Ottawa and Waterloo, Ontario, might represent Canadian examples of such cities.

Many determinants for success or failure in innovation may be related to the workings of innovation systems as selection environments for new entrepreneurial ventures. New ventures (e.g., knowledge-intensive enterprises) that have little in common with economically strong existing sectors may find that innovation systems are poorly adapted to their needs (Narula 2002). Important policy implications of these findings are thus to try to make these determinants more conducive to innovation to avoid negative lock-in situations caused by strong path dependency within innovation processes. In this context, path dependency (i.e., local economic history) will play an important role, where – as previously underlined – the challenge is to secure positive lock-ins. This is even more the case when it comes to the question of retaining economic activities, where cognitive lock-ins among policymakers and business leaders can enhance the evolutionary forces of the economy. This will prove especially important in a resource-based economy such as Canada's to secure high productivity levels (through continuous process innovations) and, thus, retain international competitiveness.

Innovativeness and Competitiveness of City-Regions

When it comes to the question of the innovativeness and competitiveness of city-regions, the constructing regional advantage (CRA) approach is highly relevant. The core arguments of the CRA approach stem from work that started in Brussels in an expert group appointed by the European Union Commission: in 2006 they launched their final report, *Constructing Regional Advantage*, as a way of taking on and combating new challenges and problems of globalization for European regions (Asheim et al. 2006). Constructing regional advantage means turning comparative advantage into competitive advantage through an explicit policy push promoting monopolistic competition based on product differentiation creating unique products. While building on the lessons from the dynamic principle of the theory of competitive advantage (Porter 1990, 1998), as well as from the innovation systems approach (Lundvall 2007 emphasizing that competitiveness can be influenced by innovation policies and supporting regulatory and institutional frameworks, the constructing advantage approach recognizes the important interplay between economic and institutional dynamics as it calls for greater attention to multi-level governance. The approach especially highlights the role of a proactive public-private partnership and the impact of the public sector and public policy support by acknowledging institutional complementarities in knowledge economies. This approach represents an improved understanding of key regional development challenges as well as better anticipation and response to the problems of globalization by addressing system failures related to the lack of connectivity in regional innovation systems (Asheim, Moodysson, and Tödtling 2011).

Innovation is the key factor in promoting competitiveness in a globalizing knowledge economy. Competition based on innovation implies choosing the high-road strategy, which is the only sustainable alternative for developed, high-cost regional and national economies, as well as for the future of developing economies. For a long time such a strategy was thought to imply promoting high-tech, R&D-intensive industries in accordance with the linear view of innovation; however, recognition has increasingly developed that a broader and more comprehensive view on innovation has to be applied to develop and retain competitiveness in diverse regions.

The EU Commission originally wanted a focus on implementing the R&D-based strategy from the Lisbon and Barcelona declarations on a regional level. It soon recognized that a no-size-fits-all approach had to be adopted due to the heterogeneity of European regions (Tödtling and Trippl 2005). Thus, a Porter perspective was adopted arguing that all industries can be innovative. The high-tech/low-tech distinction is not relevant on an industry level as a point of departure for innovation policies because R&D intensity is not the same as innovative capacity: knowledge intensity is a broader and more appropriate concept. Regions and countries should base their competitive strategy on industries they traditionally have been doing well in: that is, build on their technological path dependency to achieve positive lock-in effects. However, the CRA approach differs from Porter's cluster approach in explaining how innovation comes about in a systematic way by building on a regional innovation system approach, and with respect to the role of government or the public sector. Porter argues that innovation results when firms are co-located in a cluster where the determinants of competition are in place: thus, he lacks a causal explanation like the one Perroux (1970) applies using the notion of key industries. In contrast, the innovation system approach represents both a selection environment and a milieu for variety creation. The dynamics of the system depend on long-term relationships between industry and universities, with a strategic role played by policy. The innovation system approach represented a transition from a linear view on innovation to an interactive one, which reflects a move from science and technology policies to innovation policy that places innovation at the centre of economic development. The key role played by government is clearly illustrated by the two countries – Finland and Sweden – most explicitly applying innovation system policies. In Finland, government is a key actor implementing innovation policies through the Research and Innovation Council (formerly the Science and Technology Policy Council), while VINNOVA, the Governmental Agency for Innovation Systems, is the coordinating agency for innovation policy in Sweden. The CRA approach builds on this and emphasizes an even stronger proactive role for government and public policies in initiating public/private collaborations to promote innovation and competitiveness.

The second important policy recommendation of the CRA approach which fits the Canadian context as well is that regional advantage has to be constructed on the basis of the uniqueness of the capabilities of firms and regions rather than solely on R&D efforts (Asheim et al. 2006). This reflects recent research pointing to the complexity of modern products and innovation processes, which actualizes a differentiated knowledge base perspective (Asheim and Gertler 2005; Asheim, Coenen, Moodysson, and Vang 2007). Such a broad-based innovation policy is in line with the innovation system perspective of defining innovation as interactive learning combining an STI (Science, Technology, Innovation) and a DUI (Doing, Using, Interacting) mode of innovation (Lorenz and Lundvall 2006). Thus, the CRA approach falls nicely in line with the conclusions made by Gertler et al. in the introductory chapter of this book in emphasizing that the Canadian research suggests there is no single course for regional economic development. City-regions are advised to build on their particular inherited assets to plan for future economic prosperity. In seeking talent or in producing creative cities, no single solution can work everywhere, certainly not in a nation as large and diverse as Canada.

Theory and Policy Implications

Is talent a useful concept for theory building and policymaking? I have argued that the relevance and usefulness of the concept clearly grows if it is nuanced by applying a knowledge base approach (Asheim and Hansen 2009). As the concept is originally defined by Florida (2002), it is far too heterogeneous to be directly applicable in theory or policy. When it is differentiated according to a knowledge base approach, it is much easier to relate the concept of talent – for example – to the localization-urbanization economies discussion and to specify which type of talent cities of various sizes and characteristics realistically can try to attract. The research clearly indicates that synthetic knowledge–based workers demonstrate a preference for business climate factors such as qualified and interesting jobs rather than the night life and entertainment of large cities, while the opposite is the case for symbolic knowledge–based workers. This finding also implies that mid-sized cities and smaller towns can be attractive to talented workers in synthetic-knowledge base occupations.

Theoretically, this implies that specialized cities benefiting from localization economies, which are found in resource-based economies such as the Canadian, but also the Australian and the Nordic, can still be attractive to talent primarily bringing along a synthetic-knowledge base. Such insight will be relevant when local governments are formulating strategies for talent attraction. Some may avoid investments in cultural amenities when stimulating the business climate may prove more effective and relevant for this kind of talent.

Another policy-relevant insight from the research is that business climate and people climate are complementary and not contradictory dimensions in regional development strategies. Another way of formulating this is that policy should have the ambition to promote both competition and cohesion and, thus, secure development *in* regions as well as *of* regions. The one-sided focus on people climate and talent attraction irrespective of the realism in such strategies for different types of cities and regions, which dominated the policy agenda in the years following the publication of Florida's book in 2002, did not add much to Porter's cluster and business climate perspectives with respect to improving the economic performance and level of living conditions in cities and regions in developed economies.

Lastly, an important theoretical insight and policy implication of the role of diversity, openness, and tolerance for talent attraction is related to the increasing dependence on globally distributed knowledge networks for creativity and innovation. As argued in evolutionary economics, broader and more diverse knowledge bases provide wider scope for innovation. Moreover, for most countries the key source of such diversity in knowledge bases is found abroad. Contributing to securing the necessary diversity and variety in knowledge available for innovation will constitute an important task for policy in the years to come. This insight has relevance for developed countries' immigration policies. An open and tolerant society practising a liberal immigration policy, as is found in Canada and Sweden, will be conducive to attracting global talent, which will represent a rapidly growing competitive advantage in the globalizing knowledge economy of the future.

NOTES

1 The project "Technology, Talent, and Tolerance in European Cities: A Comparative Analysis" was organized as a European Science Foundation

"European Collaborative Research Project in the Social Sciences." Carried out over a three-year period, 2004–6, it was coordinated by Bjørn T. Asheim, Lund University, Sweden, and supervised by Meric Gertler, University of Toronto (then also affiliated with the University of Oslo).

REFERENCES

Andersen, Kristina, Hogni Kalsø Hansen, Arne Isaksen, and Mike Raunio. 2010. "Nordic city regions in the creative class debate: Putting the creative class theory to a test." *Industry and Innovation* 17 (2): 215–40. http://dx.doi.org /10.1080/13662711003633496.

Asheim, Bjørn T. 2009. "Guest editorial: Introduction to the creative class in European city regions." *Economic Geography* 85 (4): 355–62. http://dx.doi .org/10.1111/j.1944-8287.2009.01046.x.

Asheim, Bjørn T., Ron Boschma, and Philip Cooke. 2011. "Constructing regional advantage: Platform policies based on related variety and differentiated knowledge bases." *Regional Studies* 45 (7): 893–904. http://dx.doi.org /10.1080/00343404.2010.543126.

Asheim, Bjørn T., Lars Coenen, Jerker Moodysson, and Jan Vang. 2007. "Constructing knowledge-based regional advantage: Implications for regional innovation policy." *International Journal of Entrepreneurship and Innovation Management* 7 (2–5): 140–55. http://dx.doi.org/10.1504/IJEIM.2007.012879.

Asheim, Bjørn T., Lars Coenen, and Jan Vang. 2007. "Face-to-face, buzz, and knowledge bases: Sociospatial implications for learning, innovation, and innovation policy." *Environment and Planning* C 25 (5): 655–70. http://dx.doi .org/10.1068/c0648.

Asheim, Bjørn T., Phil Cooke, Jan Annerstedt, Jiri Blazek, et al. 2006. *Constructing regional advantage: Principles, perspectives, policies.* Final report from DG Research Expert Group on Constructing Regional Advantage. DG Research, European Commission, Brussels.

Asheim, Bjørn T., and Meric S. Gertler. 2005. "The geography of innovation: Regional innovation systems." In *The Oxford handbook of innovation*, ed. J. Fagerberg, D. Mowery, and R. Nelson, 291–317. Oxford: Oxford University Press.

Asheim, Bjørn T., and Hogni Kalsø Hansen. 2009. "Knowledge bases, talents and contexts: On the usefulness of the creative class approach in Sweden." *Economic Geography* 85 (4): 425–42. http://dx.doi.org/10.1111/j.1944-8287 .2009.01051.x.

Asheim, Bjørn T., Jerker Moodysson, and Franz Tödtling. 2011. "Constructing regional advantage." *European Planning Studies* 19 (7): 1133–9. http://dx.doi .org/10.1080/09654313.2011.573127.

Boschma, Ron, and Michael Fritsch. 2009. "Creative class and regional growth: Empirical evidence from seven European countries." *Economic Geography* 85 (4): 391–423. http://dx.doi.org/10.1111/j.1944-8287.2009.01048.x.

Fagerberg, Jan, and Martin Srholec. 2008. "National innovation systems, capabilities and economic development." *Research Policy* 37 (9): 1417–35. http://dx.doi.org/10.1016/j.respol.2008.06.003.

Florida, Richard. 2002. *The rise of the creative class – and how it's transforming work, leisure, community and everyday life.* New York: Basic Books.

Florida, Richard. 2006. "Where the brains are." *Atlantic Monthly*, October, 34–6. http://www.theatlantic.com/magazine/archive/2006/10/where-the-brains-are/5202.

Florida, Richard, Gary Gates, Brian Knudsen, and Kevin Stolarick. 2006. *The university and the creative economy.* http://www.creativeclass.com/rfcgdb /articles/University_andthe_Creative_Economy.pdf.

Florida, Richard, Charlotta Mellander, and Kevin Stolarick. 2008. "Inside the black box of regional development: Human capital, the creative class and tolerance." *Journal of Economic Geography* 8 (5): 615–49. http://dx.doi.org /10.1093/jeg/lbn023.

Glaeser, Edward L. 2005. Review of Richard Florida's *The rise of the creative class.* In *Regional Science and Urban Economics* 35 (5): 593–6. http://dx.doi.org/10.1016/j.regsciurbeco.2005.01.005.

Jacobs, Jane. 1969. *The economy of cities.* New York: Random House.

Krugman, Paul. 1998. "What's new about the new economic geography?" *Oxford Review of Economic Policy* 14 (2): 7–17. http://dx.doi.org/10.1093 /oxrep/14.2.7.

Laursen, Keld, and Ammon Salter. 2006. "Open for innovation: The role of openness in explaining innovation performance among UK manufacturing firms." *Strategic Management Journal* 27 (2): 131–50. http://dx.doi.org /10.1002/smj.507.

Lorenz, Edward, and Bengt-Å. Lundvall. 2006. *How Europe's economies learn: Coordinating competing models.* Oxford: Oxford University Press.

Lundvall, Bengt-Å. 2007. "National innovation systems: Analytical concept and development tool." *Industry and Innovation* 14 (1): 95–119. http://dx.doi .org/10.1080/13662710601130863.

Narula, Rajneesh. 2002. "Innovation systems and 'inertia' in R&D location: Norwegian firms and the role of systemic lock-in." *Research Policy* 31 (5): 795–816. http://dx.doi.org/10.1016/S0048-7333(01)00148-2.

Nooteboom, Bart. 2000. *Learning and innovation in organizations and economies.* Oxford: Oxford University Press.

Perroux, François. 1970. "Note on the concept of growth poles." In *Regional economics: Theory and practice,* ed. D. McKee, R.D. Dean, and W.H. Leahy, 93–103. New York: The Free Press.

Porter, Michael. 1990. *The competitive advantage of nations.* London: Macmillan.

Porter, Michael. 1998. "Clusters and the new economics of competition." *Harvard Business Review* 76 (6): 77–90. Medline:10187248.

Tödtling, Franz, and Michaela Trippl. 2005. "One size fits all? Towards a differentiated regional innovation policy approach." *Research Policy* 34 (8): 1203–19.

Törnqvist, Gunnar. 2004. *Kreativitetens geografi.* Stockholm: SNS Förlag.

Zick, Andreas, Beate Küpper, and Andreas Höveermann. 2011. *Intolerance, prejudice and discrimination: A European report.* Berlin: Friedrick Ebert-Stiftung. http://www.uni-bielefeld.de/ikg/IntolerancePrejudice.pdf.

Appendix A:
Draft Interview Guide

Each team working on the project went through an ethics review at their universities and all made some adjustments to the draft schedule to suit local conditions. The schedule was used to guide semi-structured interviews that were recorded for analysis. In some cities, the research team adapted the interview guide to create a self-administered survey instrument.

Theme: Social Foundations of Talent Attraction and Retention

Background

Talented individuals play an essential role in the learning economy. A key societal challenge is to create the conditions which attract and retain talented individuals in the city-region.

We are interested in understanding what conditions facilitate or inhibit the city-region's ability to attract and retain creative and talented individuals.

A. Questions for Highly Educated/Creative Workers

Background

Where were you born? *If outside [city name],* when did you first move to [city name]?

How would you describe your ethnic identity?

Please describe your educational history and credentials (institution, degree program, location, years).

Please describe your employment history (firm/organization, location, sector, position).

What is your current occupation?

Does your current job fully utilize your skills, training, and education?

To what extent have you moved between different kinds of sectors or occupations?

To what extent does the [city name] economy enable this kind of mobility and the kinds of opportunities available?

Attractiveness of the City Region

IF FROM OUTSIDE CITY

Why did you move to [city name]? If you worked in your field in another city, how does [city name] compare?

What characteristics of the [city name] economy and/or labour market make it an attractive place to work in your field?

What characteristics of the [city name] economy and/or labour market undermine its attractiveness as a place to work in your field?

What characteristics of living in [your city] make it an attractive place for you?

What physical assets and amenities of this area make it attractive?

How safe and secure is the community?

How affordable is [your city]? How does that play into your decision of where to live and work? Does it affect the nature of creativity in your work?

Are there particular aspects of [your city] that enhance creativity in the city?

What neighbourhoods do you find most creative? What neighbourhood do you work in now? In what ways does it facilitate creativity (or not)?

To what extent are [your city's] strengths unique to the city?

Are newcomers easily able to integrate into this region? What mechanisms are most effective for integrating them? What challenges affect the integration of newcomers? What physical features of [your city] help to attract and integrate newcomers? What associations assist newcomers to integrate?

How do civic leaders in the region respond to the diverse gender, ethnic, and cultural backgrounds that newcomers bring?

How do local associations respond to new perspectives on regional development brought by newcomers?

What characteristics of [your city] reduce its attractiveness as a place to live?

The City-Region's Ability to Retain Talent

If you were to move to another city, where would you choose to live,
and why?

How would such (a) location(s) compare to [your city] in terms of career opportunities, quality of life / quality of place?

How likely is it that you will move to another city-region within the
next three years, for the reasons just discussed?

B. Questions for Employers of Highly Educated/Creative Workers

(Could be adapted for use with Higher Education Institutions and
Research-Based Organizations.)

Background

What are your firm's primary products or services?

Please provide a brief history of the firm (year and location of establishment, founder(s), major changes in ownership since founding).

How many different sites/locations does your firm have, and where
are these [if more than one]?

How many employees (total, [city name] office(s), elsewhere)? Employment composition by Occupational category, Educational attainment.

Where are you located within [city name] and why? What aspects of
this neighbourhood facilitate creativity and innovation?

What parts of the city do your employees come from?

Attractiveness of the City Region

What are the primary sources for your highly educated/creative workers (local and non-local)? Which educational institutions? Which
competitor or supplier firms? Which cities or regions?

What proportion of your highly educated/creative workers was born
outside Canada?

Do you recruit talent from outside [your city /outside Canada]? If so,
how actively do you do so, and what mechanisms do you use?

What barriers are there to recruiting in terms of immigration policies?

Which particular locations do you target in recruitment and why?

What characteristics of the [your city] economy and/or labour market
make it an attractive place to work in your field?

What characteristics of the [your city] economy or labour market make it attractive from the perspective of the kind of people you seek to hire?

What characteristics of the [your city] economy and/or labour market undermine its attractiveness as a place to work in your field?

What characteristics of living in [your city] make it an attractive place for your highly educated/creative workers? How do these characteristics enhance your ability to attract and retain talented workers?

What characteristics of [your city's] quality of place/quality of life undermine your ability to attract and retain highly educated/creative workers?

The City Region's Ability to Retain Talent

What challenges do you currently face with respect to retaining your highly educated/creative workers? Where are the potential competing employment opportunities: primarily local or nonlocal?

If your highly educated/creative workers were to move to another city for career-related reasons, where do you think they would choose to live, and why?

How would such (a) location(s) compare to [your city] in terms of career opportunities? quality of life? quality of place?

Have you lost any highly educated/creative workers to such locations in the last three years? If so, how many? Why did those people leave?

In general, have you had a difficult time attracting and retaining talent? How do you recruit workers?

C. Additional Questions for Intermediary Organizations

Describe the goals and mandate of your organization.

What are the principal challenges facing this region, with respect to the attraction, retention, or integration of highly educated/creative workers?

In what ways does your organization promote the attraction, retention, or integration of highly educated/creative workers in the city-region?

To what extent do you focus your efforts on particular socially disadvantaged groups in this program activity? Which groups do you target for this work?

Contributors

Bjørn T. Asheim is the Chair in Economic Geography in the Department of Human Geography, and research director of the Centre for Innovation, Research, and Competence in the Learning Economy (CIRCLE) at Lund University in Sweden. In 2013 he also became professor at the University of Stavanger, Norway. He served on two ISRN project Research Advisory Boards.

Yves Bourgeois is director of the Urban and Community Studies Institute at the University of New Brunswick. His research centres on the linkages between urban growth and innovation, and connections between creativity and cultural identity formation.

Shauna Brail is senior lecturer and director of the Urban Studies Placement Program at the University of Toronto's Urban Studies Program. Her research interests in economic geography focus on the social, cultural, and economic changes associated with shifting industrial strengths of cities and with a particular interest in the cultural/creative economy.

Michael Coutanche is assistant professor in the RTA School of Media at Ryerson University where he focuses on the education of emerging screenwriters. His research interests include the occupational dynamics of Canadian screenwriters.

Sébastien Darchen is a lecturer in planning in the School of Geography, Planning, and Environmental Management at the University of Queensland. He taught previously at the Faculty of Environmental Studies, York University. He has published on development processes and the creative cities thesis in several journals, including *International Planning Studies* and *Urban Research and Practice*.

Charles H. Davis holds the E.S. Rogers Sr. Research Chair in Media Management and Entrepreneurship in the RTA School of Media at Ryerson University, where he teaches in the Master of Media Production Program, the MBA Program, and the joint Ryerson/York Program in Communication and Culture. His research interests include new product development and the political economy of media.

Betsy Donald is an associate professor of geography at Queen's University in Kingston, Ontario. She teaches and does research on the cultural economy, cities and regional development, and sustainable food systems.

Kate Geddie is a senior policy analyst in the international relations division of the Association of Universities and Colleges of Canada. She holds a doctorate in geography from the University of Toronto and recently held a post-doctoral position with the MOVE Network at the University of Lausanne, Switzerland.

Meric S. Gertler is president, professor of geography and planning, and the Goldring Chair in Canadian Studies, University of Toronto. He was co-director of the Program on Globalization and Regional Innovation Systems at the Munk School for Global Affairs. His books include *Manufacturing Culture: The Institutional Geography of Industrial Practice* and *Innovation and Social Learning*, co-edited with David A. Wolfe.

Elizabeth Godo holds a master's degree in communication and culture from Ryerson and York Universities and an Honours Bachelor of Arts in dramatic art and communication studies from the University of Windsor. She is a communications analyst at Livewire Communications and founding principal at Zeto Communications.

Jill L. Grant is professor of planning at Dalhousie University in Halifax, Nova Scotia. Her current research interests include development trends in Canadian suburbs, health and the built environment, and the factors that attract musicians and artists to Halifax. She is the author or editor of four books and dozens of articles.

Jeffry Haggett is a planner with WSP/Genivar Consulting in Halifax. He was formerly with Long Range Planning at the Regional Municipality of Wood Buffalo in Alberta. His undergraduate honours thesis in community design at Dalhousie University examined music venues in Halifax.

Heather Hall is a post-doctoral fellow in the Department of Geography at Memorial University. She earned her PhD in geography at Queen's University in Kingston, Ontario. Her research interests include the politics of regional economic development as well as planning and economic development in peripheral cities and regions.

Carolyn Hatch is a visiting scholar in the School of Planning, Design and Construction at Michigan State University and a post-doctoral fellow in the Department of Extension, MSU. She holds a doctorate in planning from the University of Toronto. Her research examines the institutional foundations of training in the North American manufacturing industry.

Brian J. Hracs is a post-doctoral research fellow in the Department of Social and Economic Geography at Uppsala University, Sweden. His research interests include the employment experiences of entrepreneurs in the creative economy and the spatial flows of talent.

Mia A. Hunt is a doctoral student of cultural geography at Royal Holloway, University of London. Her research explores city building, textures of place, and cosmopolitanism, with a current focus on the materiality, agency, and geographical imagination of everyday consumptions spaces in London.

Cooper H. Langford is Faculty Professor in Communication and Culture at the University of Calgary. His previous appointments include vice-president for research, University of Calgary, and director of physical and mathematical sciences at NSERC. His research focuses on innovation and knowledge flows.

Josh Lepawsky is associate professor of geography at Memorial University of Newfoundland. His research interests include cultural geographies of the knowledge economy and digital technology. His current work investigates the geographies of electronic waste.

Deborah Leslie is professor of geography at the University of Toronto and Canada Research Chair in the Cultural Economy. She is the author of articles on creativity and urban economic development, and on ethical and spatial dimensions of commodity chains. Recently she has been conducting research on the social dynamics of innovation in fashion and art in Toronto, and on the Cirque du Soleil in Montreal.

Ben Li has diverse interests as a policy and communication analyst at the Legislative Assembly of Alberta, as a social media consultant, and as a doctoral student at the Department of Information Processing Science at the University of Oulu, Finland. He holds degrees in biology, political science, and open-source innovation, and is studying big data research infrastructure innovations with the International Long-Term Ecological Research Network.

Jesse Morton is a planner with the Town of Bridgewater, Nova Scotia. While attending Dalhousie University's Master of Planning program, he investigated Halifax's independent music scene and the social dynamics of economic performance. After graduating in 2009, Jesse worked as a cultural planning assistant with Halifax Regional Municipality.

Peter W.B. Phillips, an international political economist, is professor of public policy in the Johnson-Shoyama Graduate School of Public Policy at the University of Saskatchewan. He undertakes research on governing transformative innovation, including biotechnology regulation and policy, innovation systems, intellectual property, supply chain management, and trade policy.

Josephine V. Rekers has a doctorate in geography from the University of Toronto and is currently a post-doctoral researcher with CIRCLE at Lund University in Sweden.

Camille D. Ryan is a former post-doctoral fellow with the University of Calgary and is now a professional research associate with the Department of Bioresource Policy, Business and Economics, College of Agriculture and Bioresources, at the University of Saskatchewan.

Jeremy Shtern is assistant professor in the School of Creative Industries at Ryerson University. He was previously with the Department of Communication at the University of Ottawa. His research focuses on the impacts of digital technologies and globalization on communication governance. He holds a PhD from the Université de Montréal.

Kevin Stolarick is the research director at the Martin Prosperity Institute at the Rotman School of Management, University of Toronto. His research interests include the relationship between firm performance and information technology and the impacts of technology, tolerance, talent, and quality of place on regional growth and prosperity.

Diane-Gabrielle Tremblay is Canada Research Chair on the Socio-Organizational Challenges of the Knowledge Economy, professor at Teluq-Université du Québec, and director of a CURA project on work life over the life course. She has been an invited professor in many universities including Paris I Sorbonne, Hanoi (Vietnam), and the European School of Management, and has published extensively.

Tara Vinodrai is associate professor at the University of Waterloo. Her research addresses innovation, creativity, labour markets, and economic development in urban economies. Her current projects examine design-led innovation in Canada and Denmark, and urban-rural linkages and governance models in sustainability and creativity-oriented regional economic development initiatives.

Graeme Webb is a doctoral student in the School of Communication at Simon Fraser University. His research interests combine political sociology with communication theory, specifically examining how communication technologies can facilitate a participatory governance paradigm at the city-region level.